Machtelt Garrels

Introduction to Linux

A Hands-On Guide

Second Edition

Fultus™ *Books*

Introduction to Linux

A Hands-On Guide

by

Machtelt Garrels

Cover design by Fultus Corporation
Cover illustration by Anna Khayrullina

ISBN 1-59682-112-4

(Second Edition)

All rights reserved.

Copyright © 2002-2007 by Machtelt Garrels

Published by Fultus Corporation

Corporate Web Site: *www.fultus.com*
Fultus eLibrary: *elibrary.fultus.com*
Online Book Superstore: *store.fultus.com*
email: *production@fultus.com*

Table of Contents

List of Figures

List of Tables

Introduction

Why this guide?

Many people still believe that learning Linux is difficult, or that only experts can understand how a Linux system works. Though there is a lot of free documentation available, the documentation is widely scattered on the Web, and often confusing, since it is usually oriented toward experienced UNIX or Linux users. Today, thanks to the advancements in development, Linux has grown in popularity both at home and at work. The goal of this guide is to show people of all ages that Linux can be simple and fun, and used for all kinds of purposes.

Who should read this book?

This guide was created as an overview of the Linux Operating System, geared toward new users as an exploration tour and getting started guide, with exercises at the end of each chapter. For more advanced trainees it can be a desktop reference, and a collection of the base knowledge needed to proceed with system and network administration. This book contains many real life examples derived from the author's experience as a Linux system and network administrator, trainer and consultant. We hope these examples will help you to get a better understanding of the Linux system and that you feel encouraged to try out things on your own.

Everybody who wants to get a "CLUE", a Command Line User Experience, with Linux (and UNIX in general) will find this book useful.

Contributions

Many thanks to all the people who shared their experiences. And especially to the Belgian Linux users for hearing me out every day and always being generous in their comments.

Also a special thought for Tabatha Marshall for doing a really thorough revision, spell check and styling, and to Eugene Crosser for spotting the errors that we two overlooked.

And thanks to all the readers who notified me about missing topics and who helped to pick out the last errors, unclear definitions and typos by going through the trouble of mailing me all their remarks. These are also the people who help me keep this guide up to date, like Filipus Klutiero who did a complete review in 2005 and 2006 and helps me getting the guide into the Debian docs collection, and Alexey Eremenko who sent me the foundation for Chapter 11.

Finally, a big thank you for the volunteers who are currently translating this document in French, Swedish, German, Farsi, Hindi and more. It is a big work that should not be underestimated; I admire your courage.

Conventions used in this document

The following typographic and usage conventions occur in this text:

Text type	Meaning
"Quoted text"	Quotes from people, quoted computer output.
terminal view	Literal computer input and output captured from the terminal, usually rendered with a light grey background.
command	Name of a command that can be entered on the command line.
VARIABLE	Name of a variable or pointer to content of a variable, as in $VARNAME.
option	Option to a command, as in "the -a option to the ls command".
argument	Argument to a command, as in "read **man ls** ".
prompt	User prompt, usually followed by a command that you type in a terminal window, like in hilda@home>**ls -l**
command options *arguments*	Command synopsis or general usage, on a separated line.
filename	Name of a file or directory, for example "Change to the/usr/bin directory."
Key	Keys to hit on the keyboard, such as "type **Q** to quit".
Button	Graphical button to click, like the OK button.
Menu->Choice	Choice to select from a graphical menu, for instance: "SelectHelp->About Mozilla in your browser."
Terminology	Important term or concept: "The Linux *kernel* is the heart of the system."
\	The backslash in a terminal view or command synopsis indicates an unfinished line. In other words, if you see a long command that is cut into multiple lines, \ means "Don't press **Enter** yet!"

Text type	Meaning
See Chapter 1, *What is Linux?*	link to related subject within this guide.

Table 1.1. Typographic and usage conventions

The following images are used:

This is a note

It contains additional information or remarks.

This is a caution

It means be careful.

This is a warning

Be *very* careful.

This is a tip

Tips and tricks.

Organization of this document

This guide is part of the Linux Documentation Project and aims to be the foundation for all other materials that you can get from the Project. As such, it provides you with the fundamental knowledge needed by anyone who wants to start working with a Linux system, while at the same time it tries to consciously avoid re-inventing the hot water. Thus, you can expect this book to be incomplete and full of links to sources of additional information on your system, on the Internet and in your system documentation.

The first chapter is an introduction to the subject on Linux; the next two discuss absolute basic commands. Chapters 4 and 5 discuss some more advanced but still basic topics. Chapter 6 is needed for continuing with the rest, since it discusses editing files, an ability you need to pass from Linux newbie to Linux user. The following chapters discuss somewhat more advanced topics that you will have to deal with in everyday Linux use.

All chapters come with exercises that will test your preparedness for the next chapter.

- Chapter 1, *What is Linux?*: What is Linux, how did it come into existence, advantages and disadvantages, what does the future hold for Linux, who should use it, installing your computer.

- Chapter 2, *Quickstart*: Getting started, connecting to the system, basic commands, where to find help.

- Chapter 3, *About files and the file system*: The filesystem, important files and directories, managing files and directories, protecting your data.

- Chapter 4, *Processes*: Understanding and managing processes, boot and shutdown procedures, postponing tasks, repetitive tasks.

- Chapter 5, *I/O redirection*: What are standard input, output and error and how are these features used from the command line.

- Chapter 6, *Text editors*: Why you should learn to work with an editor, discussion of the most common editors.

- Chapter 7, *Home sweet /home*: Configuring your graphical, text and audio environment, settings for the non-native English speaking Linux user, tips for adding extra software.

- Chapter 8, *Printers and printing*: Converting files to a printable format, getting them out of the printer, hints for solving print problems.

- Chapter 9, *Fundamental Backup Techniques*: Preparing data to be backed up, discussion of various tools, remote backup.

- Chapter 10, *Networking*: Overview of Linux networking tools and user applications, with a short discussion of the underlying service daemon programs and secure networking.

- *Chapter 11, Sound and Video*: Sound and video, including Voice over IP and sound recording is discussed in this chapter.

- Appendix A, *Where to go from here?*: Which books to read and sites to visit when you have finished reading this one.

- Appendix B, *DOS versus Linux commands*: A comparison.

- Appendix C, *Shell Features*: If you ever get stuck, these tables might be an outcome. Also a good argument when your boss insists that YOU should use HIS favorite shell.

Chapter 1
What is Linux?

Abstract

We will start with an overview of how Linux became the operating system it is today. We will discuss past and future development and take a closer look at the advantages and disadvantages of this system. We will talk about distributions, about Open Source in general and try to explain a little something about GNU.

This chapter answers questions like:

- What is Linux?

- Where and how did Linux start?

- Isn't Linux that system where everything is done in text mode?

- Does Linux have a future or is it just hype?

- What are the advantages of using Linux?

- What are the disadvantages?

- What kinds of Linux are there and how do I choose the one that fits me?

- What are the Open Source and GNU movements?

1.1 History

1.1.1 UNIX

In order to understand the popularity of Linux, we need to travel back in time, about 30 years ago...

Imagine computers as big as houses, even stadiums. While the sizes of those computers posed substantial problems, there was one thing that made this even worse: every computer had a different operating system. Software was always customized to serve a specific purpose, and software for one given system didn't run on another system. Being able to work with one system didn't automatically mean that you could work with another. It was difficult, both for the users and the system administrators.

Computers were extremely expensive then, and sacrifices had to be made even after the original purchase just to get the users to understand how they worked. The total cost per unit of computing power was enormous.

Technologically the world was not quite that advanced, so they had to live with the size for another decade. In 1969, a team of developers in the Bell Labs laboratories started working on a solution for the software problem, to address these compatibility issues. They developed a new operating system, which was

1. Simple and elegant.
2. Written in the C programming language instead of in assembly code.
3. Able to recycle code.

The Bell Labs developers named their project "UNIX."

The code recycling features were very important. Until then, all commercially available computer systems were written in a code specifically developed for one system. UNIX on the other hand needed only a small piece of that special code, which is now commonly named the kernel. This kernel is the only piece of code that needs to be adapted for every specific system and forms the base of the UNIX system. The operating system and all other functions were built around this kernel and written in a higher programming language, C. This language was especially developed for creating the UNIX system. Using this new technique, it was much easier to develop an operating system that could run on many different types of hardware.

The software vendors were quick to adapt, since they could sell ten times more software almost effortlessly. Weird new situations came in existence: imagine for instance computers from different vendors communicating in the same network, or users working on different systems without the need for extra education to use another computer. UNIX did a great deal to help users become compatible with different systems.

Throughout the next couple of decades the development of UNIX continued. More things became possible to do and more hardware and software vendors added support for UNIX to their products.

UNIX was initially found only in very large environments with mainframes and minicomputers (note that a PC is a "micro" computer). You had to work at a university, for the government or for large financial corporations in order to get your hands on a UNIX system.

But smaller computers were being developed, and by the end of the 80's, many people had home computers. By that time, there were several versions of UNIX available for the PC architecture, but none of them were truly free and more important: they were all terribly slow, so most people ran MS DOS or Windows 3.1 on their home PCs.

1.1.2 Linus and Linux

By the beginning of the 90s home PCs were finally powerful enough to run a full blown UNIX. Linus Torvalds, a young man studying computer science at the university of Helsinki, thought it would be a good idea to have some sort of freely available academic version of UNIX, and promptly started to code.

He started to ask questions, looking for answers and solutions that would help him get UNIX on his PC. Below is one of his first posts in comp.os.minix, dating from 1991:

```
From: torvalds@klaava.Helsinki.FI (Linus Benedict Torvalds)
Newsgroups: comp.os.minix
Subject: Gcc-1.40 and a posix-question
Message-ID: <1991Jul3.100050.9886@klaava.Helsinki.FI>
Date: 3 Jul 91 10:00:50 GMT
Hello netlanders,
Due to a project I'm working on (in minix), I'm interested in the posix
standard definition. Could somebody please point me to a (preferably)
machine-readable format of the latest posix rules? Ftp-sites would be nice.
```

From the start, it was Linus' goal to have a free system that was completely compliant with the original UNIX. That is why he asked for POSIX standards, POSIX still being the standard for UNIX.

In those days plug-and-play wasn't invented yet, but so many people were interested in having a UNIX system of their own, that this was only a small obstacle. New drivers became available for all kinds of new hardware, at a continuously rising speed. Almost as soon as a new piece of hardware became available, someone bought it and submitted it to the Linux test, as the system was gradually being called, releasing more free code for an ever wider range of hardware. These coders didn't stop at their PC's; every piece of hardware they could find was useful for Linux.

Back then, those people were called "nerds" or "freaks", but it didn't matter to them, as long as the supported hardware list grew longer and longer. Thanks to these people, Linux is now not only ideal to run on new PC's, but is also the system of choice for old and exotic hardware that would be useless if Linux didn't exist.

Two years after Linus' post, there were 12000 Linux users. The project, popular with hobbyists, grew steadily, all the while staying within the bounds of the POSIX standard. All the features of UNIX were added over the next couple of years, resulting in the mature operating system Linux has become today. Linux is a full UNIX clone, fit for use on workstations as well as on middle-range and high-end servers. Today, a lot of the important players on the hard- and software market each have their team of Linux developers; at your local dealer's you can even buy pre-installed Linux systems with official support - eventhough there is still a lot of hard- and software that is not supported, too.

1.1.3 Current application of Linux systems

Today Linux has joined the desktop market. Linux developers concentrated on networking and services in the beginning, and office applications have been the last barrier to be taken down. We don't like to admit that Microsoft is ruling this market, so plenty of alternatives have been started over the last couple of years to make Linux an acceptable choice as a workstation, providing an easy user interface and MS compatible office applications like word processors, spreadsheets, presentations and the like.

On the server side, Linux is well-known as a stable and reliable platform, providing database and trading services for companies like Amazon, the well-known online bookshop, US Post Office, the German army and such. Especially Internet providers and Internet service providers have grown fond of Linux as firewall, proxy- and web server, and you will find a Linux box within reach of every UNIX system administrator who appreciates a comfortable management station. Clusters of Linux machines are used in the creation of movies such as "Titanic", "Shrek" and others. In post offices, they are the nerve centers that route mail and in large search engine, clusters are used to perform internet searches.These are only a few of the thousands of heavy-duty jobs that Linux is performing day-to-day across the world.

It is also worth to note that modern Linux not only runs on workstations, mid- and high-end servers, but also on "gadgets" like PDA's, mobiles, a shipload of embedded applications and even on experimental wristwatches. This makes Linux the only operating system in the world covering such a wide range of hardware.

1.2 The user interface

1.2.1 Is Linux difficult?

Whether Linux is difficult to learn depends on the person you're asking. Experienced UNIX users will say no, because Linux is an ideal operating system for power-users and programmers, because it has been and is being developed by such people.

Everything a good programmer can wish for is available: compilers, libraries, development and debugging tools. These packages come with every standard Linux distribution. The C-compiler is included for free - as opposed to many UNIX distributions demanding licensing fees for this tool. All the documentation and manuals are there, and examples are often included to help you get started in no time. It feels like UNIX and switching between UNIX and Linux is a natural thing.

In the early days of Linux, being an expert was kind of required to start using the system. Those who mastered Linux felt better than the rest of the "lusers" who hadn't seen the light yet. It was common practice to tell a beginning user to "RTFM" (read the manuals). While the manuals were on every system, it was difficult to find the documentation, and even if someone did, explanations were in such technical terms that the new user became easily discouraged from learning the system.

The Linux-using community started to realize that if Linux was ever to be an important player on the operating system market, there had to be some serious changes in the accessibility of the system.

1.2.2 Linux for non-experienced users

Companies such as RedHat, SuSE and Mandriva have sprung up, providing packaged Linux distributions suitable for mass consumption. They integrated a great deal of graphical user interfaces (GUIs), developed by the community, in order to ease management of programs and services. As a Linux user today you have all the means of getting to know your system inside out, but it is no longer necessary to have that knowledge in order to make the system comply to your requests.

Nowadays you can log in graphically and start all required applications without even having to type a single character, while you still have the ability to access the core of the system if needed. Because of its structure, Linux allows a user to grow into the system: it equally fits new and experienced users. New users are not forced to do difficult things, while experienced users are not forced to work in the same way they did when they first started learning Linux.

While development in the service area continues, great things are being done for desktop users, generally considered as the group least likely to know how a system works. Developers of desktop applications are making incredible efforts to make the most beautiful desktops you've ever seen, or to make your Linux machine look just like your former MS Windows or MacIntosh workstation. The latest developments also include 3D acceleration support and support for USB devices, single-click updates of system and packages, and so on. Linux has these, and tries to present all available services in a logical form that ordinary people can understand. Below is a short list containing some great examples; these sites have a lot of screenshots that will give you a glimpse of what Linux on the desktop can be like:

- <http://www.gnome.org>
- <http://kde.org/screenshots/>
- <http://www.openoffice.org>
- <http://www.mozilla.org>

1.3 Does Linux have a future?

1.3.1 Open Source

The idea behind Open Source software is rather simple: when programmers can read, distribute and change code, the code will mature. People can adapt it, fix it, debug it, and they can do it at a speed that dwarfs the performance of software developers at conventional companies. This software will be more flexible and of a better quality than software that has been developed using the conventional channels, because more people have tested it in more different conditions than the closed software developer ever can.

The Open Source initiative started to make this clear to the commercial world, and very slowly, commercial vendors are starting to see the point. While lots of academics and technical people have already been convinced for 20 years now that this is the way to go, commercial vendors needed applications like the Internet to make them realize they can profit from Open Source. Now Linux has grown past the stage where it was almost exclusively an academic system, useful only to a handful of people with a technical background. Now Linux provides more than the operating system: there is an entire infrastructure supporting the chain of effort of creating an operating system, of making and testing programs for it, of bringing everything to the users, of supplying maintenance, updates and support and customizations, etcetera. Today, Linux is ready to accept the challenge of a fast-changing world.

1.3.2 Ten years of experience at your service

While Linux is probably the most well-known Open Source initiative, there is another project that contributed enormously to the popularity of the Linux operating system. This project is called SAMBA, and its achievement is the reverse engineering of the Server Message Block (SMB)/Common Internet File System (CIFS) protocol used for file- and print-serving on PC-related machines, natively supported by MS Windows NT and OS/2, and Linux. Packages are now available for almost every system and provide interconnection solutions in mixed environments using MS

Windows protocols: Windows-compatible (up to and includingWinXP) file- and print-servers.

Maybe even more successful than the SAMBA project is the Apache HTTP server project. The server runs on UNIX, Windows NT and many other operating systems. Originally known as "A PAtCHy server", based on existing code and a series of "patch files", the name for the matured code deserves to be connoted with the native American tribe of the Apache, well-known for their superior skills in warfare strategy and inexhaustible endurance. Apache has been shown to be substantially faster, more stable and more feature-full than many other web servers. Apache is run on sites that get millions of visitors per day, and while no official support is provided by the developers, the Apache user community provides answers to all your questions. Commercial support is now being provided by a number of third parties.

In the category of office applications, a choice of MS Office suite clones is available, ranging from partial to full implementations of the applications available on MS Windows workstations. These initiatives helped a great deal to make Linux acceptable for the desktop market, because the users don't need extra training to learn how to work with new systems. With the desktop comes the praise of the common users, and not only their praise, but also their specific requirements, which are growing more intricate and demanding by the day.

The Open Source community, consisting largely of people who have been contributing for over half a decade, assures Linux' position as an important player on the desktop market as well as in general IT application. Paid employees and volunteers alike are working diligently so that Linux can maintain a position in the market. The more users, the more questions. The Open Source community makes sure answers keep coming, and watches the quality of the answers with a suspicious eye, resulting in ever more stability and accessibility.

Listing all the available Linux software is beyond the scope of this guide, as there are tens of thousands of packages. Throughout this course we will present you with the most common packages, which are almost all freely available. In order to take away some of the fear of the beginning user, here's a screenshot of one of your most-wanted programs. You can see for yourself that no effort has been spared to make users who are switching from Windows feel at home:

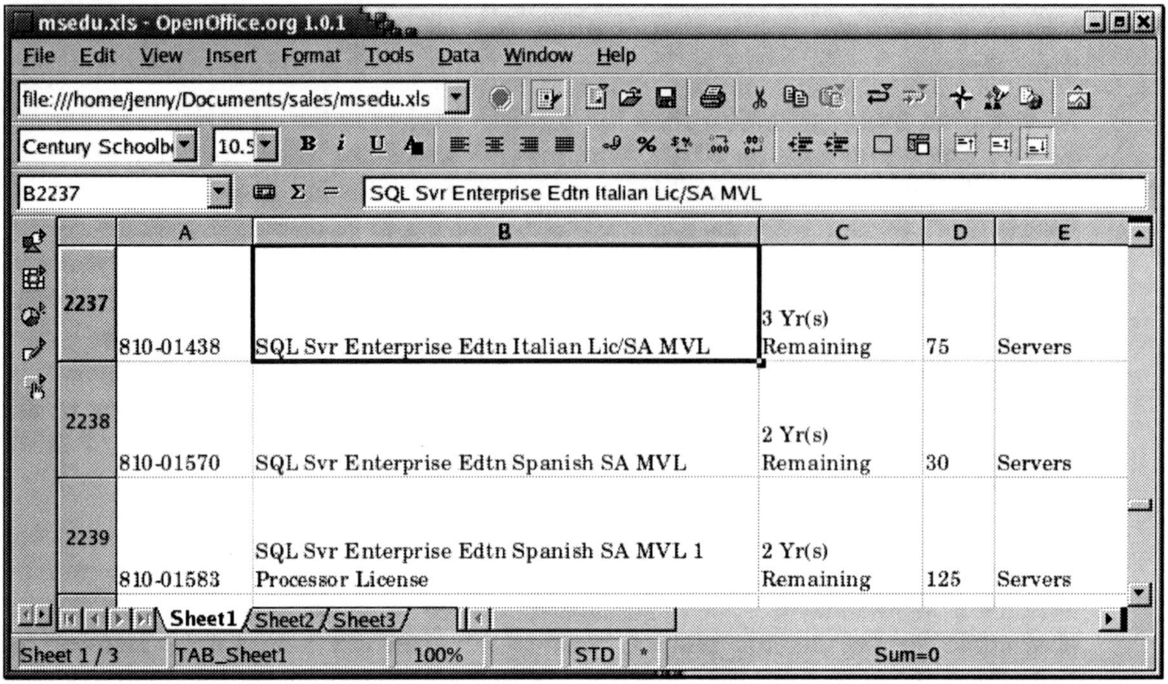

Figure 1.1. OpenOffice MS-compatible Spreadsheet

1.4   Properties of Linux

1.4.1 Linux Pros

A lot of the advantages of Linux are a consequence of Linux' origins, deeply rooted in UNIX, except for the first advantage, of course:

- Linux is free:

    As in free beer, they say. If you want to spend absolutely nothing, you don't even have to pay the price of a CD. Linux can be downloaded in its entirety from the Internet completely for free. No registration fees, no costs per user, free updates, and freely available source code in case you want to change the behavior of your system.

    Most of all, Linux is free as in free speech:

    The license commonly used is the GNU Public License (GPL). The license says that anybody who may want to do so, has the right to change Linux and eventually to redistribute a changed version, on the one condition that the code is still available after redistribution. In practice, you are free to grab a kernel image, for instance to add support for teletransportation machines or time travel and sell your new code, as long as your customers can still have a copy of that code.

- Linux is portable to any hardware platform:

A vendor who wants to sell a new type of computer and who doesn't know what kind of OS his new machine will run (say the CPU in your car or washing machine), can take a Linux kernel and make it work on his hardware, because documentation related to this activity is freely available.

- Linux was made to keep on running:

As with UNIX, a Linux system expects to run without rebooting all the time. That is why a lot of tasks are being executed at night or scheduled automatically for other calm moments, resulting in higher availability during busier periods and a more balanced use of the hardware. This property allows for Linux to be applicable also in environments where people don't have the time or the possibility to control their systems night and day.

- Linux is secure and versatile:

The security model used in Linux is based on the UNIX idea of security, which is known to be robust and of proven quality. But Linux is not only fit for use as a fort against enemy attacks from the Internet: it will adapt equally to other situations, utilizing the same high standards for security. Your development machine or control station will be as secure as your firewall.

- Linux is scalable:

From a Palmtop with 2 MB of memory to a petabyte storage cluster with hundreds of nodes: add or remove the appropriate packages and Linux fits all. You don't need a supercomputer anymore, because you can use Linux to do big things using the building blocks provided with the system. If you want to do little things, such as making an operating system for an embedded processor or just recycling your old 486, Linux will do that as well.

- The Linux OS and Linux applications have very short debug-times:

Because Linux has been developed and tested by thousands of people, both errors and people to fix them are usually found rather quickly. It sometimes happens that there are only a couple of hours between discovery and fixing of a bug.

1.4.2 Linux Cons

- There are far too many different distributions:

"Quot capites, tot rationes", as the Romans already said: the more people, the more opinions. At first glance, the amount of Linux distributions can be frightening, or ridiculous, depending on your point of view. But it also means that everyone will find what he or she needs. You don't need to be an expert to find a suitable release.

When asked, generally every Linux user will say that the best distribution is the specific version he is using. So which one should you choose? Don't worry too much about that: all releases contain more or less the same set of basic packages. On top of the basics, special third party software is added making, for example, TurboLinux more suitable for the small and medium enterprise, RedHat for servers and SuSE for workstations. However, the differences are likely to be very superficial. The best strategy is to test a couple of distributions; unfortunately not everybody has the time for this. Luckily, there is plenty of advice on the subject of choosing your Linux. A quick search on Google <http://www.google.com/linux>, using the keywords "choosing your distribution" brings up tens of links to good advise. The Installation HOWTO <http://www.tldp.org/HOWTO/Installation-HOWTO/> also discusses choosing your distribution.

- Linux is not very user friendly and confusing for beginners:

  It must be said that Linux, at least the core system, is less userfriendly to use than MS Windows and certainly more difficult than MacOS, but... In light of its popularity, considerable effort has been made to make Linux even easier to use, especially for new users. More information is being released daily, such as this guide, to help fill the gap for documentation available to users at all levels.

- Is an Open Source product trustworthy?

  How can something that is free also be reliable? Linux users have the choice whether to use Linux or not, which gives them an enormous advantage compared to users of proprietary software, who don't have that kind of freedom. After long periods of testing, most Linux users come to the conclusion that Linux is not only as good, but in many cases better and faster that the traditional solutions. If Linux were not trustworthy, it would have been long gone, never knowing the popularity it has now, with millions of users. Now users can influence their systems and share their remarks with the community, so the system gets better and better every day. It is a project that is never finished, that is true, but in an ever changing environment, Linux is also a project that continues to strive for perfection.

1.5   Linux Flavors

1.5.1 Linux and GNU

Although there are a large number of Linux implementations, you will find a lot of similarities in the different distributions, if only because every Linux machine is a box with building blocks that you may put together following your own needs and views. Installing the system is only the beginning of a longterm relationship. Just when you think you have a nice running system, Linux will stimulate your imagination and creativeness, and the more you realize what power the system can give you, the more you will try to redefine its limits.

Linux may appear different depending on the distribution, your hardware and personal taste, but the fundamentals on which all graphical and other interfaces are built, remain the same. The Linux system is based on GNU tools (Gnu's Not UNIX), which provide a set of standard ways to handle and use the system. All GNU tools are open source, so they can be installed on any system. Most distributions offer pre-compiled packages of most common tools, such as RPM packages on RedHat and Debian packages (also called deb or dpkg) on Debian, so you needn't be a programmer to install a package on your system. However, if you are and like doing things yourself, you will enjoy Linux all the better, since most distributions come with a complete set of development tools, allowing installation of new software purely from source code. This setup also allows you to install software even if it does not exist in a pre-packaged form suitable for your system.

A list of common GNU software:

- Bash: The GNU shell
- GCC: The GNU C Compiler
- GDB: The GNU Debugger
- Coreutils: a set of basic UNIX-style utilities, such as ls, cat and chmod
- Findutils: to search and find files
- Fontutils: to convert fonts from one format to another or make new fonts
- The Gimp: GNU Image Manipulation Program
- Gnome: the GNU desktop environment
- Emacs: a very powerful editor
- Ghostscript and Ghostview: interpreter and graphical frontend for PostScript files.

- GNU Photo: software for interaction with digital cameras

- Octave: a programming language, primarily intended to perform numerical computations and image processing.

- GNU SQL: relational database system

- Radius: a remote authentication and accounting server

- ...

Many commercial applications are available for Linux, and for more information about these packages we refer to their specific documentation. Throughout this guide we will only discuss freely available software, which comes (in most cases) with a GNU license.

To install missing or new packages, you will need some form of software management. The most common implementations include RPM and dpkg. RPM is the RedHat Package Manager, which is used on a variety of Linux systems, eventhough the name does not suggest this. Dpkg is the Debian package management system, which uses an interface called **apt-get**, that can manage RPM packages as well. Novell Ximian Red Carpet is a third party implementation of RPM with a graphical front-end. Other third party software vendors may have their own installation procedures, sometimes resembling the InstallShield and such, as known on MS Windows and other platforms. As you advance into Linux, you will likely get in touch with one or more of these programs.

1.5.2 GNU/Linux

The Linux kernel (the *bones* of your system, see Section 3.2.3.1) is not part of the GNU project but uses the same license as GNU software. A great majority of utilities and development tools (the *meat* of your system), which are not Linux-specific, are taken from the GNU project. Because any usable system must contain both the kernel and at least a minimal set of utilities, some people argue that such a system should be called a *GNU/Linux* system.

In order to obtain the highest possible degree of independence between distributions, this is the sort of Linux that we will discuss throughout this course. If we are not talking about a GNU/Linux system, the specific distribution, version or program name will be mentioned.

1.5.3 Which distribution should I install?

Prior to installation, the most important factor is your hardware. Since every Linux distribution contains the basic packages and can be built to meet almost any requirement (because they all use the Linux kernel), you only need to consider if the distribution will run on your hardware. LinuxPPC for example has been made to run on MacIntosh and other PowerPCs and does not run on an ordinary x86 based PC. LinuxPPC does run on the new Macs, but you can't use it for some of the older ones with ancient bus technology. Another tricky case is Sun hardware, which could be an old SPARC CPU or a newer UltraSparc, both requiring different versions of Linux.

Some Linux distributions are optimized for certain processors, such as Athlon CPUs, while they will at the same time run decent enough on the standard 486, 586 and 686 Intel processors. Sometimes distributions for special CPUs are not as reliable, since they are tested by fewer people.

Most Linux distributions offer a set of programs for generic PCs with special packages containing optimized kernels for the x86 Intel based CPUs. These distributions are well-tested and maintained on a regular basis, focusing on reliant server implementation and easy installation and update procedures. Examples are Debian, Ubuntu, Fedora, SuSE and Mandriva, which are by far the most popular Linux systems and generally considered easy to handle for the beginning user, while not blocking professionals from getting the most out of their Linux machines. Linux also runs decently on laptops and middle-range servers. Drivers for new hardware are included only after extensive testing, which adds to the stability of a system.

While the standard desktop might be Gnome on one system, another might offer KDE by default. Generally, both Gnome and KDE are available for all major Linux distributions. Other window and desktop managers are available for more advanced users.

The standard installation process allows users to choose between different basic setups, such as a workstation, where all packages needed for everyday use and development are installed, or a server installation, where different network services can be selected. Expert users can install every combination of packages they want during the initial installation process.

The goal of this guide is to apply to all Linux distributions. For your own convenience, however, it is strongly advised that beginners stick to a mainstream distribution, supporting all common hardware and applications by default. The following are very good choices for novices:

- Fedora Core <http://fedora.redhat.com/>

- Debian <http://www.debian.org/>

- SuSE Linux <http://www.suse.de/>

- Mandriva (former MandrakeSoft) <http://www.mandrake.com/>

- Knoppix <http://www.knoppix.com/>: an operating system that runs from your CD-ROM, you don't need to install anything.

Downloadable ISO-images can be obtained from LinuxISO.org <http://www.linuxiso.org/>. The main distributions can be purchased in any decent computer shop.

1.6 Summary

In this chapter, we learned that:

- Linux is an implementation of UNIX.

- The Linux operating system is written in the C programming language.

- "De gustibus et coloribus non disputandum est": there's a Linux for everyone.

- Linux uses GNU tools, a set of freely available standard tools for handling the operating system.

1.7 Exercises

A practical exercise for starters: install Linux on your PC. Read the installation manual for your distribution and/or the Installation HOWTO and do it.

 Read the docs!

Most errors stem from not reading the information provided during the install. Reading the installation messages carefully is the first step on the road to success.

Things you must know BEFORE starting a Linux installation:

- Will this distribution run on my hardware?

- Check with <http://www.ibiblio.org/mdw/HOWTO/Hardware-HOWTO/index.html> when in doubt about compatibility of your hardware.

- What kind of keyboard do I have (number of keys, layout)? What kind of mouse (serial/parallel, number of buttons)? How many MB of RAM?

- Will I install a basic workstation or a server, or will I need to select specific packages myself?

- Will I install from my hard disk, from a CD-ROM, or using the network? Should I adapt the BIOS for any of this? Does the installation method require a boot disk?

- Will Linux be the only system on this computer, or will it be a dual boot installation? Should I make a large partition in order to install virtual systems later on, or is this a virtual installation itself?

- Is this computer in a network? What is its hostname, IP address? Are there any gateway servers or other important networked machines my box should communicate with?

⚠ Linux expects to be networked

Not using the network or configuring it incorrectly may result in slow startup.

- Is this computer a gateway/router/firewall? (If you have to think about this question, it probably isn't.)

- Partitioning: let the installation program do it for you this time, we will discuss partitions in detail in Chapter 3. There is system-specific documentation available if you want to know everything about it. If your Linux distribution does not offer default partitioning, that probably means it is not suited for beginners.

- Will this machine start up in text mode or in graphical mode?

- Think of a good password for the administrator of this machine (root). Create a non-root user account (non-privileged access to the system).

- Do I need a rescue disk? (recommended)

- Which languages do I want?

The full checklist can be found at <http://www.ibiblio.org/mdw/HOWTO/Installation-HOWTO/index.html>.

In the following chapters we will find out if the installation has been successful.

Chapter 2
Quickstart

Abstract

In order to get the most out of this guide, we will immediately start with a practical chapter on connecting to the Linux system and doing some basic things.

We will discuss:

- Connecting to the system

- Disconnecting from the system

- Text and graphic mode

- Changing your password

- Navigating through the file system

- Determining file type

- Looking at text files

- Finding help

2.1 Logging in, activating the user interface and logging out

2.1.1 Introduction

In order to work on a Linux system directly, you will need to provide a user name and password. You always need to authenticate to the system. As we already mentioned in the exercise from Chapter 1, most PC-based Linux systems have two basic modes for a system to run in: either quick and sober in text console mode, which looks like DOS with mouse, multitasking and multi-user features, or in graphical mode, which looks better but eats more system resources.

2.1.2 Graphical mode

This is the default nowadays on most desktop computers. You know you will connect to the system using graphical mode when you are first asked for your user name, and then, in a new window, to type your password.

To log in, make sure the mouse pointer is in the login window, provide your user name and password to the system and click OK or press **Enter**.

Careful with that root account!

It is generally considered a bad idea to connect (graphically) using the *root* user name, the system adminstrator's account, since the use of graphics includes running a lot of extra programs, in root's case with a lot of extra permissions. To keep all risks as low as possible, use a normal user account to connect graphically. But there are enough risks to keep this in mind as a general advice, for all use of the root account: only log in as root when extra privileges are required.

After entering your user name/password combination, it can take a little while before the graphical environment is started, depending on the CPU speed of your computer, on the software you use and on your personal settings.

To continue, you will need to open a *terminal window* or *xterm* for short (X being the name for the underlying software supporting the graphical environment). This program can be found in the Applications->Utilities, System Tools or Internet menu, depending on what window manager you are using. There might be icons that you can use as a shortcut to get an xterm window as well, and clicking the right mouse button on the desktop background will usually present you with a menu containing a terminal window application.

While browsing the menus, you will notice that a lot of things can be done without entering commands via the keyboard. For most users, the good old point-'n'-click method of dealing with the computer will do. But this guide is for future network and system administrators, who will need to meddle with the heart of the system. They need a stronger tool than a mouse to handle all the tasks they will face. This tool is the shell, and when in graphical mode, we activate our shell by opening a terminal window.

The terminal window is your control panel for the system. Almost everything that follows is done using this simple but powerful text tool. A terminal window should always show a command prompt when you open one. This terminal shows a standard prompt, which displays the user's login name, and the current working directory, represented by the twiddle (~):

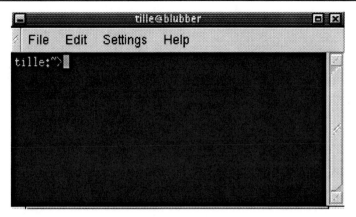

Figure 2.1. Terminal window

Another common form for a prompt is this one:

```
[user@host dir]
```

In the above example, *user* will be your login name, *hosts* the name of the machine you are working on, and *dir* an indication of your current location in the file system.

Later we will discuss prompts and their behavior in detail. For now, it suffices to know that prompts can display all kinds of information, but that they are not part of the commands you are giving to your system.

To disconnect from the system in graphical mode, you need to close all terminal windows and other applications. After that, hit the logout icon or find Log Out in the menu. Closing everything is not really necessary, and the system can do this for you, but session management might put all currently open applications back on your screen when you connect again, which takes longer and is not always the desired effect. However, this behavior is configurable.

When you see the login screen again, asking to enter user name and password, logout was successful.

 Gnome or KDE?

We mentioned both the Gnome and KDE desktops already a couple of times. These are the two most popular ways of managing your desktop, although there are many, many others. Whatever deskop you chose to work with is fine - as long as you know how to open a terminal window. However, we will continue to refer to both Gnome and KDE for the most popular ways of achieving certain tasks.

2.1.3 Text mode

You know you're in text mode when the whole screen is black, showing (in most cases white) characters. A text mode login screen typically shows some information about the machine you are working on, the name of the machine and a prompt waiting for you to log in:

```
RedHat Linux Release 8.0 (Psyche)

blast login: _
```

The login is different from a graphical login, in that you have to hit the **Enter** key after providing your user name, because there are no buttons on the screen that you can click with the mouse. Then you should type your password, followed by another **Enter**. You won't see any indication that you are entering something, not even an asterisk, and you won't see the cursor move. But this is normal on Linux and is done for security reasons.

When the system has accepted you as a valid user, you may get some more information, called the *message of the day*, which can be anything. Additionally, it is popular on UNIX systems to display a fortune cookie, which contains some general wise or unwise (this is up to you) thoughts. After that, you will be given a shell, indicated with the same prompt that you would get in graphical mode.

Don't log in as root

Also in text mode: log in as root only to do setup and configuration that absolutely requires administrator privileges, such as adding users, installing software packages, and performing network and other system configuration. Once you are finished, immediately leave the special account and resume your work as a non-privileged user. Alternatively, some systems, like Ubuntu, force you to use **sudo**, so that you do not need direct access to the administrative account.

Logging out is done by entering the **logout** command, followed by **Enter**. You are successfully disconnected from the system when you see the login screen again.

The power button

While Linux was not meant to be shut off without application of the proper procedures for halting the system, hitting the power button is equivalent to starting those procedures *on newer systems*. However, powering off an old system without going through the halting process might cause severe damage! If you want to be sure, always use the Shut down option when you log out from the graphical interface, or, when on the login screen (where you have to give your user name and password) look around for a shutdown button.

Now that we know how to connect to and disconnect from the system, we're ready for our first commands.

2.2 Absolute basics

2.2.1 The commands

These are the quickies, which we need to get started; we will discuss them later in more detail.

Command	Meaning
ls	Displays a list of files in the current working directory, like the **dir** command in DOS
cd `directory`	change directories
passwd	change the password for the current user
file `filename`	display file type of file with name `filename`
cat `textfile`	throws content of `textfile` on the screen
pwd	display present working directory
exit or logout	leave this session
man `command`	read man pages on **command**
info `command`	read Info pages on **command**
apropos `string`	search the *whatis* database for strings

Table 2.1. Quickstart commands

2.2.2 General remarks

You type these commands after the prompt, in a terminal window in graphical mode or in text mode, followed by **Enter**.

Commands can be issued by themselves, such as **ls**. A command behaves different when you specify an *option*, usually preceded with a dash (-), as in **ls -a**. The same option character may have a different meaning for another command. GNU programs take long options, preceded by two dashes (--), like **ls --all**. Some commands have no options.

The argument(s) to a command are specifications for the object(s) on which you want the command to take effect. An example is **ls** */etc*, where the directory /etc is the argument to the **ls** command. This indicates that you want to see the content of that directory, instead of the default, which would be the content of the current directory, obtained by just typing **ls** followed by **Enter**. Some commands require arguments, sometimes arguments are optional.

You can find out whether a command takes options and arguments, and which ones are valid, by checking the online help for that command, see Section 2.3.

In Linux, like in UNIX, directories are separated using forward slashes, like the ones used in web addresses (URLs). We will discuss directory structure in-depth later.

The symbols . and .. have special meaning when directories are concerned. We will try to find out about those during the exercises, and more in the next chapter.

Try to avoid logging in with or using the system administrator's account, *root*. Besides doing your normal work, most tasks, including checking the system, collecting information etc., can be executed using a normal user account with no special permissions at all. If needed, for instance when creating a new user or installing new software, the preferred way of obtaining root access is by switching user IDs, see Section 3.2.1 for an example.

Almost all commands in this book can be executed without system administrator privileges. In most cases, when issuing a command or starting a program as a non-privileged user, the system will warn you or prompt you for the root password when root access is required. Once you're done, leave the application or session that gives you root privileges immediately.

Reading documentation should become your second nature. Especially in the beginning, it is important to read system documentation, manuals for basic commands, HOWTOs and so on. Since the amount of documentation is so enormous, it is impossible to include all related documentation. This book will try to guide you to the most appropriate documentation on every subject discussed, in order to stimulate the habit of reading the man pages.

2.2.3 Using Bash features

Several special key combinations allow you to do things easier and faster with the GNU shell, Bash, which is the default on almost any Linux system, see Section 3.2.3.2. Below is a list of the most commonly used features; you are strongly suggested to make a habit out of using them, so as to get the most out of your Linux experience from the very beginning.

Key or key combination	Function
Ctrl+A	Move cursor to the beginning of the command line.
Ctrl+C	End a running program and return the prompt, see Chapter 4.

Key or key combination	Function
Ctrl+D	Log out of the current shell session, equal to typing **exit** or **logout**.
Ctrl+E	Move cursor to the end of the command line.
Ctrl+H	Generate backspace character.
Ctrl+L	Clear this terminal.
Ctrl+R	Search command history, see Section 3.3.3.4.
Ctrl+Z	Suspend a program, see Chapter 4.
ArrowLeft and ArrowRight	Move the cursor one place to the left or right on the command line, so that you can insert characters at other places than just at the beginning and the end.
ArrowUp and ArrowDown	Browse history. Go to the line that you want to repeat, edit details if necessary, and press **Enter** to save time.
Shift+PageUp and Shift+PageDown	Browse terminal buffer (to see text that has "scrolled off" the screen).
Tab	Command or filename completion; when multiple choices are possible, the system will either signal with an audio or visual bell, or, if too many choices are possible, ask you if you want to see them all.
TabTab	Shows file or command completion possibilities.

Table 2.2. Key combinations in Bash

The last two items in the above table may need some extra explanantions. For instance, if you want to change into the directory directory_with_a_very_long_name, you are not going to type that very long name, no. You just type on the command line **cd dir**, then you press **Tab** and the shell completes the name for you, if no other files are starting with the same three characters. Of course, if there are no other items starting with "d", then you might just as wel type **cd d** and then **Tab**. If more than one file starts with the same characters, the shell will signal this to you, upon which you can hit **Tab** twice with short interval, and the shell presents the choices you have:

```
your_prompt> cd st
starthere       stuff           stuffit
```

In the above example, if you type "a" after the first two characters and hit **Tab** again, no other possibilities are left, and the shell completes the directory name, without you having to type the string "rthere":

```
your_prompt> cd starthere
```

Of course, you'll still have to hit **Enter** to accept this choice.

In the same example, if you type "u", and then hit **Tab**, the shell will add the "ff" for you, but then it protests again, because multiple choices are possible. If you type **Tab Tab** again, you'll see the choices; if you type one or more characters that make the choice unambiguous to the system, and **Tab** again, or **Enter** when you've reach the end of the file name that you want to choose, the shell completes the file name and changes you into that directory - if indeed it is a directory name.

This works for all file names that are arguments to commands.

The same goes for command name completion. Typing **ls** and then hitting the **Tab** key twice, lists all the commands in your PATH (see Section 3.2.1) that start with these two characters:

```
your_prompt> ls
ls             lsdev      lspci      lsraid        lsw
lsattr         lsmod      lspgpot    lss16toppm
lsb_release    lsof       lspnp      lsusb
```

2.3 Getting help

2.3.1 Be warned

GNU/Linux is all about becoming more self-reliant. And as usual with this system, there are several ways to achieve the goal. A common way of getting help is finding someone who knows, and however patient and peace-loving the Linux-using community will be, almost everybody will expect you to have tried one or more of the methods in this section before asking them, and the ways in which this viewpoint is expressed may be rather harsh if you prove not to have followed this basic rule.

2.3.2 The man pages

A lot of beginning users fear the man (manual) pages, because they are an overwhelming source of documentation. They are, however, very structured, as you will see from the example below on: **man man**.

Reading man pages is usually done in a terminal window when in graphical mode, or just in text mode if you prefer it. Type the command like this at the prompt, followed by **Enter**:

```
yourname@yourcomp ~> man man
```

The documentation for **man** will be displayed on your screen after you press **Enter**:

```
man(1)                                                            man(1)



NAME
 man - format and display the on-line manual pages
 manpath - determine user's search path for man pages

SYNOPSIS
 man [-acdfFhkKtwW] [--path] [-m system] [-p string] [-C config_file]
 [-M pathlist] [-P pager] [-S section_list] [section] name ...


DESCRIPTION
 man formats and displays the on-line manual pages.  If you specify
 section, man only looks in that section of the manual.
 name is normally the name of the manual page, which is typically the
 name of a  command, function, or file.  However, if name contains a
 slash (/) then man interprets it as a file specification, so that you
 can do man ./foo.5 or even man /cd/foo/bar.1.gz.

 See  below  for  a  description  of where man looks for the manual
 page files.

OPTIONS
 -C  config_file
lines 1-27
```

Browse to the next page using the space bar. You can go back to the previous page using the b-key. When you reach the end, **man** will usually quit and you get the prompt back. Type **q** if you want to leave the man page before reaching the end, or if the viewer does not quit automatically at the end of the page.

Pagers

The available key combinations for manipulating the man pages depend on the *pager* used in your distribution. Most distributions use **less** to view the man pages and to scroll around. See Section 3.3.4.2 for more info on pagers.

Each man page usually contains a couple of standard sections, as we can see from the **man man** example:

- The first line contains the name of the command you are reading about, and the id of the section in which this man page is located. The man pages are ordered in chapters. Commands are likely to have multiple man pages, for example the man page from the user section, the man page from the system admin section, and the man page from the programmer section.

- The name of the command and a short description are given, which is used for building an index of the man pages. You can look for any given search string in this index using the **apropos** command.

- The synopsis of the command provides a technical notation of all the options and/or arguments this command can take. You can think of an option as a way of executing the command. The argument is what you execute it on. Some commands have no options or no arguments. Optional options and arguments are put in between "[" and "]" to indicate that they can be left out.

- A longer description of the command is given.

- Options with their descriptions are listed. Options can usually be combined. If not so, this section will tell you about it.

- Environment describes the shell variables that influence the behavior of this command (not all commands have this).

- Sometimes sections specific to this command are provided.

- A reference to other man pages is given in the "SEE ALSO" section. In between parentheses is the number of the man page section in which to find this command. Experienced users often switch to the "SEE ALSO" part using the / command followed by the search string SEE and press **Enter**.

- Usually there is also information about known bugs (anomalies) and where to report new bugs you may find.

- There might also be author and copyright information.

Some commands have multiple man pages. For instance, the **passwd** command has a man page in section 1 and another in section 5. By default, the man page with the lowest number is shown. If you want to see another section than the default, specify it after the **man** command:

```
man 5 passwd
```

If you want to see all man pages about a command, one after the other, use the -a to man:

```
man -a passwd
```

This way, when you reach the end of the first man page and press **SPACE** again, the man page from the next section will be displayed.

2.3.3 More info

2.3.3.1 The Info pages

In addition to the man pages, you can read the Info pages about a command, using the **info** command. These usually contain more recent information and are somewhat easier to use. The man pages for some commands refer to the Info pages.

Get started by typing **info** *info* in a terminal window:

```
File: info.info,  Node: Top,  Next: Getting Started,  Up: (dir)

Info: An Introduction
*********************

   Info is a program, which you are using now, for reading
documentation of computer programs.  The GNU Project distributes most
of its on-line manuals in the Info format, so you need a program called
"Info reader" to read the manuals.  One of such programs you are using
now.

   If you are new to Info and want to learn how to use it, type the
command `h' now.  It brings you to a programmed instruction sequence.

   To learn advanced Info commands, type `n' twice.  This brings you to
`Info for Experts', skipping over the `Getting Started' chapter.

* Menu:

* Getting Started::          Getting started using an Info reader.
* Advanced Info::            Advanced commands within Info.
* Creating an Info File::    How to make your own Info file.
--zz-Info: (info.info.gz)Top, 24 lines --Top----------------------------
Welcome to Info version 4.2. Type C-h for help, m for menu item.
```

Use the arrow keys to browse through the text and move the cursor on a line starting with an asterisk, containing the keyword about which you want info, then hit **Enter**. Use the **P** and **N** keys to go to the previous or next subject. The space bar will move you one page further, no matter whether this starts a new subject or an Info page for another command. Use **Q** to quit. The **info** program has more information.

2.3.3.2 The whatis and apropos commands

A short index of explanations for commands is available using the **whatis** command, like in the examples below:

```
[your_prompt] whatis ls
ls                  (1)  - list directory contents
```

This displays short information about a command, and the first section in the collection of man pages that contains an appropriate page.

If you don't know where to get started and which man page to read, **apropos** gives more information. Say that you don't know how to start a browser, then you could enter the following command:

```
another prompt> apropos browser
Galeon [galeon](1)  - gecko-based GNOME web browser
lynx            (1)  - a general purpose distributed information browser
                      for the World Wide Web
ncftp           (1)  - Browser program for the File Transfer Protocol
opera           (1)  - a graphical web browser
pilot           (1)  - simple file system browser in the style of the
                      Pine Composer
pinfo           (1)  - curses based lynx-style info browser
pinfo [pman]    (1)  - curses based lynx-style info browser
viewres         (1x) - graphical class browser for Xt
```

After pressing **Enter** you will see that a lot of browser related stuff is on your machine: not only web browsers, but also file and FTP browsers, and browsers for documentation. If you have development packages installed, you may also have the accompanying man pages dealing with writing programs having to do with browsers. Generally, a command with a man page in section one, so one marked with "(1)", is suitable for trying out as a user. The user who issued the above **apropos** might consequently try to start the commands **galeon**, **lynx** or **opera**, since these clearly have to do with browsing the world wide web.

2.3.3.3   The --help option

Most GNU commands support the `--help`, which gives a short explanation about how to use the command and a list of available options. Below is the output of this option with the **cat** command:

```
userprompt@host: cat --help
Usage: cat [OPTION] [FILE]...
Concatenate FILE(s), or standard input, to standard output.

  -A, --show-all            equivalent to -vET
  -b, --number-nonblank     number nonblank output lines
  -e                        equivalent to -vE
  -E, --show-ends           display $ at end of each line
  -n, --number              number all output lines
  -s, --squeeze-blank       never more than one single blank line
  -t                        equivalent to -vT
  -T, --show-tabs           display TAB characters as ^I
  -u                        (ignored)
  -v, --show-nonprinting    use ^ and M- notation, except for LFD and TAB
      --help      display this help and exit
      --version   output version information and exit

With no FILE, or when FILE is -, read standard input.

Report bugs to <bug-textutils@gnu.org>.
```

2.3.3.4   Graphical help

Don't despair if you prefer a graphical user interface. Konqueror, the default KDE file manager, provides painless and colourful access to the man and Info pages. You may want to try "info:info" in the *Location* address bar, and you will get a browsable Info page about the **info** command. Similarly, "man:ls" will present you with the man page for the **ls** command. You even get command name completion: you will see the man pages for all the commands starting with "ls" in a scroll-down menu. Entering "info:/dir" in the address location toolbar displays all the Info pages, arranged in utility categories. Excellent Help content, including the Konqueror Handbook. Start up from the menu or by typing the command **konqueror** in a terminal window, followed by **Enter**; see the screenshot below.

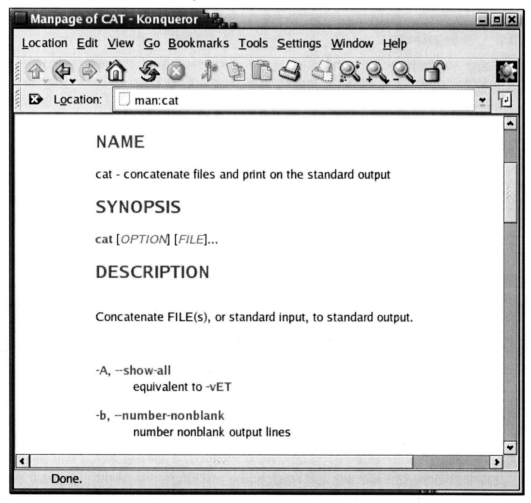

Figure 2.2. Konqueror as help browser

The Gnome Help Browser is very user friendly as well. You can start it selecting Applications->Help from the Gnome menu, by clicking the lifeguard icon on your desktop or by entering the command **gnome-help** in a terminal window. The system documentation and man pages are easily browsable with a plain interface.

The **nautilus** file manager provides a searchable index of the man and Info pages, they are easily browsable and interlinked. Nautilus is started from the command line, or clicking your home directory icon, or from the Gnome menu.

The big advantage of GUIs for system documentation is that all information is completely interlinked, so you can click through in the "SEE ALSO" sections and wherever links to other man pages appear, and thus browse and acquire knowledge without interruption for hours at the time.

2.3.3.5   Exceptions

Some commands don't have separate documentation, because they are part of another command. **cd**, **exit**, **logout** and **pwd** are such exceptions. They are part of your shell program and are called *shell built-in* commands. For information about these, refer to the man or info page of your shell. Most beginning Linux users have a Bash shell. See Section 3.2.3.2 for more about shells.

If you have been changing your original system configuration, it might also be possible that man pages are still there, but not visible because your shell environment has changed. In that case, you will need to check the MANPATH variable. How to do this is explained in Section 7.2.1.2.

Some programs or packages only have a set of instructions or references in the directory /usr/share/doc. See Section 3.3.4 to display.

In the worst case, you may have removed the documentation from your system by accident (hopefully by accident, because it is a very bad idea to do this on purpose). In that case, first try to make sure that there is really nothing appropriate left using a search tool, read on in Section 3.3.3. If so, you may have to re-install the package that contains the command to which the documentation applied, see Section 7.5.

2.4   Summary

Linux traditionally operates in text mode or in graphical mode. Since CPU power and RAM are not the cost anymore these days, every Linux user can afford to work in graphical mode and will usually do so. This does not mean that you don't have to know about text mode: we will work in the text environment throughout this course, using a terminal window.

Linux encourages its users to acquire knowledge and to become independent. Inevitably, you will have to read a lot of documentation to achieve that goal; that is why, as you will notice, we refer to extra documentation for almost every command, tool and problem listed in this book. The more docs you read, the easier it will become and the faster you will leaf through manuals. Make reading documentation a habit as soon as possible. When you don't know the answer to a problem, refering to the documentation should become a second nature.

We already learned some commands:

These are the quickies, which we need to get started; we will discuss them later in more detail.

Command	Meaning
apropos	Search information about a command or subject.
cat	Show content of one or more files.
cd	Change into another directory.
exit	Leave a shell session.
file	Get information about the content of a file.
info	Read Info pages about a command.
logout	Leave a shell session.
ls	List directory content.
man	Read manual pages of a command.
passwd	Change your password.
pwd	Display the current working directory.

Table 2.3. New commands in Chapter 2: Basics

2.5 Exercises

Most of what we learn is by making mistakes and by seeing how things can go wrong. These exercises are made to get you to read some error messages. The order in which you do these exercises is important.

Don't forget to use the Bash features on the command line: try to do the exercises typing as few characters as possible!

2.5.1 Connecting and disconnecting

- Determine whether you are working in text or in graphical mode.

I am working in text/graphical mode. (cross out what's not applicable)

- Log in with the user name and password you made for yourself during the installation.

- Log out.

- Log in again, using a non-existent user name

  -> What happens?

2.5.2 Passwords

Log in again with your user name and password.

- Change your password into *P6p3.aa!* and hit the **Enter** key.

  -> What happens?

- Try again, this time enter a password that is ridiculously easy, like *123* or *aaa*.

  -> What happens?

- Try again, this time don't enter a password but just hit the **Enter** key.

  -> What happens?

- Try the command **psswd** instead of **passwd**

  -> What happens?

New password

Unless you change your password back again to what it was before this exercise, it will be "P6p3.aa!". Change your password after this exercise!

Note that some systems might not allow to recycle passwords, i.e. restore the original one within a certain amount of time or a certain amount of password changes, or both.

2.5.3 Directories

These are some exercises to help you get the feel.

- Enter the command **cd blah**

  -> What happens?

- Enter the command **cd ..**

  Mind the space between "cd" and ".."! Use the **pwd** command.

-> What happens?

- List the directory contents with the **ls** command.

  -> What do you see?

  -> What do you think these are?

  -> Check using the **pwd** command.

- Enter the **cd** command.

  -> What happens?

- Repeat step 2 two times.

  -> What happens?

- Display the content of this directory.

- Try the command **cd root**

  -> What happens?

  -> To which directories do you have access?

- Repeat step 4.

Do you know another possibility to get where you are now?

2.5.4 Files

- Change directory to / and then to etc. Type **ls**; if the output is longer than your screen, make the window longer, or try **Shift+PageUp** and **Shift+PageDown**.

  The file inittab contains the answer to the first question in this list. Try the **file** command on it.

  -> The file type of my inittab is .....

- Use the command **cat inittab** and read the file.

  -> What is the default mode of your computer?

- Return to your home directory using the **cd** command.

- Enter the command **file .**

  -> Does this help to find the meaning of "."?

- Can you look at "." using the **cat** command?

- Display help for the **cat** program, using the `--help` option. Use the option for numbering of output lines to count how many users are listed in the file `/etc/passwd`.

2.5.5 Getting help

- Read **man** *intro*

- Read **man** *ls*

- Read **info** *passwd*

- Enter the **apropos pwd** command.

- Try **man** or **info** on **cd**.

  -> How would you find out more about **cd**?

- Read **ls** `--help` and try it out.

Chapter 3
About files and the file system

Abstract

After the initial exploration in Chapter 2, we are ready to discuss the files and directories on a Linux system in more detail. Many users have difficulties with Linux because they lack an overview of what kind of data is kept in which locations. We will try to shine some light on the organization of files in the file system.

We will also list the most important files and directories and use different methods of viewing the content of those files, and learn how files and directories can be created, moved and deleted.

After completion of the exercises in this chapter, you will be able to:

- Describe the layout of a Linux file system
- Display and set paths
- Describe the most important files, including kernel and shell
- Find lost and hidden files
- Create, move and delete files and directories
- Display contents of files
- Understand and use different link types
- Find out about file properties and change file permissions

3.1 General overview of the Linux file system

3.1.1 Files

3.1.1.1 General

A simple description of the UNIX system, also applicable to Linux, is this:

"On a UNIX system, everything is a file; if something is not a file, it is a process."

This statement is true because there are special files that are more than just files (named pipes and sockets, for instance), but to keep things simple, saying that everything is a file is an acceptable generalization. A Linux system, just like UNIX, makes no difference between a file and a directory, since a directory is just a file containing names of other files. Programs, services, texts, images, and so forth, are all files. Input and output devices, and generally all devices, are considered to be files, according to the system.

In order to manage all those files in an orderly fashion, man likes to think of them in an ordered tree-like structure on the hard disk, as we know from MS-DOS (Disk Operating System) for instance. The large branches contain more branches, and the branches at the end contain the tree's leaves or normal files. For now we will use this image of the tree, but we will find out later why this is not a fully accurate image.

3.1.1.2   Sorts of files

Most files are just files, called *regular* files; they contain normal data, for example text files, executable files or programs, input for or output from a program and so on.

While it is reasonably safe to suppose that everything you encounter on a Linux system is a file, there are some exceptions.

- *Directories*: files that are lists of other files.

- *Special files*: the mechanism used for input and output. Most special files are in /dev, we will discuss them later.

- *Links*: a system to make a file or directory visible in multiple parts of the system's file tree. We will talk about links in detail.

- *(Domain) sockets*: a special file type, similar to TCP/IP sockets, providing inter-process networking protected by the file system's access control.

- *Named pipes*: act more or less like sockets and form a way for processes to communicate with each other, without using network socket semantics.

The -l option to **ls** displays the file type, using the first character of each input line:

```
jaime:~/Documents> ls -l
total 80
-rw-rw-r--   1 jaime    jaime    31744 Feb 21 17:56 intro Linux.doc
-rw-rw-r--   1 jaime    jaime    41472 Feb 21 17:56 Linux.doc
drwxrwxr-x   2 jaime    jaime     4096 Feb 25 11:50 course
```

This table gives an overview of the characters determining the file type:

Symbol	Meaning
-	Regular file
d	Directory
l	Link
c	Special file
s	Socket
p	Named pipe
b	Block device

Table 3.1. File types in a long list

In order not to always have to perform a long listing for seeing the file type, a lot of systems by default don't issue just **ls**, but **ls -F**, which suffixes file names with one of the characters "/=*|@" to indicate the file type. To make it extra easy on the beginning user, both the -F and --color options are usually combined, see Section 3.3.1.1. We will use **ls -F** throughout this document for better readability.

As a user, you only need to deal directly with plain files, executable files, directories and links. The special file types are there for making your system do what you demand from it and are dealt with by system administrators and programmers.

Now, before we look at the important files and directories, we need to know more about partitions.

3.1.2 About partitioning

3.1.2.1 Why partition?

Most people have a vague knowledge of what partitions are, since every operating system has the ability to create or remove them. It may seem strange that Linux uses more than one partition on the same disk, even when using the standard installation procedure, so some explanation is called for.

One of the goals of having different partitions is to achieve higher data security in case of disaster. By dividing the hard disk in partitions, data can be grouped and separated. When an accident occurs, only the data in the partition that got the hit will be damaged, while the data on the other partitions will most likely survive.

This principle dates from the days when Linux didn't have journaled file systems and power failures might have lead to disaster. The use of partitions remains for security and robustness reasons, so a breach on one part of the system doesn't automatically mean that the whole computer is in danger. This is currently the most important reason for partitioning. A simple example: a user creates a script, a program or a web application that starts filling up the disk. If the disk contains only one big partition, the entire system will stop functioning if the disk is full. If the user stores the data on a separate partition, then only that (data) partition will be affected, while the system partitions and possible other data partitions keep functioning.

Mind that having a journaled file system only provides data security in case of power failure and sudden disconnection of storage devices. This does not protect your data against bad blocks and logical errors in the file system. In those cases, you should use a RAID (Redundant Array of Inexpensive Disks) solution.

3.1.2.2   Partition layout and types

There are two kinds of major partitions on a Linux system:

- *data partition*: normal Linux system data, including the *root partition* containing all the data to start up and run the system; and

- *swap partition*: expansion of the computer's physical memory, extra memory on hard disk.

Most systems contain a root partition, one or more data partitions and one or more swap partitions. Systems in mixed environments may contain partitions for other system data, such as a partition with a FAT or VFAT file system for MS Windows data.

Most Linux systems use **fdisk** at installation time to set the partition type. As you may have noticed during the exercise from Chapter 1, this usually happens automatically. On some occasions, however, you may not be so lucky. In such cases, you will need to select the partition type manually and even manually do the actual partitioning. The standard Linux partitions have number 82 for swap and 83 for data, which can be journaled (ext3) or normal (ext2, on older systems). The **fdisk** utility has built-in help, should you forget these values.

Apart from these two, Linux supports a variety of other file system types, such as the relatively new Reiser file system, JFS, NFS, FATxx and many other file systems natively available on other (proprietary) operating systems.

The standard root partition (indicated with a single forward slash, /) is about 100-500 MB, and contains the system configuration files, most basic commands and server programs, system libraries, some temporary space and the home directory of the administrative user. A standard installation requires about 250 MB for the root partition.

Swap space (indicated with *swap*) is only accessible for the system itself, and is hidden from view during normal operation. Swap is the system that ensures, like on normal UNIX systems, that you can keep on working, whatever happens. On Linux, you will virtually never see irritating messages like *Out of memory, please close some applications first and try again*, because of this extra memory. The swap or virtual memory procedure has long been adopted by operating systems outside the UNIX world by now.

Using memory on a hard disk is naturally slower than using the real memory chips of a computer, but having this little extra is a great comfort. We will learn more about swap when we discuss processes in Chapter 4.

Linux generally counts on having twice the amount of physical memory in the form of swap space on the hard disk. When installing a system, you have to know how you are going to do this. An example on a system with 512 MB of RAM:

- 1st possibility: one swap partition of 1 GB
- 2nd possibility: two swap partitions of 512 MB
- 3rd possibility: with two hard disks: 1 partition of 512 MB on each disk.

The last option will give the best results when a lot of I/O is to be expected.

Read the software documentation for specific guidelines. Some applications, such as databases, might require more swap space. Others, such as some handheld systems, might not have any swap at all by lack of a hard disk. Swap space may also depend on your kernel version.

The kernel is on a separate partition as well in many distributions, because it is the most important file of your system. If this is the case, you will find that you also have a */boot* partition, holding your kernel(s) and accompanying data files.

The rest of the hard disk(s) is generally divided in data partitions, although it may be that all of the non-system critical data resides on one partition, for example when you perform a standard workstation installation. When non-critical data is separated on different partitions, it usually happens following a set pattern:

- a partition for user programs (*/usr*)
- a partition containing the users' personal data (*/home*)
- a partition to store temporary data like print- and mail-queues (*/var*)
- a partition for third party and extra software (*/opt*)

Once the partitions are made, you can only add more. Changing sizes or properties of existing partitions is possible but not advisable.

The division of hard disks into partitions is determined by the system administrator. On larger systems, he or she may even spread one partition over several hard disks, using the appropriate software. Most distributions allow for standard setups optimized for workstations (average users) and for general server purposes, but also accept customized partitions. During the installation process you can define your own partition layout using either your distribution specific tool, which is usually a straight forward graphical interface, or **fdisk**, a text-based tool for creating partitions and setting their properties.

A workstation or client installation is for use by mainly one and the same person. The selected software for installation reflects this and the stress is on common user packages, such as nice desktop themes, development tools, client programs for E-mail, multimedia software, web and other services. Everything is put together on one large partition, swap space twice the amount of RAM is added and your generic workstation is complete, providing the largest amount of disk space possible for personal use, but with the disadvantage of possible data integrity loss during problem situations.

On a server, system data tends to be separate from user data. Programs that offer services are kept in a different place than the data handled by this service. Different partitions will be created on such systems:

- a partition with all data necessary to boot the machine
- a partition with configuration data and server programs
- one or more partitions containing the server data such as database tables, user mails, an ftp archive etc.
- a partition with user programs and applications
- one or more partitions for the user specific files (home directories)
- one or more swap partitions (virtual memory)

Servers usually have more memory and thus more swap space. Certain server processes, such as databases, may require more swap space than usual; see the specific documentation for detailed information. For better performance, swap is often divided into different swap partitions.

3.1.2.3 Mount points

All partitions are attached to the system via a mount point. The mount point defines the place of a particular data set in the file system. Usually, all partitions are connected through the *root* partition. On this partition, which is indicated with the slash (/), directories are created. These empty directories will be the starting point of the partitions that are attached to them. An example: given a partition that holds the following directories:

```
videos/        cd-images/  pictures/
```

We want to attach this partition in the filesystem in a directory called /opt/media. In order to do this, the system administrator has to make sure that the directory /opt/media exists on the system. Preferably, it should be an empty directory. How this is done is explained later on in this chapter. Then, using the **mount** command, the administrator can attach the partition to the system. When you look at the content of the formerly empty directory /opt/media, it will contain the files and directories that are on the mounted medium (hard disk or partition of a hard disk, CD, DVD, flash card, USB or other storage device).

During system startup, all the partitions are thus mounted, as described in the file /etc/fstab. Some partitions are not mounted by default, for instance if they are not constantly connected to the system, such like the storage used by your digital camera. If well configured, the device will be mounted as soon as the system notices that it is connected, or it can be user-mountable, i.e. you don't need to be system administrator to attach and detach the device to and from the system. There is an example in Section 9.3.

On a running system, information about the partitions and their mount points can be displayed using the **df** command (which stands for *disk full* or *disk free*). In Linux, **df** is the GNU version, and supports the -h or *human readable* option which greatly improves readability. Note that commercial UNIX machines commonly have their own versions of **df** and many other commands. Their behavior is usually the same, though GNU versions of common tools often have more and better features.

The **df** command only displays information about active non-swap partitions. These can include partitions from other networked systems, like in the example below where the home directories are mounted from a file server on the network, a situation often encountered in corporate environments.

```
freddy:~> df -h
Filesystem          Size  Used Avail Use% Mounted on
/dev/hda8           496M  183M  288M  39% /
/dev/hda1           124M  8.4M  109M   8% /boot
/dev/hda5            19G   15G  2.7G  85% /opt
/dev/hda6           7.0G  5.4G  1.2G  81% /usr
/dev/hda7           3.7G  2.7G  867M  77% /var
fs1:/home           8.9G  3.7G  4.7G  44% /.automount/fs1/root/home
```

3.1.3 More file system layout

3.1.3.1 Visual

For convenience, the Linux file system is usually thought of in a tree structure. On a standard Linux system you will find the layout generally follows the scheme presented below.

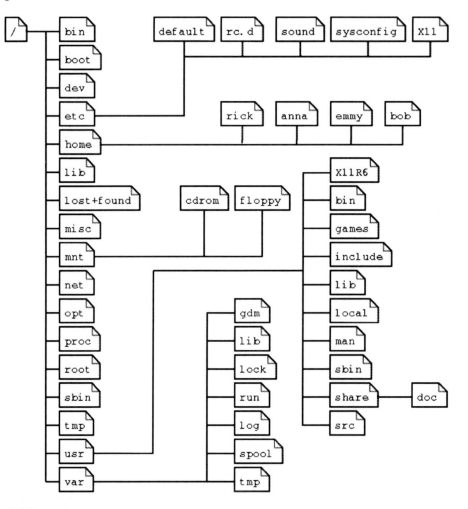

Figure 3.1. Linux file system layout

This is a layout from a RedHat system. Depending on the system admin, the operating system and the mission of the UNIX machine, the structure may vary, and directories may be left out or added at will. The names are not even required; they are only a convention.

The tree of the file system starts at the trunk or *slash*, indicated by a forward slash (/). This directory, containing all underlying directories and files, is also called the *root directory* or "the root" of the file system.

Directories that are only one level below the root directory are often preceded by a slash, to indicate their position and prevent confusion with other directories that could have the same name. When starting with a new system, it is always a good idea to take a look in the root directory. Let's see what you could run into:

```
emmy:~> cd /
emmy:/> ls
bin/    dev/   home/    lib/          misc/   opt/   root/   tmp/   var/
boot/   etc/   initrd/  lost+found/   mnt/    proc/  sbin/   usr/
```

Directory	Content
/bin	Common programs, shared by the system, the system administrator and the users.
/boot	The startup files and the kernel, vmlinuz. In some recent distributions also grub data. Grub is the GRand Unified Boot loader and is an attempt to get rid of the many different boot-loaders we know today.
/dev	Contains references to all the CPU peripheral hardware, which are represented as files with special properties.
/etc	Most important system configuration files are in /etc, this directory contains data similar to those in the Control Panel in Windows
/home	Home directories of the common users.
/initrd	(on some distributions) Information for booting. Do not remove!
/lib	Library files, includes files for all kinds of programs needed by the system and the users.
/lost+found	Every partition has a lost+found in its upper directory. Files that were saved during failures are here.
/misc	For miscellaneous purposes.
/mnt	Standard mount point for external file systems, e.g. a CD-ROM or a digital camera.
/net	Standard mount point for entire remote file systems
/opt	Typically contains extra and third party software.
/proc	A virtual file system containing information about system resources. More information about the meaning of the files in proc is obtained by entering the command **man proc** in a terminal window. The file

Directory	Content
	`proc.txt` discusses the virtual file system in detail.
/root	The administrative user's home directory. Mind the difference between /, the root directory and /root, the home directory of the *root* user.
/sbin	Programs for use by the system and the system administrator.
/tmp	Temporary space for use by the system, cleaned upon reboot, so don't use this for saving any work!
/usr	Programs, libraries, documentation etc. for all user-related programs.
/var	Storage for all variable files and temporary files created by users, such as log files, the mail queue, the print spooler area, space for temporary storage of files downloaded from the Internet, or to keep an image of a CD before burning it.

Table 3.2. Subdirectories of the root directory

How can you find out which partition a directory is on? Using the **df** command with a dot (.) as an option shows the partition the current directory belongs to, and informs about the amount of space used on this partition:

```
sandra:/lib> df -h .
Filesystem        Size  Used Avail Use% Mounted on
/dev/hda7         980M  163M  767M  18% /
```

As a general rule, every directory under the root directory is on the root partition, unless it has a separate entry in the full listing from **df** (or **df -h** with no other options).

Read more in **man *hier*.**

3.1.3.2   The file system in reality

For most users and for most common system administration tasks, it is enough to accept that files and directories are ordered in a tree-like structure. The computer, however, doesn't understand a thing about trees or tree-structures.

Every partition has its own file system. By imagining all those file systems together, we can form an idea of the tree-structure of the entire system, but it is not as simple as that. In a file system, a file is represented by an *inode*, a kind of serial number containing information about the actual data that makes up the file: to whom this file belongs, and where is it located on the hard disk.

Every partition has its own set of inodes; throughout a system with multiple partitions, files with the same inode number can exist.

Each inode describes a data structure on the hard disk, storing the properties of a file, including the physical location of the file data. When a hard disk is initialized to accept data storage, usually during the initial system installation process or when adding extra disks to an existing system, a fixed number of inodes per partition is created. This number will be the maximum amount of files, of all types (including directories, special files, links etc.) that can exist at the same time on the partition. We typically count on having 1 inode per 2 to 8 kilobytes of storage.

At the time a new file is created, it gets a free inode. In that inode is the following information:

- Owner and group owner of the file.
- File type (regular, directory, ...)
- Permissions on the file Section 3.4.1
- Date and time of creation, last read and change.
- Date and time this information has been changed in the inode.
- Number of links to this file (see later in this chapter).
- File size
- An address defining the actual location of the file data.

The only information not included in an inode, is the file name and directory. These are stored in the special directory files. By comparing file names and inode numbers, the system can make up a tree-structure that the user understands. Users can display inode numbers using the -i option to ls. The inodes have their own separate space on the disk.

3.2 Orientation in the file system

3.2.1 The path

When you want the system to execute a command, you almost never have to give the full path to that command. For example, we know that the **ls** command is in the /bin directory (check with **which -a** *ls*), yet we don't have to enter the command **/bin/ls** for the computer to list the content of the current directory.

The PATH environment variable takes care of this. This variable lists those directories in the system where executable files can be found, and thus saves the user a lot of typing and memorizing locations of commands. So the path naturally contains a lot of directories containing bin somewhere in their names, as the user below demonstrates. The **echo** command is used to display the content ("$") of the variable PATH:

```
rogier:> echo $PATH
/opt/local/bin:/usr/X11R6/bin:/usr/bin:/usr/sbin/:/bin
```

In this example, the directories /opt/local/bin, /usr/X11R6/bin, /usr/bin, /usr/sbin and /bin are subsequently searched for the required program. As soon as a match is found, the search is stopped, even if not every directory in the path has been searched. This can lead to strange situations. In the first example below, the user knows there is a program called **sendsms** to send an SMS message, and another user on the same system can use it, but she can't. The difference is in the configuration of the PATH variable:

```
[jenny@blob jenny]$ sendsms
bash: sendsms: command not found
[jenny@blob jenny]$ echo $PATH
/bin:/usr/bin:/usr/bin/X11:/usr/X11R6/bin:/home/jenny/bin
[jenny@blob jenny]$ su - tony
Password:
tony:~>which sendsms
sendsms is /usr/local/bin/sendsms

tony:~>echo $PATH
/home/tony/bin.Linux:/home/tony/bin:/usr/local/bin:/usr/local/sbin:\
/usr/X11R6/bin:/usr/bin:/usr/sbin:/bin:/sbin
```

Note the use of the **su** (switch user) facility, which allows you to run a shell in the environment of another user, on the condition that you know the user's password.

A backslash indicates the continuation of a line on the next, without an **Enter** separating one line from the other.

In the next example, a user wants to call on the **wc** (word count) command to check the number of lines in a file, but nothing happens and he has to break off his action using the **Ctrl+C** combination:

```
jumper:~> wc -l test

(Ctrl-C)
jumper:~> which wc
wc is hashed (/home/jumper/bin/wc)

jumper:~> echo $PATH
/home/jumper/bin:/usr/local/bin:/usr/local/sbin:/usr/X11R6/bin:\
/usr/bin:/usr/sbin:/bin:/sbin
```

The use of the **which** command shows us that this user has a `bin`-directory in his home directory, containing a program that is also called **wc**. Since the program in his home directory is found first when searching the paths upon a call for **wc**, this "home-made" program is executed, with input it probably doesn't understand, so we have to stop it. To resolve this problem there are several ways (there are always several ways to solve a problem in UNIX/Linux): one answer could be to rename the user's **wc** program, or the user can give the full path to the exact command he wants, which can be found by using the `-a` option to the **which** command.

If the user uses programs in the other directories more frequently, he can change his path to look in his own directories last:

```
jumper:~> export PATH=/usr/local/bin:/usr/local/sbin:/usr/X11R6/bin:\
/usr/bin:/usr/sbin:/bin:/sbin:/home/jumper/bin
```

Changes are not permanent

Note that when using the export command in a shell, the changes are temporary and only valid for this session (until you log out). Opening new sessions, even while the current one is still running, will not result in a new path in the new session. We will see in Section 7.2 how we can make these kinds of changes to the environment permanent, adding these lines to the shell configuration files.

3.2.2 Absolute and relative paths

A path, which is the way you need to follow in the tree structure to reach a given file, can be described as starting from the trunk of the tree (the / or root directory). In that case, the path starts with a slash and is called an absolute path, since there can be no mistake: only one file on the system can comply.

In the other case, the path doesn't start with a slash and confusion is possible between `~/bin/wc` (in the user's home directory) and `bin/wc` in `/usr`, from the previous example. Paths that don't start with a slash are always relative.

In relative paths we also use the . and .. indications for the current and the parent directory. A couple of practical examples:

- When you want to compile source code, the installation documentation often instructs you to run the command *./***configure**, which runs the *configure* program located in the current directory (that came with the new code), as opposed to running another configure program elsewhere on the system.

- In HTML files, relative paths are often used to make a set of pages easily movable to another place:

```
<img alt="Garden with trees" src="../images/garden.jpg">
```

- Notice the difference one more time:

```
theo:~> ls /mp3
ls: /mp3: No such file or directory
theo:~>ls mp3/
oriental/  pop/  sixties/
```

3.2.3 The most important files and directories

3.2.3.1   The kernel

The kernel is the heart of the system. It manages the communication between the underlying hardware and the peripherals. The kernel also makes sure that processes and daemons (server processes) are started and stopped at the exact right times. The kernel has a lot of other important tasks, so many that there is a special kernel-development mailing list on this subject only, where huge amounts of information are shared. It would lead us too far to discuss the kernel in detail. For now it suffices to know that the kernel is the most important file on the system.

3.2.3.2   The shell

3.2.3.2.1 What is a shell?

When I was looking for an appropriate explanation on the concept of a *shell*, it gave me more trouble than I expected. All kinds of definitions are available, ranging from the simple comparison that "the shell is the steering wheel of the car", to the vague definition in the Bash manual which says that "bash is an sh-compatible command language interpreter," or an even more obscure expression, "a shell manages the interaction between the system and its users". A shell is much more than that.

A shell can best be compared with a way of talking to the computer, a language. Most users do know that other language, the point-and-click language of the desktop. But in that language the computer is leading the conversation, while the user has the passive role of picking tasks from the ones presented. It is very difficult for a programmer to include all options and possible uses of a command in the GUI-format. Thus, GUIs are almost always less capable than the command or commands that form the backend.

The shell, on the other hand, is an advanced way of communicating with the system, because it allows for two-way conversation and taking initiative. Both partners in the communication are equal, so new ideas can be tested. The shell allows the user to handle a system in a very flexible way. An additional asset is that the shell allows for task automation.

3.2.3.2.2 Shell types

Just like people know different languages and dialects, the computer knows different shell types:

- **sh** or Bourne Shell: the original shell still used on UNIX systems and in UNIX related environments. This is the basic shell, a small program with few features. When in POSIX-compatible mode, **bash** will emulate this shell.

- **bash** or Bourne Again SHell: the standard GNU shell, intuitive and flexible. Probably most advisable for beginning users while being at the same time a powerful tool for the advanced and professional user. On Linux, **bash** is the standard shell for common users. This shell is a so-called *superset* of the Bourne shell, a set of add-ons and plug-ins. This means that the Bourne Again SHell is compatible with the Bourne shell: commands that work in **sh**, also work in **bash**. However, the reverse is not always the case. All examples and exercises in this book use **bash**.

- **csh** or C Shell: the syntax of this shell resembles that of the C programming language. Sometimes asked for by programmers.

- **tcsh** or Turbo C Shell: a superset of the common C Shell, enhancing user-friendliness and speed.

- **ksh** or the Korn shell: sometimes appreciated by people with a UNIX background. A superset of the Bourne shell; with standard configuration a nightmare for beginning users.

The file /etc/shells gives an overview of known shells on a Linux system:

```
mia:~> cat /etc/shells
/bin/bash
/bin/sh
/bin/tcsh
/bin/csh
```

 Fake Bourne shell

Note that /bin/sh is usually a link to Bash, which will execute in Bourne shell compatible mode when called on this way.

Your default shell is set in the /etc/passwd file, like this line for user *mia*:

```
mia:L2NOfqdlPrHwE:504:504:Mia Maya:/home/mia:/bin/bash
```

To switch from one shell to another, just enter the name of the new shell in the active terminal. The system finds the directory where the name occurs using the PATH settings, and since a shell is an executable file (program), the current shell activates it and it gets executed. A new prompt is usually shown, because each shell has its typical appearance:

```
mia:~> tcsh
[mia@post21 ~]$
```

3.2.3.2.3 Which shell am I using?

If you don't know which shell you are using, either check the line for your account in /etc/passwd or type the command

echo $SHELL

3.2.3.3 Your home directory

Your home directory is your default destination when connecting to the system. In most cases it is a subdirectory of /home, though this may vary. Your home directory may be located on the hard disk of a remote file server; in that case your home directory may be found in /nethome/your_user_name. In another case the system administrator may have opted for a less comprehensible layout and your home directory may be on /disk6/HU/07/jgillard.

Whatever the path to your home directory, you don't have to worry too much about it. The correct path to your home directory is stored in the HOME environment variable, in case some program needs it. With the **echo** command you can display the content of this variable:

```
orlando:~> echo $HOME
/nethome/orlando
```

You can do whatever you like in your home directory. You can put as many files in as many directories as you want, although the total amount of data and files is naturally limited because of the hardware and size of the partitions, and sometimes because the system administrator has applied a quota system. Limiting disk usage was common practice when hard disk space was still expensive. Nowadays, limits are almost exclusively applied in large environments. You can see for yourself if a limit is set using the **quota** command:

```
pierre@lamaison:/> quota -v
Diskquotas for user pierre (uid 501): none
```

In case quotas have been set, you get a list of the limited partitions and their specific limitations. Exceeding the limits may be tolerated during a grace period with fewer or no restrictions at all. Detailed information can be found using the **info** *quota* or **man** *quota* commands.

No Quota?

If your system can not find the **quota**, then no limitation of file system usage is being applied.

Your home directory is indicated by a tilde (~), shorthand for /path_to_home/user_name. This same path is stored in the HOME variable, so you don't have to do anything to activate it. A simple application: switch from /var/music/albums/arno/2001 to images in your home directory using one elegant command:

```
rom:/var/music/albums/arno/2001> cd ~/images

rom:~/images> pwd
/home/rom/images
```

Later in this chapter we will talk about the commands for managing files and directories in order to keep your home directory tidy.

3.2.4 The most important configuration files

As we mentioned before, most configuration files are stored in the /etc directory. Content can be viewed using the **cat** command, which sends text files to the standard output (usually your monitor). The syntax is straight forward:

```
cat file1 file2 ... fileN
```

In this section we try to give an overview of the most common configuration files. This is certainly not a complete list. Adding extra packages may also add extra configuration files in /etc. When reading the configuration files, you will find that they are usually quite well commented and self-explanatory. Some files also have man pages which contain extra documentation, such as **man** *group*.

File	Information/service
aliases	Mail aliases file for use with the Sendmail and Postfix mail server. Running a mail server on each and every system has long been common use in the UNIX world, and almost every Linux distribution still comes with a Sendmail package. In this file local user names are matched with real names as they occur in E-mail addresses, or with other local addresses.
apache	Config files for the Apache web server.
bashrc	The system-wide configuration file for the Bourne Again SHell. Defines functions and aliases for all users. Other shells may have their own system-wide config files, like cshrc.

File	Information/service
`crontab` and the `cron.*` directories	Configuration of tasks that need to be executed periodically - backups, updates of the system databases, cleaning of the system, rotating logs etc.
`default`	Default options for certain commands, such as **useradd**.
`filesystems`	Known file systems: ext3, vfat, iso9660 etc.
`fstab`	Lists partitions and their *mount points*.
`ftp*`	Configuration of the ftp-server: who can connect, what parts of the system are accessible etc.
`group`	Configuration file for user groups. Use the shadow utilities **groupadd**, **groupmod** and **groupdel** to edit this file. Edit manually only if you really know what you are doing.
`hosts`	A list of machines that can be contacted using the network, but without the need for a domain name service. This has nothing to do with the system's network configuration, which is done in `/etc/sysconfig`.
`inittab`	Information for booting: mode, number of text consoles etc.
`issue`	Information about the distribution (release version and/or kernel info).
`ld.so.conf`	Locations of library files.
`lilo.conf`, `silo.conf`, `aboot.conf` etc.	Boot information for the LInux LOader, the system for booting that is now gradually being replaced with GRUB.
`logrotate.*`	Rotation of the logs, a system preventing the collection of huge amounts of log files.
`mail`	Directory containing instructions for the behavior of the mail server.
`modules.conf`	Configuration of modules that enable special features (drivers).
`motd`	Message Of The Day: Shown to everyone who connects to the system (in text mode), may be used by the system admin to announce system services/maintenance etc.
`mtab`	Currently mounted file systems. It is advised to never edit this file.

File	Information/service
nsswitch.conf	Order in which to contact the name resolvers when a process demands resolving of a host name.
pam.d	Configuration of authentication modules.
passwd	Lists local users. Use the shadow utilities **useradd**, **usermod** and **userdel** to edit this file. Edit manually only when you really know what you are doing.
printcap	Outdated but still frequently used printer configuration file. Don't edit this manually unless you really know what you are doing.
profile	System wide configuration of the shell environment: variables, default properties of new files, limitation of resources etc.
rc*	Directories defining active services for each run level.
resolv.conf	Order in which to contact DNS servers (Domain Name Servers only).
sendmail.cf	Main config file for the Sendmail server.
services	Connections accepted by this machine (open ports).
sndconfig and sound	Configuration of the sound card and sound events.
ssh	Directory containing the config files for secure shell client and server.
sysconfig	Directory containing the system configuration files: mouse, keyboard, network, desktop, system clock, power management etc. (specific to RedHat)
X11	Settings for the graphical server, X. RedHat uses XFree, which is reflected in the name of the main configuration file, XFree86Config. Also contains the general directions for the window managers available on the system, for example **gdm**, **fvwm**, **twm**, etc.
xinetd.*	Configuration files for Internet services that are run from the system's (extended) Internet services daemon (servers that don't run an independent daemon).

Table 3.3. Most common configuration files

Throughout this guide we will learn more about these files and study some of them in detail.

3.2.5 The most common devices

Devices, generally every peripheral attachment of a PC that is not the CPU itself, is presented to the system as an entry in the /dev directory. One of the advantages of this UNIX-way of handling devices is that neither the user nor the system has to worry much about the specification of devices.

Users that are new to Linux or UNIX in general are often overwhelmed by the amount of new names and concepts they have to learn. That is why a list of common devices is included in this introduction.

Name	Device
cdrom	CD drive
console	Special entry for the currently used console.
cua*	Serial ports
dsp*	Devices for sampling and recording
fd*	Entries for most kinds of floppy drives, the default is /dev/fd0, a floppy drive for 1.44 MB floppies.
hd[a-t] [1-16]	Standard support for IDE drives with maximum amount of partitions each.
ir*	Infrared devices
isdn*	Management of ISDN connections
js*	Joystick(s)
lp*	Printers
mem	Memory
midi*	midi player
mixer* and music	Idealized model of a mixer (combines or adds signals)
modem	Modem
mouse (also msmouse, logimouse, psmouse, input/mice, psaux)	All kinds of mouses
null	Bottomless garbage can
par*	Entries for parallel port support

Name	Device
pty*	Pseudo terminals
radio*	For Radio Amateurs (HAMs).
ram*	boot device
sd*	SCSI disks with their partitions
sequencer	For audio applications using the synthesizer features of the sound card (MIDI-device controller)
tty*	Virtual consoles simulating vt100 terminals.
usb*	USB card and scanner
video*	For use with a graphics card supporting video.

Table 3.4. Common devices

3.2.6 The most common variable files

In the /var directory we find a set of directories for storing specific non-constant data (as opposed to the ls program or the system configuration files, which change relatively infrequently or never at all). All files that change frequently, such as log files, mailboxes, lock files, spoolers etc. are kept in a subdirectory of /var.

As a security measure these files are usually kept in separate parts from the main system files, so we can keep a close eye on them and set stricter permissions where necessary. A lot of these files also need more permissions than usual, like /var/tmp, which needs to be writable for everyone. A lot of user activity might be expected here, which might even be generated by anonymous Internet users connected to your system. This is one reason why the /var directory, including all its subdirectories, is usually on a separate partition. This way, there is for instance no risk that a mail bomb, for instance, fills up the rest of the file system, containing more important data such as your programs and configuration files.

/var/tmp and /tmp

Files in /tmp can be deleted without notice, by regular system tasks or because of a system reboot. On some (customized) systems, also /var/tmp might behave unpredictably. Nevertheless, since this is not the case by default, we advise to use the /var/tmp directory for saving temporary files. When in doubt, check with your system administrator. If you manage your own system, you can be reasonably sure that this is a safe place if you did not consciously change settings on /var/tmp (as root, a normal user can not do this).

Whatever you do, try to stick to the privileges granted to a normal user - don't go saving files directly under the root (/) of the file system, don't put them in /usr or some subdirectory or in another reserved place. This pretty much limits your access to safe file systems.

One of the main security systems on a UNIX system, which is naturally implemented on every Linux machine as well, is the log-keeping facility, which logs all user actions, processes, system events etc. The configuration file of the so-called *syslogdaemon* determines which and how long logged information will be kept. The default location of all logs is /var/log, containing different files for access log, server logs, system messages etc.

In /var we typically find server data, which is kept here to separate it from critical data such as the server program itself and its configuration files. A typical example on Linux systems is /var/www, which contains the actual HTML pages, scripts and images that a web server offers. The FTP-tree of an FTP server (data that can be downloaded by a remote client) is also best kept in one of /var's subdirectories. Because this data is publicly accessible and often changeable by anonymous users, it is safer to keep it here, away from partitions or directories with sensitive data.

On most workstation installations, /var/spool will at least contain an at and a cron directory, containing scheduled tasks. In office environments this directory usually contains lpd as well, which holds the print queue(s) and further printer configuration files, as well as the printer log files.

On server systems we will generally find /var/spool/mail, containing incoming mails for local users, sorted in one file per user, the user's "inbox". A related directory is mqueue, the spooler area for unsent mail messages. These parts of the system can be very busy on mail servers with a lot of users. News servers also use the /var/spool area because of the enormous amounts of messages they have to process.

The /var/lib/rpm directory is specific to RPM-based (RedHat Package Manager) distributions; it is where RPM package information is stored. Other package managers generally also store their data somewhere in /var.

3.3 Manipulating files

3.3.1 Viewing file properties

3.3.1.1 More about ls

Besides the name of the file, ls can give a lot of other information, such as the file type, as we already discussed. It can also show permissions on a file, file size, inode number, creation date and time, owners and amount of links to the file. With the -a option to **ls**, files that are normally hidden from view can be displayed as well. These are files that have a name starting with a dot. A couple of typical examples include the configuration files in your home directory. When you've worked with a certain system for a while, you will notice that tens of files and directories have been created that are not automatically listed in a directory index. Next to that, every directory contains a file named just dot (.) and one with two dots (..), which are used in combination with their inode number to determine the directory's position in the file system's tree structure.

You should really read the Info pages about **ls**, since it is a very common command with a lot of useful options. Options can be combined, as is the case with most UNIX commands and their options. A common combination is **ls -al**; it shows a long list of files and their properties as well as the destinations that any symbolic links point to. **ls -latr** displays the same files, only now in reversed order of the last change, so that the file changed most recently occurs at the bottom of the list. Here are a couple of examples:

```
krissie:~/mp3> ls
Albums/   Radio/   Singles/   gene/   index.html

krissie:~/mp3> ls -a
./     .thumbs   Radio      gene/
../    Albums/   Singles/   index.html

krissie:~/mp3> ls -l Radio/
total 8
drwxr-xr-x    2 krissie krissie   4096 Oct 30  1999 Carolina/
drwxr-xr-x    2 krissie krissie   4096 Sep 24  1999 Slashdot/

krissie:~/mp3> ls -ld Radio/
drwxr-xr-x    4 krissie krissie   4096 Oct 30  1999 Radio/

krissie:~/mp3> ls -ltr
total 20
drwxr-xr-x    4 krissie krissie   4096 Oct 30  1999 Radio/
-rw-r--r--    1 krissie krissie    453 Jan  7  2001 index.html
drwxrwxr-x   30 krissie krissie   4096 Oct 20 17:32 Singles/
drwxr-xr-x    2 krissie krissie   4096 Dec  4 23:22 gene/
drwxrwxr-x   13 krissie krissie   4096 Dec 21 11:40 Albums/
```

On most Linux versions **ls** is *aliased* to color-ls by default. This feature allows to see the file type without using any options to **ls**. To achieve this, every file type has its own color. The standard scheme is in /etc/DIR_COLORS:

Color	File type
blue	directories

Color	File type
red	compressed archives
white	text files
pink	images
cyan	links
yellow	devices
green	executables
flashing red	broken links

Table 3.5. Color-ls default color scheme

More information is in the man page. The same information was in earlier days displayed using suffixes to every non-standard file name. For mono-color use (like printing a directory listing) and for general readability, this scheme is still in use:

Character	File type
nothing	regular file
/	directory
*	executable file
@	link
=	socket
|	named pipe

Table 3.6. Default suffix scheme for ls

A description of the full functionality and features of the **ls** command can be read with **info** *coreutils ls*.

3.3.1.2 More tools

To find out more about the kind of data we are dealing with, we use the **file** command. By applying certain tests that check properties of a file in the file system, magic numbers and language tests, **file** tries to make an educated guess about the format of a file. Some examples:

```
mike:~> file Documents/
Documents/: directory

mike:~> file high-tech-stats.pdf
```

```
high-tech-stats.pdf: PDF document, version 1.2

mike:~> file Nari-288.rm
Nari-288.rm: RealMedia file

mike:~> file bijlage10.sdw
bijlage10.sdw: Microsoft Office Document

mike:~> file logo.xcf
logo.xcf: GIMP XCF image data, version 0, 150 x 38, RGB Color

mike:~> file cv.txt
cv.txt: ISO-8859 text

mike:~> file image.png
image.png: PNG image data, 616 x 862, 8-bit grayscale, non-interlaced

mike:~> file figure
figure: ASCII text

mike:~> file me+tux.jpg
me+tux.jpg: JPEG image data, JFIF standard 1.01, resolution (DPI),
            "28 Jun 1999", 144 x 144

mike:~> file 42.zip.gz
42.zip.gz: gzip compressed data, deflated, original filename,
           `42.zip', last modified: Thu Nov  1 23:45:39 2001, os: Unix

mike:~> file vi.gif
vi.gif: GIF image data, version 89a, 88 x 31

mike:~> file slide1
slide1: HTML document text

mike:~> file template.xls
template.xls: Microsoft Office Document

mike:~> file abook.ps
abook.ps: PostScript document text conforming at level 2.0

mike:~> file /dev/log
/dev/log: socket

mike:~> file /dev/hda
/dev/hda: block special (3/0)
```

The **file** command has a series of options, among others the -z option to look into compressed files. See **info** *file* for a detailed description. Keep in mind that the results of **file** are not absolute, it is only a guess. In other words, **file** can be tricked.

✎ **Why all the fuss about file types and formats?**

Shortly, we will discuss a couple of command-line tools for looking at *plain text files*. These tools will not work when used on the wrong type of files. In the worst case, they will crash your terminal and/or make a lot of beeping noises. If this happens to you, just close the terminal session and start a new one. But try to avoid it, because it is usually very disturbing for other people.

3.3.2 Creating and deleting files and directories

3.3.2.1 Making a mess...

... Is not a difficult thing to do. Today almost every system is networked, so naturally files get copied from one machine to another. And especially when working in a graphical environment, creating new files is a piece of cake and is often done without the approval of the user. To illustrate the problem, here's the full content of a new user's directory, created on a standard RedHat system:

```
[newuser@blob user]$ ls -al
total 32
drwx------   3 user     user         4096 Jan 16 13:32 .
drwxr-xr-x   6 root     root         4096 Jan 16 13:32 ..
-rw-r--r--   1 user     user           24 Jan 16 13:32 .bash_logout
-rw-r--r--   1 user     user          191 Jan 16 13:32 .bash_profile
-rw-r--r--   1 user     user          124 Jan 16 13:32 .bashrc
drwxr-xr-x   3 user     user         4096 Jan 16 13:32 .kde
-rw-r--r--   1 user     user         3511 Jan 16 13:32 .screenrc
-rw-------   1 user     user           61 Jan 16 13:32 .xauthDqztLr
```

On first sight, the content of a "used" home directory doesn't look that bad either:

```
olduser:~> ls
app-defaults/  crossover/     Fvwm@       mp3/        OpenOffice.org638/
articles/      Desktop/       GNUstep/    Nautilus/   staroffice6.0/
bin/           Desktop1/      images/     nqc/        training/
brol/          desktoptest/   Machines@   ns_imap/    webstart/
C/             Documents/     mail/       nsmail/     xml/
closed/        Emacs@         Mail/       office52/   Xrootenv.0
```

But when all the directories and files starting with a dot are included, there are 185 items in this directory. This is because most applications have their own directories and/or files, containing user-specific settings, in the home directory of that user. Usually these files are created the first time you start an application. In some cases you will be notified when a non-existent directory needs to be created, but most of the time everything is done automatically.

Furthermore, new files are created seemingly continuously because users want to save files, keep different versions of their work, use Internet applications, and download files and attachments to their local machine. It doesn't stop. It is clear that one definitely needs a scheme to keep an overview on things.

In the next section, we will discuss our means of keeping order. We only discuss text tools available to the shell, since the graphical tools are very intuitive and have the same look and feel as the well known point-and-click MS Windows-style file managers, including graphical help functions and other features you expect from this kind of applications. The following list is an overview of the most popular file managers for GNU/Linux. Most file managers can be started from the menu of your desktop manager, or by clicking your home directory icon, or from the command line, issuing these commands:

- **nautilus**: The default file manager in Gnome, the GNU desktop. Excellent documentation about working with this tool can be found at <http://www. gnome.org>.

- **konqueror**: The file manager typically used on a KDE desktop. The handbook is at <http://docs.kde.org>.

- **mc**: Midnight Commander, the Unix file manager after the fashion of Norton Commander. All documentation available from <http://gnu.org/ directory/> or a mirror, such as <http://www.ibiblio.org>.

These applications are certainly worth giving a try and usually impress newcomers to Linux, if only because there is such a wide variety: these are only the most popular tools for managing directories and files, and many other projects are being developed. Now let's find out about the internals and see how these graphical tools use common UNIX commands.

3.3.2.2 The tools

3.3.2.2.1 Creating directories

A way of keeping things in place is to give certain files specific default locations by creating directories and subdirectories (or folders and sub-folders if you wish). This is done with the **mkdir** command:

```
richard:~> mkdir archive

richard:~> ls -ld archive
drwxrwxrwx  2 richard richard          4096 Jan 13 14:09 archive/
```

Creating directories and subdirectories in one step is done using the -p option:

```
richard:~> cd archive

richard:~/archive> mkdir 1999 2000 2001
```

```
richard:~/archive> ls
1999/  2000/  2001/

richard:~/archive> mkdir 2001/reports/Restaurants-Michelin/
mkdir: cannot create directory `2001/reports/Restaurants-Michelin/':
No such file or directory

richard:~/archive> mkdir -p 2001/reports/Restaurants-Michelin/

richard:~/archive> ls 2001/reports/
Restaurants-Michelin/
```

If the new file needs other permissions than the default file creation permissions, the new access rights can be set in one move, still using the **mkdir** command, see the Info pages for more. We are going to discuss access modes in the next section on file security.

The name of a directory has to comply with the same rules as those applied on regular file names. One of the most important restrictions is that you can't have two files with the same name in one directory (but keep in mind that Linux is, like UNIX, a case sensitive operating system). There are virtually no limits on the length of a file name, but it is usually kept shorter than 80 characters, so it can fit on one line of a terminal. You can use any character you want in a file name, although it is advised to exclude characters that have a special meaning to the shell. When in doubt, check with Appendix C.

3.3.2.2.2 Moving files

Now that we have properly structured our home directory, it is time to clean up unclassified files using the **mv** command:

```
richard:~/archive> mv ../report[1-4].doc reports/Restaurants-Michelin/
```

This command is also applicable when renaming files:

```
richard:~> ls To_Do
-rw-rw-r--    1 richard richard       2534 Jan 15 12:39 To_Do

richard:~> mv To_Do done

richard:~> ls -l done
-rw-rw-r--    1 richard richard       2534 Jan 15 12:39 done
```

It is clear that only the name of the file changes. All other properties remain the same.

Detailed information about the syntax and features of the **mv** command can be found in the man or Info pages. The use of this documentation should always be your first reflex when confronted with a problem. The answer to your problem is likely to be in the system documentation. Even experienced users read man pages every day, so beginning users should read them all the time. After a while, you will get to know the most common options to the common commands, but you will still need the documentation as a primary source of information. Note that the information contained in the HOWTOs, FAQs, man pages and such is slowly being merged into the Info pages, which are today the most up-to-date source of online (as in readily available on the system) documentation.

3.3.2.2.3 Copying files

Copying files and directories is done with the **cp** command. A useful option is recursive copy (copy all underlying files and subdirectories), using the -R option to **cp**. The general syntax is

cp [-R] fromfile tofile

As an example the case of user *newguy*, who wants the same Gnome desktop settings user *oldguy* has. One way to solve the problem is to copy the settings of *oldguy* to the home directory of *newguy*:

```
victor:~> cp -R ../oldguy/.gnome/ .
```

This gives some errors involving file permissions, but all the errors have to do with private files that *newguy* doesn't need anyway. We will discuss in the next part how to change these permissions in case they really are a problem.

3.3.2.2.4 Removing files

Use the **rm** command to remove single files, **rmdir** to remove empty directories. (Use **ls -a** to check whether a directory is empty or not). The **rm** command also has options for removing non-empty directories with all their subdirectories, read the Info pages for these rather dangerous options.

How empty can a directory be?

It is normal that the directories . (dot) and .. (dot-dot) can't be removed, since they are also necessary in an empty directory to determine the directories ranking in the file system hierarchy.

On Linux, just like on UNIX, there is no garbage can - at least not for the shell, although there are plenty of solutions for graphical use. So once removed, a file is really gone, and there is generally no way to get it back unless you have backups, or you are really fast and have a real good system administrator. To protect the beginning user from this malice, the interactive behavior of the **rm**, **cp** and **mv** commands can be activated using the -i option. In that case the system won't immediately act upon request. Instead it will ask for confirmation, so it takes an additional click on the **Enter** key to inflict the damage:

```
mary:~> rm -ri archive/
rm: descend into directory `archive'? y
rm: descend into directory `archive/reports'? y
rm: remove directory `archive/reports'? y
rm: descend into directory `archive/backup'? y
rm: remove `archive/backup/sysbup200112.tar'? y
rm: remove directory `archive/backup'? y
rm: remove directory `archive'? y
```

We will discuss how to make this option the default in Chapter 7, which discusses customizing your shell environment.

3.3.3 Finding files

3.3.3.1   Using shell features

In the example on moving files we already saw how the shell can manipulate multiple files at once. In that example, the shell finds out automatically what the user means by the requirements between the square braces "[" and "]". The shell can substitute ranges of numbers and upper or lower case characters alike. It also substitutes as many characters as you want with an asterisk, and only one character with a question mark.

All sorts of substitutions can be used simultaneously; the shell is very logical about it. The Bash shell, for instance, has no problem with expressions like **ls** *dirname/*/*/*[2-3]*.

In other shells, the asterisk is commonly used to minimize the efforts of typing: people would enter **cd** *dir** instead of **cd** **directory**. In Bash however, this is not necessary because the GNU shell has a feature called file name completion. It means that you can type the first few characters of a command (anywhere) or a file (in the current directory) and if no confusion is possible, the shell will find out what you mean. For example in a directory containing many files, you can check if there are any files beginning with the letter A just by typing **ls** *A* and pressing the **Tab** key twice, rather than pressing **Enter**. If there is only one file starting with "A", this file will be shown as the argument to **ls** (or any shell command, for that matter) immediately.

3.3.3.2   Which

A very simple way of looking up files is using the **which** command, to look in the directories listed in the user's search path for the required file. Of course, since the search path contains only paths to directories containing executable programs, **which** doesn't work for ordinary files. The **which** command is useful when troubleshooting "Command not Found" problems. In the example below, user *tina* can't use the **acroread** program, while her colleague has no troubles whatsoever on the same system. The problem is similar to the PATH problem in the previous part: Tina's colleague tells her that he can see the required program in /opt/acroread/bin, but this directory is not in her path:

```
tina:~> which acroread
/usr/bin/which: no acroread in (/bin:/usr/bin:/usr/bin/X11)
```

The problem can be solved by giving the full path to the command to run, or by re-exporting the content of the PATH variable:

```
tina:~> export PATH=$PATH:/opt/acroread/bin
```

```
tina:~> echo $PATH
/bin:/usr/bin:/usr/bin/X11:/opt/acroread/bin
```

Using the **which** command also checks to see if a command is an alias for another command:

```
gerrit:~> which -a ls
ls is aliased to `ls -F --color=auto'
ls is /bin/ls
```

3.3.3.3 Find and locate

These are the real tools, used when searching other paths beside those listed in the search path. The **find** tool, known from UNIX, is very powerful, which may be the cause of a somewhat more difficult syntax. GNU **find**, however, deals with the syntax problems. This command not only allows you to search file names, it can also accept file size, date of last change and other file properties as criteria for a search. The most common use is for finding file names:

find <path> -name *<searchstring>*

This can be interpreted as "Look in all files and subdirectories contained in a given path, and print the names of the files containing the search string in their name" (not in their content).

Another application of **find** is for searching files of a certain size, as in the example below, where user *peter* wants to find all files in the current directory or one of its subdirectories, that are bigger than 5 MB:

```
peter:~> find . -size +5000k
psychotic_chaos.mp3
```

If you dig in the man pages, you will see that **find** can also perform operations on the found files. A common example is removing files. It is best to first test without the -exec option that the correct files are selected, after that the command can be rerun to delete the selected files. Below, we search for files ending in .tmp:

```
peter:~>  find . -name "*.tmp" -exec rm {} \;

peter:~>
```

☞ **Optimize!**

This command will call on **rm** as many times as a file answering the requirements is found. In the worst case, this might be thousands or millions of times. This is quite a load on your system.

A more realistic way of working would be the use of a pipe (|) and the **xargs** tool with **rm** as an argument. This way, the **rm** command is only called when the command line is full, instead of for every file. See Chapter 5 for more on using I/O redirection to ease everyday tasks.

Later on (in 1999 according to the man pages, after 20 years of **find**), **locate** was developed. This program is easier to use, but more restricted than **find**, since its output is based on a file index database that is updated only once every day. On the other hand, a search in the **locate** database uses less resources than **find** and therefore shows the results nearly instantly.

Most Linux distributions use **slocate** these days, security enhanced locate, the modern version of **locate** that prevents users from getting output they have no right to read. The files in *root*'s home directory are such an example, these are not normally accessible to the public. A user who wants to find someone who knows about the C shell may issue the command **locate .cshrc**, to display all users who have a customized configuration file for the C shell. Supposing the users *root* and *jenny* are running C shell, then only the file /home/jenny/.cshrc will be displayed, and not the one in *root*'s home directory. On most systems, **locate** is a symbolic link to the **slocate** program:

```
billy:~> ls -l /usr/bin/locate
lrwxrwxrwx 1 root slocate  7 Oct 28 14:18 /usr/bin/locate -> slocate*
```

User *tina* could have used **locate** to find the application she wanted:

```
tina:~> locate acroread
/usr/share/icons/hicolor/16x16/apps/acroread.png
/usr/share/icons/hicolor/32x32/apps/acroread.png
/usr/share/icons/locolor/16x16/apps/acroread.png
/usr/share/icons/locolor/32x32/apps/acroread.png
/usr/local/bin/acroread
/usr/local/Acrobat4/Reader/intellinux/bin/acroread
/usr/local/Acrobat4/bin/acroread
```

Directories that don't contain the name `bin` can't contain the program - they don't contain executable files. There are three possibilities left. The file in `/usr/local/bin` is the one *tina* would have wanted: it is a link to the shell script that starts the actual program:

```
tina:~> file /usr/local/bin/acroread
/usr/local/bin/acroread: symbolic link to ../Acrobat4/bin/acroread

tina:~> file /usr/local/Acrobat4/bin/acroread
/usr/local/Acrobat4/bin/acroread: Bourne shell script text executable

tina:~> file /usr/local/Acrobat4/Reader/intellinux/bin/acroread
/usr/local/Acrobat4/Reader/intellinux/bin/acroread: ELF 32-bit LSB
executable, Intel 80386, version 1, dynamically linked (uses
shared libs), not stripped
```

In order to keep the path as short as possible, so the system doesn't have to search too long every time a user wants to execute a command, we add `/usr/local/bin` to the path and not the other directories, which only contain the binary files of one specific program, while `/usr/local/bin` contains other useful programs as well.

Again, a description of the full features of **find** and **locate** can be found in the Info pages.

3.3.3.4 The grep command

3.3.3.4.1 General line filtering

A simple but powerful program, **grep** is used for filtering input lines and returning certain patterns to the output. There are literally thousands of applications for the **grep** program. In the example below, *jerry* uses **grep** to see how he did the thing with **find**:

```
jerry:~> grep -a find .bash_history
find . -name userinfo
man find
find ../ -name common.cfg
```

Search history

Also useful in these cases is the search function in **bash**, activated by pressing **Ctrl+R** at once, such as in the example where we want to check how we did that last **find** again:

```
thomas ~> ^R
(reverse-i-search)`find': find `/home/thomas` -name *.xml
```

Type your search string at the search prompt. The more characters you type, the more restricted the search gets. This reads the command history for this shell session (which is written to .bash_history in your home directory when you quit that session). The most recent occurrence of your search string is shown. If you want to see previous commands containing the same string, type **Ctrl+R** again.

See the Info pages on **bash** for more.

All UNIXes with just a little bit of decency have an online dictionary. So does Linux. The dictionary is a list of known words in a file named words, located in /usr/share/dict. To quickly check the correct spelling of a word, no graphical application is needed:

```
william:~> grep pinguin /usr/share/dict/words

william:~> grep penguin /usr/share/dict/words
penguin
penguins
```

Dictionary vs. word list

Some distributions offer the **dict** command, which offers more features than simply searching words in a list.

Who is the owner of that home directory next to mine? Hey, there's his telephone number!

```
lisa:~> grep gdbruyne /etc/passwd
gdbruyne:x:981:981:Guy Debruyne, tel 203234:/home/gdbruyne:/bin/bash
```

And what was the E-mail address of Arno again?

```
serge:~/mail> grep -i arno *
sent-mail: To: <Arno.Hintjens@celeb.com>
sent-mail: On Mon, 24 Dec 2001, Arno.Hintjens@celeb.com wrote:
```

find and **locate** are often used in combination with **grep** to define some serious queries. For more information, see Chapter 5 on I/O redirection.

3.3.3.4.2 Special characters

Characters that have a special meaning to the shell have to be *escaped*. The escape character in Bash is backslash, as in most shells; this takes away the special meaning of the following character. The shell knows about quite some special characters, among the most common /, ., ? and *. A full list can be found in the Info pages and documentation for your shell.

For instance, say that you want to display the file "*" instead of all the files in a directory, you would have to use

less *

The same goes for filenames containing a space:

```
cat This\ File
```

3.3.4 More ways to view file content

3.3.4.1 General

Apart from **cat**, which really doesn't do much more than sending files to the standard output, there are other tools to view file content.

The easiest way of course would be to use graphical tools instead of command line tools. In the introduction we already saw a glimpse of an office application, OpenOffice.org. Other examples are the GIMP (start up with **gimp** from the command line), the GNU Image Manipulation Program; **xpdf** to view Portable Document Format files (PDF); GhostView (**gv**) for viewing PostScript files; Mozilla/FireFox, **links** (a text mode browser), Konqueror, Opera and many others for web content; XMMS, CDplay and others for multimedia file content; AbiWord, Gnumeric, KOffice etc. for all kinds of office applications and so on. There are thousands of Linux applications; to list them all would take days.

Instead we keep concentrating on shell- or text-mode applications, which form the basics for all other applications. These commands work best in a text environment on files containing text. When in doubt, check first using the **file** command.

So let's see what text tools we have that are useful to look inside files.

Font problems

Plain text tools such as the ones we will now be discussing, often have problems with "plain" text files because of the font encoding used in those files. Special characters, such as accented alphabetical characters, Chinese characters and other characters from languages using different character sets than the default *en_US* encoding and so on, are then displayed the wrong way or replaced by unreadable rubbish. These problems are discussed in Section 7.4.

3.3.4.2 "less is more"

Undoubtedly you will hear someone say this phrase sooner or later when working in a UNIX environment. A little bit of UNIX history explains this:

- First there was **cat**. Output was streamed in an uncontrollable way.

- Then there was **pg**, which may still be found on older UNIXes. This command puts text to the output one page at the time.

- The **more** program was a revised version of **pg**. This command is still available on every Linux system.

- **less** is the GNU version of more and has extra features allowing highlighting of search strings, scrolling back etc. The syntax is very simple:

  less `name_of_file`

  More information is located in the Info pages.

You already know about pagers by now, because they are used for viewing the man pages.

3.3.4.3   The head and tail commands

These two commands display the n first/last lines of a file respectively. To see the last ten commands entered:

```
tony:~> tail -10 .bash_history
locate configure | grep bin
man bash
cd
xawtv &
grep usable /usr/share/dict/words
grep advisable /usr/share/dict/words
info quota
man quota
echo $PATH
frm
```

head works similarly. The **tail** command has a handy feature to continuously show the last n lines of a file that changes all the time. This `-f` option is often used by system administrators to check on log files. More information is located in the system documentation files.

3.3.5 Linking files

3.3.5.1   Link types

Since we know more about files and their representation in the file system, understanding links (or shortcuts) is a piece of cake. A link is nothing more than a way of matching two or more file names to the same set of file data. There are two ways to achieve this:

- Hard link: Associate two or more file names with the same inode. Hard links share the same data blocks on the hard disk, while they continue to behave as independent files.

There is an immediate disadvantage: hard links can't span partitions, because inode numbers are only unique within a given partition.

- Soft link or symbolic link (or for short: symlink): a small file that is a pointer to another file. A symbolic link contains the path to the target file instead of a physical location on the hard disk. Since inodes are not used in this system, soft links can span across partitions.

The two link types behave similar, but are not the same, as illustrated in the scheme below:

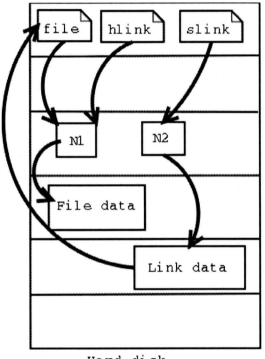

Figure 3.2. Hard and soft link mechanism

Note that removing the target file for a symbolic link makes the link useless.

Each regular file is in principle a hardlink. Hardlinks can not span across partitions, since they refer to inodes, and inode numbers are only unique within a given partition.

It may be argued that there is a third kind of link, the *user-space* link, which is similar to a shortcut in MS Windows. These are files containing meta-data which can only be interpreted by the graphical file manager. To the kernel and the shell these are just normal files. They may end in a *.desktop* or *.lnk* suffix; an example can be found in `~/.gnome-desktop`:

```
[dupont@boulot .gnome-desktop]$ cat La\ Maison\ Dupont
[Desktop Entry]
Encoding=Legacy-Mixed
Name=La Maison Dupont
Type=X-nautilus-home
X-Nautilus-Icon=temp-home
URL=file:///home/dupont
```

This example is from a KDE desktop:

```
[lena@venus Desktop]$ cat camera
[Desktop Entry]
Dev=/dev/sda1
FSType=auto
Icon=memory
MountPoint=/mnt/camera
Type=FSDevice
X-KDE-Dynamic-Device=true
```

Creating this kind of link is easy enough using the features of your graphical environment. Should you need help, your system documentation should be your first resort.

In the next section, we will study the creation of UNIX-style symbolic links using the command line.

3.3.5.2 Creating symbolic links

The symbolic link is particularly interesting for beginning users: they are fairly obvious to see and you don't need to worry about partitions.

The command to make links is **ln**. In order to create symlinks, you need to use the `-s` option:

ln `-s targetfile linkname`

In the example below, user *freddy* creates a link in a subdirectory of his home directory to a directory on another part of the system:

```
freddy:~/music> ln -s /opt/mp3/Queen/ Queen

freddy:~/music> ls -l
lrwxrwxrwx  1 freddy  freddy  17 Jan 22 11:07 Queen -> /opt/mp3/Queen
```

Symbolic links are always very small files, while hard links have the same size as the original file.

The application of symbolic links is widespread. They are often used to save disk space, to make a copy of a file in order to satisfy installation requirements of a new program that expects the file to be in another location, they are used to fix scripts that suddenly have to run in a new environment and can generally save a lot of work. A system admin may decide to move the home directories of the users to a new location, `disk2` for instance, but if he wants everything to work like before, like the `/etc/passwd` file, with a minimum of effort he will create a symlink from `/home` to the new location `/disk2/home`.

3.4 File security

3.4.1 Access rights: Linux's first line of defense

The Linux security model is based on the one used on UNIX systems, and is as rigid as the UNIX security model (and sometimes even more), which is already quite robust. On a Linux system, every file is owned by a user and a group user. There is also a third category of users, those that are not the user owner and don't belong to the group owning the file. For each category of users, read, write and execute permissions can be granted or denied.

We already used the *long* option to list files using the **ls -l** command, though for other reasons. This command also displays file permissions for these three user categories; they are indicated by the nine characters that follow the first character, which is the file type indicator at the beginning of the file properties line. As seen in the examples below, the first three characters in this series of nine display access rights for the actual user that owns the file. The next three are for the group owner of the file, the last three for other users. The permissions are always in the same order: read, write, execute for the user, the group and the others. Some examples:

```
marise:~> ls -l To_Do
-rw-rw-r--   1 marise   users       5 Jan 15 12:39 To_Do
marise:~> ls -l /bin/ls
-rwxr-xr-x   1 root     root    45948 Aug  9 15:01 /bin/ls*
```

The first file is a regular file (first dash). Users with user name *marise* or users belonging to the group *users* can read and write (change/move/delete) the file, but they can't execute it (second and third dash). All other users are only allowed to read this file, but they can't write or execute it (fourth and fifth dash).

The second example is an executable file, the difference: everybody can run this program, but you need to be *root* to change it.

The Info pages explain how the **ls** command handles display of access rights in detail, see the section *What information is listed.*

For easy use with commands, both access rights or modes and user groups have a code. See the tables below.

Code	Meaning
0 or -	The access right that is supposed to be on this place is not granted.
4 or r	read access is granted to the user category defined in this place
2 or w	write permission is granted to the user category defined in this place
1 or x	execute permission is granted to the user category defined in this place

Table 3.7. Access mode codes

Code	Meaning
u	user permissions
g	group permissions
o	permissions for others

Table 3.8. User group codes

This straight forward scheme is applied very strictly, which allows a high level of security even without network security. Among other functions, the security scheme takes care of user access to programs, it can serve files on a need-to-know basis and protect sensitive data such as home directories and system configuration files.

You should know what your user name is. If you don't, it can be displayed using the **id** command, which also displays the default group you belong to and eventually other groups of which you are a member:

```
tilly:~> id
uid=504(tilly) gid=504(tilly) groups=504(tilly),100(users),2051(org)
```

Your user name is also stored in the environment variable USER:

```
tilly:~> echo $USER
tilly
```

3.4.2 The tools

3.4.2.1   The chmod command

A normal consequence of applying strict file permissions, and sometimes a nuisance, is that access rights will need to be changed for all kinds of reasons. We use the **chmod** command to do this, and eventually *to chmod* has become an almost acceptable English verb, meaning the changing of the access mode of a file. The **chmod** command can be used with alphanumeric or numeric options, whatever you like best.

The example below uses alphanumeric options in order to solve a problem that commonly occurs with new users:

```
asim:~> ./hello
bash: ./hello: bad interpreter: Permission denied

asim:~> cat hello
#!/bin/bash
echo "Hello, World"

asim:~> ls -l hello
-rw-rw-r--    1 asim     asim       32 Jan 15 16:29 hello

asim:~> chmod u+x hello

asim:~> ./hello
Hello, World

asim:~> ls -l hello
-rwxrw-r--    1 asim     asim       32 Jan 15 16:29 hello*
```

The + and - operators are used to grant or deny a given right to a given group. Combinations separated by commas are allowed. The Info and man pages contain useful examples. Here's another one, which makes the file from the previous example a private file to user *asim*:

```
asim:~> chmod u+rwx,go-rwx hello

asim:~> ls -l hello
-rwx------    1 asim     asim       32 Jan 15 16:29 hello*
```

The kind of problem resulting in an error message saying that permission is denied somewhere is usually a problem with access rights in most cases. Also, comments like, "It worked yesterday," and "When I run this as root it works," are most likely caused by the wrong file permissions.

When using **chmod** with numeric arguments, the values for each granted access right have to be counted together per group. Thus we get a 3-digit number, which is the symbolic value for the settings **chmod** has to make. The following table lists the most common combinations:

Command	Meaning
chmod *400* file	To protect a file against accidental overwriting.
chmod *500*	To protect yourself from accidentally removing, renaming or

Command	Meaning
directory	moving files from this directory.
chmod *600* file	A private file only changeable by the user who entered this command.
chmod *644* file	A publicly readable file that can only be changed by the issuing user.
chmod *660* file	Users belonging to your group can change this files, others don't have any access to it at all.
chmod *700* file	Protects a file against any access from other users, while the issuing user still has full access.
chmod *755* directory	For files that should be readable and executable by others, but only changeable by the issuing user.
chmod *775* file	Standard file sharing mode for a group.
chmod *777* file	Everybody can do everything to this file.

Table 3.9. File protection with chmod

If you enter a number with less than three digits as an argument to **chmod**, omitted characters are replaced with zeros starting from the left. There is actually a fourth digit on Linux systems, that precedes the first three and sets special access modes. Everything about these and many more are located in the Info pages.

3.4.2.2 Logging on to another group

When you type **id** on the command line, you get a list of all the groups that you can possibly belong to, preceded by your user name and ID and the group name and ID that you are currently connected with. However, on many Linux systems you can only be actively logged in to one group at the time. By default, this active or *primary group* is the one that you get assigned from the /etc/passwd file. The fourth field of this file holds users' primary group ID, which is looked up in the /etc/group file. An example:

```
asim:~> id
uid=501(asim) gid=501(asim) groups=100(users),501(asim),3400(web)

asim:~> grep asim /etc/passwd
asim:x:501:501:Asim El Baraka:/home/asim:/bin/bash

asim:~> grep 501 /etc/group
asim:x:501:
```

The fourth field in the line from /etc/passwd contains the value "501", which represents the group *asim* in the above example. From /etc/group we can get the name matching this group ID. When initially connecting to the system, this is the group that *asim* will belong to.

✎ User private group scheme

In order to allow more flexibility, most Linux systems follow the so-called *user private group scheme*, that assigns each user primarily to his or her own group. This group is a group that only contains this particular user, hence the name "private group". Usually this group has the same name as the user login name, which can be a bit confusing.

Apart from his own private group, user *asim* can also be in the groups *users* and *web*. Because these are secondary groups to this user, he will need to use the **newgrp** to log into any of these groups. In the example, *asim* needs to create files that are owned by the group *web*.

```
asim:/var/www/html> newgrp web

asim:/var/www/html> id
uid=501(asim) gid=3400(web) groups=100(users),501(asim),3400(web)
```

When *asim* creates new files now, they will be in group ownership of the group *web* instead of being owned by the group *asim*:

```
asim:/var/www/html> touch test

asim:/var/www/html> ls -l test
-rw-rw-r--   1 asim web    0 Jun 10 15:38 test
```

Logging in to a new group prevents you from having to use **chown** (see Section 3.4.2.4) or calling your system administrator to change ownerships for you.

See the manpage for **newgrp** for more information.

3.4.2.3   The file mask

When a new file is saved somewhere, it is first subjected to the standard security procedure. Files without permissions don't exist on Linux. The standard file permission is determined by the *mask* for new file creation. The value of this mask can be displayed using the **umask** command:

```
bert:~> umask
0002
```

Instead of adding the symbolic values to each other, as with **chmod**, for calculating the permission on a new file they need to be subtracted from the total possible access rights. In the example above, however, we see 4 values displayed, yet there are only 3 permission categories: *user*, *group* and *other*. The first zero is part of the special file attributes settings, which we will discuss in Section 3.4.2.4 and Section 4.1.6. It might just as well be that this first zero is not displayed on your system when entering the **umask** command, and that you only see 3 numbers representing the default file creation mask.

Each UNIX-like system has a system function for creating new files, which is called each time a user uses a program that creates new files, for instance, when downloading a file from the Internet, when saving a new text document and so on. This function creates both new files and new directories. Full read, write and execute permission is granted to everybody when creating a new directory. When creating a new file, this function will grant read and write permissions for everybody, but set execute permissions to none for all user categories. This, before the mask is applied, a directory has permissions *777* or *rwxrwxrwx*, a plain file *666* or *rw-rw-rw-*.

The *umask* value is subtracted from these default permissions after the function has created the new file or directory. Thus, a directory will have permissions of *775* by default, a file *664*, if the mask value is *(0)002*. This is demonstrated in the example below:

```
bert:~> mkdir newdir

bert:~> ls -ld newdir
drwxrwxr-x    2 bert      bert         4096 Feb 28 13:45 newdir/

bert:~> touch newfile

bert:~> ls -l newfile
-rw-rw-r--    1 bert      bert            0 Feb 28 13:52 newfile
```

If you log in to another group using the **newgrp** command, the mask remains unchanged. Thus, if it is set to *002*, files and directories that you create while being in the new group will also be accessible to the other members of that group; you don't have to use **chmod**.

The *root* user usually has stricter default file creation permissions:

```
[root@estoban root]# umask
022
```

These defaults are set system-wide in the shell resource configuration files, for instance /etc/bashrc or /etc/profile. You can change them in your own shell configuration file, see Chapter 7 on customizing your shell environment.

3.4.2.4 Changing user and group ownership

When a file is owned by the wrong user or group, the error can be repaired with the **chown** (change owner) and **chgrp** (change group) commands. Changing file ownership is a frequent system administrative task in environments where files need to be shared in a group. Both commands are very flexible, as you can find out by using the `--help` option.

The **chown** command can be applied to change both user and group ownership of a file, while **chgrp** only changes group ownership. Of course the system will check if the user issuing one of these commands has sufficient permissions on the file(s) she wants to change.

In order to only change the user ownership of a file, use this syntax:

chown *newuser* **file**

If you use a colon after the user name (see the Info pages), group ownership will be changed as well, to the primary group of the user issuing the command. On a Linux system, each user has his own group, so this form can be used to make files private:

```
jacky:~> id
uid=1304(jacky) gid=(1304) groups=1304(jacky),2034(pproject)

jacky:~> ls -l my_report
-rw-rw-r-- 1 jacky    project       29387 Jan 15 09:34 my_report

jacky:~> chown jacky: my_report

jacky:~> chmod o-r my_report

jacky:~> ls -l my_report
-rw-rw---- 1 jacky    jacky         29387 Jan 15 09:34 my_report
```

If *jacky* would like to share this file, without having to give everybody permission to write it, he can use the **chgrp** command:

```
jacky:~> ls -l report-20020115.xls
-rw-rw---- 1 jacky    jacky    45635 Jan 15 09:35 report-20020115.xls

jacky:~> chgrp project report-20020115.xls

jacky:~> chmod o= report-20020115.xls

jacky:~> ls -l report-20020115.xls
-rw-rw---- 1 jacky    project 45635 Jan 15 09:35 report-20020115.xls
```

This way, users in the group *project* will be able to work on this file. Users not in this group have no business with it at all.

Both **chown** and **chgrp** can be used to change ownership recursively, using the -R option. In that case, all underlying files and subdirectories of a given directory will belong to the given user and/or group.

Restrictions

On most systems, the use of the **chown** and **chgrp** commands is restricted for non-privileged users. If you are not the administrator of the system, you can not change user nor group ownerships for security reasons. If the usage of these commands would not be restricted, malicious users could assign ownership of files to other users and/or groups and change behavior of those users' environments and even cause damage to other users' files.

3.4.2.5 Special modes

For the system admin to not be bothered solving permission problems all the time, special access rights can be given to entire directories, or to separate programs. There are three special modes:

- Sticky bit mode: After execution of a job, the command is kept in the system memory. Originally this was a feature used a lot to save memory: big jobs are loaded into memory only once. But these days memory is inexpensive and there are better techniques to manage it, so it is not used anymore for its optimizing capabilities on single files. When applied to an entire directory, however, the sticky bit has a different meaning. In that case, a user can only change files in this directory when she is the user owner of the file or when the file has appropriate permissions. This feature is used on directories like /var/tmp, that have to be accessible for everyone, but where it is not appropriate for users to change or delete each other's data. The sticky bit is indicated by a *t* at the end of the file permission field:

```
mark:~> ls -ld /var/tmp
drwxrwxrwt   19 root       root         8192 Jan 16 10:37 /var/tmp/
```

  The sticky bit is set using the command **chmod o+t directory**. The historic origin of the "t" is in UNIX' *save Text access* feature.

- SUID (set user ID) and SGID (set group ID): represented by the character *s* in the user or group permission field. When this mode is set on an executable file, it will run with the user and group permissions on the file instead of with those of the user issuing the command, thus giving access to system resources. We will discuss this further in Chapter 4.

- SGID (set group ID) on a directory: in this special case every file created in the directory will have the same group owner as the directory itself (while normal behavior would be that new files are owned by the users who create them). This way, users don't need to worry about file ownership when sharing directories:

```
mimi:~> ls -ld /opt/docs
drwxrws---  4 root     users          4096 Jul 25 2001 docs/

mimi:~> ls -l /opt/docs
-rw-rw----  1 mimi     users        345672 Aug 30 2001-Council.doc
```

This is the standard way of sharing files in UNIX.

Existing files are left unchanged!

Files that are being moved to a SGID directory but were created elsewhere keep their original user and group owner. This may be confusing.

3.5 Summary

On UNIX, as on Linux, all entities are in some way or another presented to the system as files with the appropriate file properties. Use of (predefined) paths allows the users and the system admin to find, read and manipulate files.

We've made our first steps toward becoming an expert: we discussed the real and the fake structure of the file system, and we know about the Linux file security model, as well as several other security precautions that are taken on every system by default.

The shell is the most important tool for interaction with the system. We learned several shell commands in this chapter, which are listed in the table below.

Command	Meaning
bash	GNU shell program.
cat file(s)	Send content of file(s) to standard output.
cd directory	Enter directory. cd is a bash built-in command.
chgrp newgroup file(s)	Change the group ownership of file(s) to newgroup
chmod mode file(s)	Change access permissions on file(s)
chown newowner [:[newgroup]] file(s)	Change file owner and group ownership.
cp sourcefile targetfile	Copy sourcefile to targetfile.
df file	Reports on used disk space on the partition containing file.

Command	Meaning
echo *string*	Display a line of text
export	Part of **bash** that announces variables and their values to the system.
file `filename`	Determine file type of `filename`.
find *path expression*	Find files in the file system hierarchy
grep *PATTERN* `file`	Print lines in `file` containing the search pattern.
head `file`	Send the first part of `file` to standard output
id	Prints real and effective user name and groups.
info *command*	Read documentation about **command**.
less `file`	View `file` with a powerful viewer.
ln `targetfile linkname`	Make a link with name `linkname` to `targetfile`.
locate *searchstring*	Print all accessible files matching the search pattern.
ls `file(s)`	Prints directory content.
man *command*	Format and display online (system) manual pages for **command**.
mkdir `newdir`	Make a new empty directory.
mv `oldfile newfile`	Rename or move `oldfile`.
newgrp *groupname*	Log in to a new group.
pwd	Print the present or current working directory.
quota	Show disk usage and limits.
rm `file`	Removes files and directories.
rmdir `file`	Removes directories.
tail `file`	Print the last part of `file`.
umask [*value*]	Show or change new file creation mode.
wc `file`	Counts lines, words and characters in `file`.
which *command*	Shows the full path to **command**.

Table 3.10. New commands in Chapter 3: Files and the file system

We also stressed the fact that you should READ THE MAN PAGES. This documentation is your first-aid kit and contains the answers to many questions. The above list contains the basic commands that you will use on a daily basis, but they can do much more than the tasks we've discussed here. Reading the documentation will give you the control you need.

Last but not least, a handy overview of file permissions:

Who\What	r(ead)	w(rite)	(e)x(ecute)
u(ser)	4	2	1
g(roup)	4	2	1
o(ther)	4	2	1

Table 3.11. File permissions

3.6 Exercises

Just login with your common user ID.

3.6.1 Partitions

- On which partition is your home directory?
- How many partitions are on your system?
- What is the total size of your Linux installation?

3.6.2 Paths

- Display your search path.
- Export a senseless path by entering, for instance, **export PATH=blah** and try listing directory content.
- What is the path to your home directory? How would another user reach your home directory starting from his own home directory, using a relative path?
- Go to the tmp directory in /var.
- Now go to share in /usr using only one command. Change to doc. What is your present working directory?

3.6.3 Tour of the system

- Change to the /proc directory.
- What CPU(s) is the system running on?
- How much RAM does it currently use?

- How much swap space do you have?
- What drivers are loaded?
- How many hours has the system been running?
- Which filesystems are known by your system?
- Change to `/etc/rc.d` | `/etc/init.d` | `/etc/runlevels` and choose the directory appropriate for your run level.
- What services should be running in this level?
- Which services run in graphical mode that don't run in text mode?
- Change to `/etc`
- How long does the system keep the log file in which user logins are monitored?
- Which release are you running?
- Are there any issues or messages of the day?
- How many users are defined on your system? Don't count them, let the computer do it for you!
- How many groups?
- Where is the time zone information kept?
- Are the HOWTOs installed on your system?
- Change to `/usr/share/doc`.
- Name three programs that come with the GNU *coreutils* package.
- Which version of **bash** is installed on this system?

3.6.4 Manipulating files

- Create a new directory in your home directory.
- Can you move this directory to the same level as your home directory?
- Copy all XPM files from `/usr/share/pixmaps` to the new directory. What does XPM mean?
- List the files in reverse alphabetical order.
- Change to your home directory. Create a new directory and copy all the files of the `/etc` directory into it. Make sure that you also copy the files and directories which are in the subdirectories of `/etc`! (recursive copy)

- Change into the new directory and make a directory for files starting with an upper case character and one for files starting with a lower case character. Move all the files to the appropriate directories. Use as few commands as possible.

- Remove the remaining files.

- Delete the directory and its entire content using a single command.

- Use **grep** to find out which script starts the Font Server in the graphical run level.

- Where is the *sendmail* server program?

- Make a symbolic link in your home directory to /var/tmp. Check that it really works.

- Make another symbolic link in your home directory to this link. Check that it works. Remove the first link and list directory content. What happened to the second link?

3.6.5 File permissions

- Can you change file permissions on /home?

- What is your standard file creation mode?

- Change ownership of /etc to your own user and group.

- Change file permissions of ~/.bashrc so that only you and your primary group can read it.

- Issue the command **locate root**. Do you notice anything special?

- Make a symbolic link to /root. Can it be used?

Chapter 4
Processes

Next to files, processes are the most important things on a UNIX/Linux system. In this chapter, we will take a closer look at those processes. We will learn more about:

- Multi-user processing and multi-tasking

- Process types

- Controlling processes with different signals

- Process attributes

- The life cycle of a process

- System startup and shutdown

- SUID and SGID

- System speed and response

- Scheduling processes

- The Vixie cron system

- How to get the most out of your system

4.1   Processes inside out

4.1.1 Multi-user and multi-tasking

Now that we are more used to our environment and we are able to communicate a little bit with our system, it is time to study the processes we can start in more detail. Not every command starts a single process. Some commands initiate a series of processes, such as **mozilla**; others, like **ls**, are executed as a single command.

Furthermore, Linux is based on UNIX, where it has been common policy to have multiple users running multiple commands, at the same time and on the same system. It is obvious that measures have to be taken to have the CPU manage all these processes, and that functionality has to be provided so users can switch between processes. In some cases, processes will have to continue to run even when the user who started them logs out. And users need a means to reactivate interrupted processes.

We will explain the structure of Linux processes in the next sections.

4.1.2 Process types

4.1.2.1   Interactive processes

Interactive processes are initialized and controlled through a terminal session. In other words, there has to be someone connected to the system to start these processes; they are not started automatically as part of the system functions. These processes can run in the foreground, occupying the terminal that started the program, and you can't start other applications as long as this process is running in the foreground. Alternatively, they can run in the background, so that the terminal in which you started the program can accept new commands while the program is running. Until now, we mainly focussed on programs running in the foreground - the length of time taken to run them was too short to notice - but viewing a file with the **less** command is a good example of a command occupying the terminal session. In this case, the activated program is waiting for you to do something. The program is still connected to the terminal from where it was started, and the terminal is only useful for entering commands this program can understand. Other commands will just result in errors or unresponsiveness of the system.

While a process runs in the background, however, the user is not prevented from doing other things in the terminal in which he started the program, while it is running.

The shell offers a feature called *job control* which allows easy handling of multiple processes. This mechanism switches processes between the foreground and the background. Using this system, programs can also be started in the background immediately.

Running a process in the background is only useful for programs that don't need user input (via the shell). Putting a job in the background is typically done when execution of a job is expected to take a long time. In order to free the issuing terminal after entering the command, a trailing ampersand is added. In the example, using graphical mode, we open an extra terminal window from the existing one:

```
billy:~> xterm &
[1] 26558

billy:~> jobs
[1]+  Running                 xterm &
```

The full job control features are explained in detail in the **bash** Info pages, so only the frequently used job control applications are listed here:

(part of) command	Meaning
regular_command	Runs this command in the foreground.
command &	Run this command in the background (release the terminal)
jobs	Show commands running in the background.
Ctrl+Z	Suspend (stop, but not quit) a process running in the foreground (suspend).
Ctrl+C	Interrupt (terminate and quit) a process running in the foreground.
%n	Every process running in the background gets a number assigned to it. By using the % expression a job can be referred to using its number, for instance **fg %2**.
bg	Reactivate a suspended program in the background.
fg	Puts the job back in the foreground.
kill	End a process (also see Shell Builtin Commands in the Info pages of **bash**)

Table 4.1. Controlling processes

More practical examples can be found in the exercises.

Most UNIX systems are likely to be able to run **screen**, which is useful when you actually want another shell to execute commands. Upon calling **screen**, a new session is created with an accompanying shell and/or commands as specified, which you can then put out of the way. In this new session you may do whatever it is you want to do. All programs and operations will run independent of the issuing shell. You can then detach this session, while the programs you started in it continue to run, even when you log out of the originating shell, and pick your *screen* up again any time you like.

This program originates from a time when virtual consoles were not invented yet, and everything needed to be done using one text terminal. To addicts, it still has meaning in Linux, even though we've had virtual consoles for almost ten years.

4.1.2.2 Automatic processes

Automatic or batch processes are not connected to a terminal. Rather, these are tasks that can be queued into a spooler area, where they wait to be executed on a FIFO (first-in, first-out) basis. Such tasks can be executed using one of two criteria:

- At a certain date and time: done using the **at** command, which we will discuss in the second part of this chapter.

- At times when the total system load is low enough to accept extra jobs: done using the **batch** command. By default, tasks are put in a queue where they wait to be executed until the system load is lower than 0.8. In large environments, the system administrator may prefer batch processing when large amounts of data have to be processed or when tasks demanding a lot of system resources have to be executed on an already loaded system. Batch processing is also used for optimizing system performance.

4.1.2.3 Daemons

Daemons are server processes that run continuously. Most of the time, they are initialized at system startup and then wait in the background until their service is required. A typical example is the networking daemon, *xinetd*, which is started in almost every boot procedure. After the system is booted, the network daemon just sits and waits until a client program, such as an FTP client, needs to connect.

4.1.3 Process attributes

A process has a series of characteristics, which can be viewed with the **ps** command:

- The process ID or PID: a unique identification number used to refer to the process.

- The parent process ID or PPID: the number of the process (PID) that started this process.

- Nice number: the degree of friendliness of this process toward other processes (not to be confused with process priority, which is calculated based on this nice number and recent CPU usage of the process).

- Terminal or TTY: terminal to which the process is connected.

- User name of the real and effective user (RUID and EUID): the owner of the process. The real owner is the user issuing the command, the effective user is the one determining access to system resources. RUID and EUID are usually the same, and the process has the same access rights the issuing user would have. An example to clarify this: the browser **mozilla** in /usr/bin is owned by user *root*:

```
theo:~> ls -l /usr/bin/mozilla
-rwxr-xr-x  1 root    root         4996 Nov 20 18:28 /usr/bin/mozilla*

theo:~> mozilla &
[1] 26595

theo:~> ps -af
UID      PID  PPID C STIME TTY      TIME CMD
theo   26601 26599 0 15:04 pts/5 00:00:00 /usr/lib/mozilla/mozilla-bin
theo   26613 26569 0 15:04 pts/5 00:00:00 ps -af
```

When user *theo* starts this program, the process itself and all processes started by the initial process, will be owned by user *theo* and not by the system administrator. When **mozilla** needs access to certain files, that access will be determined by *theo*'s permissions and not by *root*'s.

• Real and effective group owner (RGID and EGID): The real group owner of a process is the primary group of the user who started the process. The effective group owner is usually the same, except when SGID access mode has been applied to a file.

4.1.4 Displaying process information

The **ps** command is one of the tools for visualizing processes. This command has several options which can be combined to display different process attributes.

With no options specified, **ps** only gives information about the current shell and eventual processes:

```
theo:~> ps
  PID TTY          TIME CMD
 4245 pts/7    00:00:00 bash
 5314 pts/7    00:00:00 ps
```

Since this does not give enough information - generally, at least a hundred processes are running on your system - we will usually select particular processes out of the list of all processes, using the **grep** command in a *pipe*, see Section 5.1.2.1, as in this line, which will select and display all processes owned by a particular user:

ps -ef | grep *username*

This example shows all processes with a process name of **bash**, the most common login shell on Linux systems:

```
theo:> ps auxw | grep bash
brenda   31970  0.0  0.3  6080 1556 tty2   S  Feb23   0:00 -bash
root     32043  0.0  0.3  6112 1600 tty4   S  Feb23   0:00 -bash
theo     32581  0.0  0.3  6384 1864 pts/1  S  Feb23   0:00 bash
theo     32616  0.0  0.3  6396 1896 pts/2  S  Feb23   0:00 bash
theo     32629  0.0  0.3  6380 1856 pts/3  S  Feb23   0:00 bash
```

```
theo       2214  0.0  0.3  6412 1944 pts/5  S  16:18  0:02 bash
theo       4245  0.0  0.3  6392 1888 pts/7  S  17:26  0:00 bash
theo       5427  0.0  0.1  3720  548 pts/7  S  19:22  0:00 grep bash
```

In these cases, the **grep** command finding lines containing the string *bash* is often displayed as well on systems that have a lot of idletime. If you don't want this to happen, use the **pgrep** command.

Bash shells are a special case: this process list also shows which ones are login shells (where you have to give your username and password, such as when you log in in textmode or do a remote login, as opposed to non-login shells, started up for instance by clicking a terminal window icon). Such login shells are preceded with a dash (-).

 |?

We will explain about the | operator in the next chapter, see Chapter 5.

More info can be found the usual way: **ps --help** or **man *ps***. GNU **ps** supports different styles of option formats; the above examples don't contain errors.

Note that **ps** only gives a momentary state of the active processes, it is a one-time recording. The **top** program displays a more precise view by updating the results given by **ps** (with a bunch of options) once every five seconds, generating a new list of the processes causing the heaviest load periodically, meanwhile integrating more information about the swap space in use and the state of the CPU, from the proc file system:

```
12:40pm up 9 days, 6:00, 4 users, load average: 0.21, 0.11, 0.03
89 processes: 86 sleeping, 3 running, 0 zombie, 0 stopped
CPU states:  2.5% user,  1.7% system,  0.0% nice, 95.6% idle
Mem:   255120K av, 239412K used,  15708K free,    756K shrd,  22620K buff
Swap: 1050176K av,  76428K used, 973748K free,  82756K cached

  PID USER     PRI NI SIZE   RSS SHARE STAT %CPU %MEM TIME COMMAND
 5005 root      14  0 91572  15M 11580 R    1.9  6.0  7:53 X
19599 jeff      14  0  1024 1024   796 R    1.1  0.4  0:01 top
19100 jeff       9  0  5288 4948  3888 R    0.5  1.9  0:24 gnome-terminal
19328 jeff       9  0 37884  36M 14724 S    0.5 14.8  1:30 mozilla-bin
    1 root       8  0   516  472   464 S    0.0  0.1  0:06 init
    2 root       9  0     0    0     0 SW   0.0  0.0  0:02 keventd
    3 root       9  0     0    0     0 SW   0.0  0.0  0:00 kapm-idled
    4 root      19 19     0    0     0 SWN  0.0  0.0  0:00 ksoftirqd_CPU0
    5 root       9  0     0    0     0 SW   0.0  0.0  0:33 kswapd
    6 root       9  0     0    0     0 SW   0.0  0.0  0:00 kreclaimd
    7 root       9  0     0    0     0 SW   0.0  0.0  0:00 bdflush
    8 root       9  0     0    0     0 SW   0.0  0.0  0:05 kupdated
    9 root      -1-20     0    0     0 SW<  0.0  0.0  0:00 mdrecoveryd
   13 root       9  0     0    0     0 SW   0.0  0.0  0:01 kjournald
   89 root       9  0     0    0     0 SW   0.0  0.0  0:00 khubd
```

```
 219 root      9  0       0     0      0 SW    0.0   0.0   0:00 kjournald
 220 root      9  0       0     0      0 SW    0.0   0.0   0:00 kjournald
```

The first line of **top** contains the same information displayed by the **uptime** command:

```
jeff:~> uptime
  3:30pm, up 12 days, 23:29, 6 users, load average: 0.01, 0.02, 0.00
```

The data for these programs is stored among others in /var/run/utmp (information about currently connected users) and in the virtual file system /proc, for example /proc/loadavg (average load information). There are all sorts of graphical applications to view this data, such as the Gnome System Monitor and *lavaps*. Over at FreshMeat <http://www.freshmeat.net/> and SourceForge <http://www.sourceforge.org/> you will find tens of applications that centralize this information along with other server data and logs from multiple servers on one (web) server, allowing monitoring of the entire IT infrastructure from one workstation.

The relations between processes can be visualized using the **pstree** command:

```
sophie:~> pstree
init-+-amd
     |-apmd
     |-2*[artsd]
     |-atd
     |-crond
     |-deskguide_apple
     |-eth0
     |-gdm---gdm-+-X
     |           `-gnome-session-+-Gnome
     |                           |-ssh-agent
     |                           `-true
     |-geyes_applet
     |-gkb_applet
     |-gnome-name-serv
     |-gnome-smproxy
     |-gnome-terminal-+-bash---vim
     |                |-bash
     |                |-bash---pstree
     |                |-bash---ssh
     |                |-bash---mozilla-bin---mozilla-bin---3*[mozilla-bin]
     |                `-gnome-pty-helper
     |-gpm
     |-gweather
     |-kapm-idled
     |-3*[kdeinit]
     |-keventd
     |-khubd
     |-5*[kjournald]
     |-klogd
     |-lockd---rpciod
     |-lpd
```

```
    |-mdrecoveryd
    |-6*[mingetty]
    |-8*[nfsd]
    |-nscd---nscd---5*[nscd]
    |-ntpd
    |-3*[oafd]
    |-panel
    |-portmap
    |-rhnsd
    |-rpc.mountd
    |-rpc.rquotad
    |-rpc.statd
    |-sawfish
    |-screenshooter_a
    |-sendmail
    |-sshd---sshd---bash---su---bash
    |-syslogd
    |-tasklist_applet
    |-vmnet-bridge
    |-xfs
    `-xinetd-ipv6
```

The -u and -a options give additional information. For more options and what they do, refer to the Info pages.

In the next section, we will see how one process can create another.

4.1.5 Life and death of a process

4.1.5.1   Process creation

A new process is created because an existing process makes an exact copy of itself. This child process has the same environment as its parent, only the process ID number is different. This procedure is called *forking*.

After the forking process, the address space of the child process is overwritten with the new process data. This is done through an *exec* call to the system.

The *fork-and-exec* mechanism thus switches an old command with a new, while the environment in which the new program is executed remains the same, including configuration of input and output devices, environment variables and priority. This mechanism is used to create all UNIX processes, so it also applies to the Linux operating system. Even the first process, **init**, with process ID 1, is forked during the boot procedure in the so-called *bootstrapping* procedure.

This scheme illustrates the fork-and-exec mechanism. The process ID changes after the fork procedure:

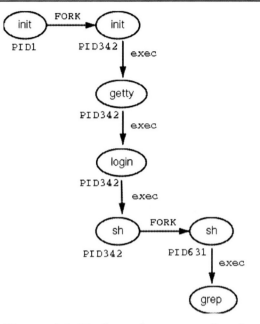

Figure 4.1. Fork-and-exec mechanism

There are a couple of cases in which **init** becomes the parent of a process, while the process was not started by **init**, as we already saw in the **pstree** example. Many programs, for instance, *daemonize* their child processes, so they can keep on running when the parent stops or is being stopped. A window manager is a typical example; it starts an **xterm** process that generates a shell that accepts commands. The window manager then denies any further responsibility and passes the child process to **init**. Using this mechanism, it is possible to change window managers without interrupting running applications.

Every now and then things go wrong, even in good families. In an exceptional case, a process might finish while the parent does not wait for the completion of this process. Such an unburied process is called a *zombie* process.

4.1.5.2 Ending processes

When a process ends normally (it is not killed or otherwise unexpectedly interrupted), the program returns its *exit status* to the parent. This exit status is a number returned by the program providing the results of the program's execution. The system of returning information upon executing a job has its origin in the C programming language in which UNIX has been written.

The return codes can then be interpreted by the parent, or in scripts. The values of the return codes are program-specific. This information can usually be found in the man pages of the specified program, for example the **grep** command returns -1 if no matches are found, upon which a message on the lines of "No files found" can be printed. Another example is the Bash builtin command **true**, which does nothing except return an exit status of 0, meaning success.

4.1.5.3 Signals

Processes end because they receive a signal. There are multiple signals that you can send to a process. Use the **kill** command to send a signal to a process. The command **kill -1** shows a list of signals. Most signals are for internal use by the system, or for programmers when they write code. As a user, you will need the following signals:

Signal name	Signal number	Meaning
SIGTERM	15	Terminate the process in an orderly way.
SIGINT	2	Interrupt the process. A process can ignore this signal.
SIGKILL	9	Interrupt the process. A process can not ignore this signal.
SIGHUP	1	For daemons: reread the configuration file.

Table 4.2. Common signals

You can read more about default actions that are taken when sending a signal to a process in **man 7 signal**.

4.1.6 SUID and SGID

As promised in the previous chapter, we will now discuss the special modes SUID and SGID in more detail. These modes exist to provide normal users the ability to execute tasks they would normally not be able to do because of the tight file permission scheme used on UNIX based systems. In the ideal situation special modes are used as sparsely as possible, since they include security risks. Linux developers have generally tried to avoid them as much as possible. The Linux **ps** version, for example, uses the information stored in the /proc file system, which is accessible to everyone, thus avoiding exposition of sensitive system data and resources to the general public. Before that, and still on older UNIX systems, the **ps** program needed access to files such as /dev/mem and /dev/kmem, which had disadvantages because of the permissions and ownerships on these files:

```
rita:~> ls -l /dev/*mem
crw-r-----    1 root     kmem       1,    2 Aug 30 22:30 /dev/kmem
crw-r-----    1 root     kmem       1,    1 Aug 30 22:30 /dev/mem
```

With older versions of **ps**, it was not possible to start the program as a common user, unless special modes were applied to it.

While we generally try to avoid applying any special modes, it is sometimes necessary to use an SUID. An example is the mechanism for changing passwords. Of course users will want to do this themselves instead of having their password set by the system administrator. As we know, user names and passwords are listed in the /etc/passwd file, which has these access permissions and owners:

```
bea:~> ls -l /etc/passwd
-rw-r--r--    1 root     root         1267 Jan 16 14:43 /etc/passwd
```

Still, users need to be able to change their own information in this file. This is achieved by giving the **passwd** program special permissions:

```
mia:~> which passwd
passwd is /usr/bin/passwd

mia:~> ls -l /usr/bin/passwd
-r-s--x--x    1 root     root        13476 Aug  7 06:03 /usr/bin/passwd*
```

When called, the **passwd** command will run using the access permissions of *root*, thus enabling a common user to edit the password file which is owned by the system admin.

SGID modes on a file don't occur nearly as frequently as SUID, because SGID often involves the creation of extra groups. In some cases, however, we have to go through this trouble in order to build an elegant solution (don't worry about this too much - the necessary groups are usually created upon installation). This is the case for the **write** and **wall** programs, which are used to send messages to other users' terminals (ttys). The **write** command writes a message to a single user, while **wall** writes to all connected users.

Sending text to another user's terminal or graphical display is normally not allowed. In order to bypass this problem, a group has been created, which owns all terminal devices. When the **write** and **wall** commands are granted SGID permissions, the commands will run using the access rights as applicable to this group, *tty* in the example. Since this group has write access to the destination terminal, also a user having no permissions to use that terminal in any way can send messages to it.

In the example below, user *joe* first finds out on which terminal his correspondent is connected, using the **who** command. Then he sends her a message using the **write** command. Also illustrated are the access rights on the **write** program and on the terminals occupied by the receiving user: it is clear that others than the user owner have no permissions on the device, except for the group owner, which can write to it.

```
joe:~> which write
write is /usr/bin/write

joe:~> ls -l /usr/bin/write
-rwxr-sr-x    1 root     tty          8744 Dec  5 00:55 /usr/bin/write*
```

```
joe:~> who
jenny      tty1      Jan 23 11:41
jenny      pts/1     Jan 23 12:21 (:0)
jenny      pts/2     Jan 23 12:22 (:0)
jenny      pts/3     Jan 23 12:22 (:0)
joe        pts/0     Jan 20 10:13 (lo.callhost.org)

joe:~> ls -l /dev/tty1
crw--w----  1 jenny   tty  4,    1 Jan 23 11:41 /dev/tty1

joe:~> write jenny tty1
hey Jenny, shall we have lunch together?
^C
```

User *jenny* gets this on her screen:

```
Message from joe@lo.callhost.org on ptys/1 at 12:36 ...
hey Jenny, shall we have lunch together?
EOF
```

After receiving a message, the terminal can be cleared using the **Ctrl+L** key combination. In order to receive no messages at all (except from the system administrator), use the **mesg** command. To see which connected users accept messages from others use **who -w**. All features are fully explained in the Info pages of each command.

Group names may vary

The group scheme is specific to the distribution. Other distributions may use other names or other solutions.

4.2   Boot process, Init and shutdown

4.2.1 Introduction

One of the most powerful aspects of Linux concerns its open method of starting and stopping the operating system, where it loads specified programs using their particular configurations, permits you to change those configurations to control the boot process, and shuts down in a graceful and organized way.

Beyond the question of controlling the boot or shutdown process, the open nature of Linux makes it much easier to determine the exact source of most problems associated with starting up or shutting down your system. A basic understanding of this process is quite beneficial to everybody who uses a Linux system.

A lot of Linux systems use **lilo**, the LInux LOader for booting operating systems. We will only discuss GRUB, however, which is easier to use and more flexible. Should you need information about **lilo**, refer to the man pages and HOWTOs. Both systems support dual boot installations, we refer to the HOWTOs on this subject for practical examples and background information.

4.2.2 The boot process

When an x86 computer is booted, the processor looks at the end of the system memory for the BIOS (Basic Input/Output System) and runs it. The BIOS program is written into permanent read-only memory and is always available for use. The BIOS provides the lowest level interface to peripheral devices and controls the first step of the boot process.

The BIOS tests the system, looks for and checks peripherals, and then looks for a drive to use to boot the system. Usually it checks the floppy drive (or CD-ROM drive on many newer systems) for bootable media, if present, and then it looks to the hard drive. The order of the drives used for booting is usually controlled by a particular BIOS setting on the system. Once Linux is installed on the hard drive of a system, the BIOS looks for a Master Boot Record (MBR) starting at the first sector on the first hard drive, loads its contents into memory, then passes control to it.

This MBR contains instructions on how to load the GRUB (or LILO) boot-loader, using a pre-selected operating system. The MBR then loads the boot-loader, which takes over the process (if the boot-loader is installed in the MBR). In the default Red Hat Linux configuration, GRUB uses the settings in the MBR to display boot options in a menu. Once GRUB has received the correct instructions for the operating system to start, either from its command line or configuration file, it finds the necessary boot file and hands off control of the machine to that operating system.

4.2.3 GRUB features

This boot method is called *direct loading* because instructions are used to directly load the operating system, with no intermediary code between the boot-loaders and the operating system's main files (such as the kernel). The boot process used by other operating systems may differ slightly from the above, however. For example, Microsoft's DOS and Windows operating systems completely overwrite anything on the MBR when they are installed without incorporating any of the current MBR's configuration. This destroys any other information stored in the MBR by other operating systems, such as Linux. The Microsoft operating systems, as well as various other proprietary operating systems, are loaded using a chain loading boot method. With this method, the MBR points to the first sector of the partition holding the operating system, where it finds the special files necessary to actually boot that operating system.

GRUB supports both boot methods, allowing you to use it with almost any operating system, most popular file systems, and almost any hard disk your BIOS can recognize.

GRUB contains a number of other features; the most important include:

- GRUB provides a true command-based, pre-OS environment on x86 machines to allow maximum flexibility in loading operating systems with certain options or gathering information about the system.

- GRUB supports Logical Block Addressing (LBA) mode, needed to access many IDE and all SCSI hard disks. Before LBA, hard drives could encounter a 1024-cylinder limit, where the BIOS could not find a file after that point.

- GRUB's configuration file is read from the disk every time the system boots, preventing you from having to write over the MBR every time you change the boot options.

A full description of GRUB may be found by issuing the **info *grub*** command or at the GRUB site <http://www.gnu.org/software/grub/>. The Linux Documentation Project has a "Multiboot with GRUB Mini-HOWTO" <http://www.tldp.org/ HOWTO/mini/Multiboot-with-GRUB.html>.

4.2.4 Init

The kernel, once it is loaded, finds **init** in `sbin` and executes it.

When **init** starts, it becomes the parent or grandparent of all of the processes that start up automatically on your Linux system. The first thing **init** does, is reading its initialization file, `/etc/inittab`. This instructs **init** to read an initial configuration script for the environment, which sets the path, starts swapping, checks the file systems, and so on. Basically, this step takes care of everything that your system needs to have done at system initialization: setting the clock, initializing serial ports and so forth.

Then **init** continues to read the `/etc/inittab` file, which describes how the system should be set up in each run level and sets the default *run level*. A run level is a configuration of processes. All UNIX-like systems can be run in different process configurations, such as the single user mode, which is referred to as run level 1 or run level S (or s). In this mode, only the system administrator can connect to the system. It is used to perform maintenance tasks without risks of damaging the system or user data. Naturally, in this configuration we don't need to offer user services, so they will all be disabled. Another run level is the reboot run level, or run level 6, which shuts down all running services according to the appropriate procedures and then restarts the system.

Use the **who** to check what your current run level is:

```
willy@ubuntu:~$ who -r
     run-level 2 2006-10-17 23:22          last=S
```

More about run levels in the next section, see Section 4.2.5.

After having determined the default run level for your system, **init** starts all of the background processes necessary for the system to run by looking in the appropriate rc directory for that run level. **init** runs each of the kill scripts (their file names start with a K) with a stop parameter. It then runs all of the start scripts (their file names start with an S) in the appropriate run level directory so that all services and applications are started correctly. In fact, you can execute these same scripts manually after the system is finished booting with a command like **/etc/init.d/httpd** *stop* or **service** *httpd* *stop* logged in as *root*, in this case stopping the web server.

Special case

Note that on system startup, the scripts in rc2.d and rc3.d are usually executed. In that case, no services are stopped (at least not permanently). There are only services that are started.

None of the scripts that actually start and stop the services are located in /etc/rc<x>.d. Rather, all of the files in /etc/rc<x>.d are symbolic links that point to the actual scripts located in /etc/init.d. A symbolic link is nothing more than a file that points to another file, and is used in this case because it can be created and deleted without affecting the actual scripts that kill or start the services. The symbolic links to the various scripts are numbered in a particular order so that they start in that order. You can change the order in which the services start up or are killed by changing the name of the symbolic link that refers to the script that actually controls the service. You can use the same number multiple times if you want a particular service started or stopped right before or after another service, as in the example below, listing the content of /etc/rc5.d, where **crond** and **xfs** are both started from a linkname starting with "S90". In this case, the scripts are started in alphabetical order.

```
[jean@blub /etc/rc5.d] ls
K15httpd@       K45named@       S08ipchains@    S25netfs@       S85gpm@
K16rarpd@       K46radvd@       S08iptables@    S26apmd@        S90crond@
K20nfs@         K61ldap@        S09isdn@        S28autofs@      S90xfs@
K20rstatd@      K65identd@      S10network@     S30nscd@        S95anacron@
K20rusersd@     K74ntpd@        S12syslog@      S55sshd@        S95atd@
K20rwalld@      K74ypserv@      S13portmap@     S56rawdevices@  S97rhnsd@
K20rwhod@       K74ypxfrd@      S14nfslock@     S56xinetd@      S99local@
K25squid@       K89bcm5820@     S17keytable@    S60lpd@
K34yppasswdd@   S05kudzu@       S20random@      S80sendmail@
```

After **init** has progressed through the run levels to get to the default run level, the /etc/inittab script forks a **getty** process for each virtual console (login prompt in text mode). **getty** opens tty lines, sets their modes, prints the login prompt, gets the user's name, and then initiates a login process for that user. This allows users to authenticate themselves to the system and use it. By default, most systems offer 6 virtual consoles, but as you can see from the inittab file, this is configurable.

/etc/inittab can also tell **init** how it should handle a user pressing **Ctrl+Alt+Delete** at the console. As the system should be properly shut down and restarted rather than immediately power-cycled, **init** is told to execute the command **/sbin/shutdown -t3 -r *now***, for instance, when a user hits those keys. In addition, /etc/inittab states what **init** should do in case of power failures, if your system has a UPS unit attached to it.

On most RPM-based systems the graphical login screen is started in run level 5, where /etc/inittab runs a script called /etc/X11/prefdm. The prefdm script runs the preferred X display manager, based on the contents of the /etc/sysconfig/desktop directory. This is typically **gdm** if you run GNOME or **kdm** if you run KDE, but they can be mixed, and there's also the **xdm** that comes with a standard X installation.

But there are other possibilities as well. On Debian, for instance, there is an initscript for each of the display managers, and the content of the /etc/X11/default-display-manager is used to determine which one to start. More about the graphical interface can be read in Section 7.3. Ultimately, your system documentation will explain the details about the higher level aspects of **init**.

The /etc/default and/or /etc/sysconfig directories contain entries for a range of functions and services, these are all read at boot time. The location of the directory containing system defaults might be somewhat different depending on your Linux distribution.

Besides the graphical user environment, a lot of other services may be started as well. But if all goes well, you should be looking at a login prompt or login screen when the boot process has finished.

Other procedures

We explained how SysV **init** works on x86 based machines. Startup procedures may vary on other architectures and distributions. Other systems may use the BSD-style **init**, where startup files are not split up into multiple /etc/rc<LEVEL>.d directories. It might also be possible that your system uses /etc/rc.d/init.d instead of /etc/init.d.

4.2.5 Init run levels

The idea behind operating different services at different run levels essentially revolves around the fact that different systems can be used in different ways. Some services cannot be used until the system is in a particular state, or *mode*, such as being ready for more than one user or having networking available.

There are times in which you may want to operate the system in a lower mode. Examples are fixing disk corruption problems in run level 1 so no other users can possibly be on the system, or leaving a server in run level 3 without an X session running. In these cases, running services that depend upon a higher system mode to function does not make sense because they will not work correctly anyway. By already having each service assigned to start when its particular run level is reached, you ensure an orderly start up process, and you can quickly change the mode of the machine without worrying about which services to manually start or stop.

Available run levels are generally described in /etc/inittab, which is partially shown below:

```
#
# inittab   This file describes how the INIT process should set up
#           the system in a certain run-level.

# Default run level. The run levels are:
#   0 - halt (Do NOT set initdefault to this)
#   1 - Single user mode
#   2 - Multiuser, without NFS
#   (The same as 3, if you do not have networking)
#   3 - Full multiuser mode
#   4 - unused
#   5 - X11
#   6 - reboot (Do NOT set initdefault to this)
#
id:5:initdefault:
<--cut-->
```

Feel free to configure unused run levels (commonly run level 4) as you see fit. Many users configure those run levels in a way that makes the most sense for them while leaving the standard run levels as they are by default. This allows them to quickly move in and out of their custom configuration without disturbing the normal set of features at the standard run levels.

If your machine gets into a state where it will not boot due to a bad /etc/inittab or will not let you log in because you have a corrupted /etc/passwd file (or if you have simply forgotten your password), boot into single-user mode.

No graphics?

When you are working in text mode because you didn't get presented a graphical login screen on the console of your machine, you can normally switch to console 7 or up to have a graphical login. If this is not the case, check the current run level using the command **who -r**. If it is set to something else than the original default from /etc/inittab, chances are that the system does not start up in graphical mode by default. Contact your system administrator or read **man init** in that case. Note that switching run levels is done preferably using the **telinit** command; switching from a text to a graphical console or vice versa does not involve a run level switch.

The discussion of run levels, scripts and configurations in this guide tries to be as general as possible. Lots of variations exist. For instance, Gentoo Linux stores scripts in /etc/run levels. Other systems might first run through (a) lower run level(s) and execute all the scripts in there before arriving at the final run level and executing those scripts. Refer to your system documentation for more information. You might also read through the scripts that are refered to in /etc/inittab to get a better comprehension of what happens on your system.

4.2.5.1 Tools

The **chkconfig** or **update-rc.d** utilities, when installed on your system, provide a simple command-line tool for maintaining the /etc/init.d directory hierarchy. These relieve system administrators from having to directly manipulate the numerous symbolic links in the directories under /etc/rc[x].d.

In addition, some systems offer the **ntsysv** tool, which provides a text-based interface; you may find this easier to use than **chkconfig**'s command-line interface. On SuSE Linux, you will find the **yast** and **insserv** tools. For Mandrake easy configuration, you may want to try DrakConf, which allows among other features switching between run levels 3 and 5. In Mandriva this became the Mandriva Linux Control Center.

Most distributions provide a graphical user interface for configuring processes, check with your system documentation.

All of these utilities must be run as root. The system administrator may also manually create the appropriate links in each run level directory in order to start or stop a service in a certain run level.

4.2.6 Shutdown

UNIX was not made to be shut down, but if you really must, use the **shutdown** command. After completing the shutdown procedure, the -h option will halt the system, while -r will reboot it.

The **reboot** and **halt** commands are now able to invoke **shutdown** if run when the system is in run levels 1-5, and thus ensure proper shutdown of the system,but it is a bad habit to get into, as not all UNIX/Linux versions have this feature.

If your computer does not power itself down, you should not turn off the computer until you see a message indicating that the system is halted or finished shutting down, in order to give the system the time to unmount all partitions. Being impatient may cause data loss.

4.3 Managing processes

4.3.1 Work for the system admin

While managing system resources, including processes, is a task for the local system administrator, it doesn't hurt a common user to know something about it, especially where his or her own processes and their optimal execution are concerned.

We will explain a little bit on a theoretical level about system performance, though not as far as hardware optimization and such. Instead, we will study the daily problems a common user is confronted with, and actions such a user can take to optimally use the resources available. As we learn in the next section, this is mainly a matter of thinking before acting.

Figure 4.2. Can't you go faster?

4.3.2 How long does it take?

Bash offers a built-in **time** command that displays how long a command takes to execute. The timing is highly accurate and can be used on any command. In the example below, it takes about a minute and a half to make this book:

```
tilly:~/xml/src> time make
Output written on abook.pdf (222 pages, 1619861 bytes).
Transcript written on abook.log.

real    1m41.056s
user    1m31.190s
sys 0m1.880s
```

The GNU **time** command in /usr/bin (as opposed to the shell built-in version) displays more information that can be formatted in different ways. It also shows the exit status of the command, and the total elapsed time. The same command as the above using the independent **time** gives this output:

```
tilly:~/xml/src> /usr/bin/time make
Output written on abook.pdf (222 pages, 1595027 bytes).
Transcript written on abook.log.

Command exited with non-zero status 2
88.87user 1.74system 1:36.21elapsed 94%CPU
                (0avgtext+0avgdata 0maxresident)k
0inputs+0outputs (2192major+30002minor)pagefaults 0swaps
```

Refer again to the Info pages for all the information.

4.3.3 Performance

To a user, performance means quick execution of commands. To a system manager, on the other hand, it means much more: the system admin has to optimize system performance for the whole system, including users, all programs and daemons. System performance can depend on a thousand tiny things which are not accounted for with the **time** command:

- the program executing is badly written or doesn't use the computer appropriately

- access to disks, controllers, display, all kinds of interfaces, etc.

- reachability of remote systems (network performance)

- amount of users on the system, amount of users actually working simultaneously

- time of day

- ...

4.3.4 Load

In short: the load depends on what is normal for your system. My old P133 running a firewall, SSH server, file server, a route daemon, a sendmail server, a proxy server and some other services doesn't complain with 7 users connected; the load is still 0 on average. Some (multi-CPU) systems I've seen were quite happy with a load of 67. There is only one way to find out - check the load regularly if you want to know what's normal. If you don't, you will only be able to measure system load from the response time of the command line, which is a very rough measurement since this speed is influenced by a hundred other factors.

Keep in mind that different systems will behave different with the same load average. For example, a system with a graphics card supporting hardware acceleration will have no problem rendering 3D images, while the same system with a cheap VGA card will slow down tremendously while rendering. My old P133 will become quite uncomfortable when I start the X server, but on a modern system you hardly notice the difference in the system load.

4.3.5 Can I do anything as a user?

A big environment can slow you down. If you have lots of environment variables set (instead of shell variables), long search paths that are not optimized (errors in setting the path environment variable) and such, the system will need more time to search and read data.

In X, window managers and desktop environments can be real CPU-eaters. A really fancy desktop comes with a price, even when you can download it for free, since most desktops provide add-ons ad infinitum. Modesty is a virtue if you don't buy a new computer every year.

4.3.5.1 Priority

The priority or importance of a job is defined by it's *nice* number. A program with a high nice number is friendly to other programs, other users and the system; it is not an important job. The lower the nice number, the more important a job is and the more resources it will take without sharing them.

Making a job nicer by increasing its nice number is only useful for processes that use a lot of CPU time (compilers, math applications and such). Processes that always use a lot of I/O time are automatically rewarded by the system and given a higher priority (a lower nice number), for example keyboard input always gets highest priority on a system.

Defining the priority of a program is done with the **nice** command.

Most systems also provide the BSD **renice** command, which allows you to change the *niceness* of a running command. Again, read the man page for your system-specific information.

 Interactive programs

It is NOT a good idea to **nice** or **renice** an interactive program or a job running in the foreground.

Use of these commands is usually a task for the system administrator. Read the man page for more info on extra functionality available to the system administrator.

4.3.5.2   CPU resources

On every Linux system, many programs want to use the CPU(s) at the same time, even if you are the only user on the system. Every program needs a certain amount of cycles on the CPU to run. There may be times when there are not enough cycles because the CPU is too busy. The **uptime** command is wildly inaccurate (it only displays averages, you have to know what is normal), but far from being useless. There are some actions you can undertake if you think your CPU is to blame for the unresponsiveness of your system:

- Run heavy programs when the load is low. This may be the case on your system during the night. See next section for scheduling.

- Prevent the system from doing unnecessary work: stop daemons and programs that you don't use, use **locate** instead of a heavy **find**, ...

- Run big jobs with a low priority

If none of these solutions are an option in your particular situation, you may want to upgrade your CPU. On a UNIX machine this is a job for the system admin.

4.3.5.3   Memory resources

When the currently running processes expect more memory than the system has physically available, a Linux system will not crash; it will start paging, or *swapping*, meaning the process uses the memory on disk or in swap space, moving contents of the physical memory (pieces of running programs or entire programs in the case of swapping) to disk, thus reclaiming the physical memory to handle more processes. This slows the system down enormously since access to disk is much slower than access to memory. The **top** command can be used to display memory and swap use. Systems using glibc offer the **memusage** and **memusagestat** commands to visualize memory usage.

If you find that a lot of memory and swap space are being used, you can try:

- Killing, stopping or renicing those programs that use a big chunk of memory

- Adding more memory (and in some cases more swap space) to the system.

- Tuning system performance, which is beyond the scope of this document. See the reading list in Appendix A for more.

4.3.5.4   I/O resources

While I/O limitations are a major cause of stress for system admins, the Linux system offers rather poor utilities to measure I/O performance. The **ps**, **vmstat** and **top** tools give some indication about how many programs are waiting for I/O; **netstat** displays network interface statistics, but there are virtually no tools available to measure the I/O response to system load, and the **iostat** command gives a brief overview of general I/O usage. Various graphical front-ends exist to put the output of these commands in a humanly understandable form.

Each device has its own problems, but the bandwidth available to network interfaces and the bandwidth available to disks are the two primary causes of bottlenecks in I/O performance.

Network I/O problems:

- Network overload:

  The amount of data transported over the network is larger than the network's capacity, resulting in slow execution of every network related task for all users. They can be solved by cleaning up the network (which mainly involves disabling protocols and services that you don't need) or by reconfiguring the network (for example use of subnets, replacing hubs with switches, upgrading interfaces and equipment).

- Network integrity problems:

  Occurs when data is transferred incorrectly. Solving this kind of problem can only be done by isolating the faulty element and replacing it.

Disk I/O problems:

- per-process transfer rate too low:

  Read or write speed for a single process is not sufficient.

- aggregate transfer rate too low:

  The maximum total bandwidth that the system can provide to all programs that run is not enough.

This kind of problem is more difficult to detect, and usually takes extra hardware in order to re-divide data streams over buses, controllers and disks, if overloaded hardware is cause of the problem. One solution to solve this is a RAID array configuration optimized for input and output actions. This way, you get to keep the same hardware. An upgrade to faster buses, controlers and disks is usually the other option.

If overload is not the cause, maybe your hardware is gradually failing, or not well connected to the system. Check contacts, connectors and plugs to start with.

4.3.5.5   Users

Users can be divided in several classes, depending on their behavior with resource usage:

- Users who run a (large) number of small jobs: you, the beginning Linux user, for instance.

- Users who run relatively few but large jobs: users running simulations, calculations, emulators or other programs that eat a lot of memory, and usually these users have accompanying large data files.

- Users who run few jobs but use a lot of CPU time (developers and the like).

You can see that system requirements may vary for each class of users, and that it can be hard to satisfy everyone. If you are on a multi-user system, it is useful (and fun) to find out habits of other users and the system, in order to get the most out of it for your specific purposes.

4.3.5.6   Graphical tools

For the graphical environment, there are a whole bunch of monitoring tools available. Below is a screen shot of the Gnome System Monitor, which has features for displaying and searching process information, and monitoring system resources:

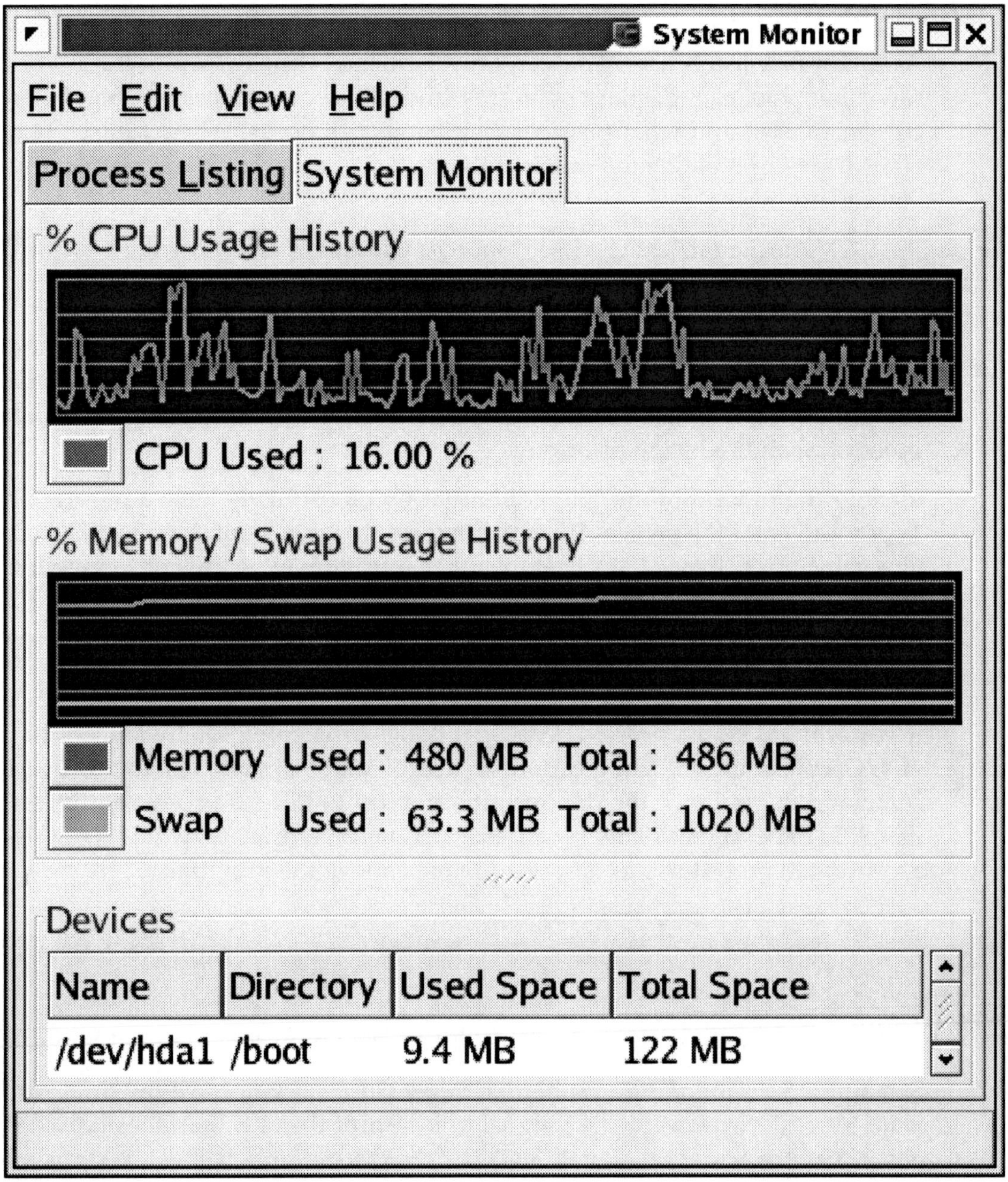

Figure 4.3. Gnome System Monitor

There are also a couple of handy icons you can install in the task bar, such as a disk, memory and load monitor. **xload** is another small X application for monitoring system load. Find your favorite!

4.3.5.7   Interrupting your processes

As a non-privileged user, you can only influence your own processes. We already saw how you can display processes and filter out processes that belong to a particular user, and what possible restrictions can occur. When you see that one of your processes is eating too much of the system's resources, there are two things that you can do:

1.   Make the process use less resources without interrupting it;

2.   Stop the process altogether.

In the case that you want the process to continue to run, but you also want to give the other processes on the system a chance, you can **renice** the process. Appart from using the **nice** or **renice** commands, **top** is an easy way of spotting the troublesome process(es) and reducing priority.

Identify the process in the "NI" column, it will most likely have a negative priority. Type **r** and enter the process ID of the process that you want to renice. Then enter the nice value, for instance "20". That means that from now on, this process will take 1/5 of the CPU cycles at the most.

Examples of processes that you want to keep on running are emulators, virtual machines, compilers and so on.

If you want to stop a process because it hangs or is going totally berserk in the way of I/O consumption, file creation or use of other system resources, use the **kill** command. If you have the opportunity, first try to kill the process softly, sending it the *SIGTERM* signal. This is an instruction to terminate whatever it is doing, according to procedures as described in the code of the program:

```
joe:~> ps -ef | grep mozilla
joe    25822    1   0 Mar11 ?      00:34:04 /usr/lib/mozilla-1.4.1/mozilla-

joe:~> kill -15 25822
```

In the example above, user *joe* stopped his Mozilla browser because it hung.

Some processes are a little bit harder to get rid of. If you have the time, you might want to send them the SIGINT signal to interrupt them. If that does not do the trick either, use the strongest signal, SIGKILL. In the example below, *joe* stops a Mozilla that is frozen:

```
joe:~> ps -ef | grep mozilla
joe    25915    1   0 Mar11 ?      00:15:06 /usr/lib/mozilla-1.4.1/mozilla-

joe:~> kill -9 25915
```

```
joe:~> ps -ef | grep 25915
joe 2634 32273 0 18:09 pts/4    00:00:00 grep 25915
```

In such cases, you might want to check that the process is really dead, using the **grep** filter again on the PID. If this only returns the **grep** process, you can be sure that you succeeded in stopping the process.

Among processes that are hard to kill is your shell. And that is a good thing: if they would be easy to kill, you woud loose your shell every time you type **Ctrl-C** on the command line accidentally, since this is equivalent to sending a SIGINT.

 UNIX without pipes is almost unthinkable

The usage of pipes (|) for using output of one command as input of another is explained in the next chapter, Chapter 5.

In a graphical environment, the **xkill** program is very easy to use. Just type the name of the command, followed by an **Enter** and select the window of the application that you want to stop. It is rather dangerous because it sends a SIGKILL by default, so only use it when an application hangs.

4.4   Scheduling processes

4.4.1 Use that idle time!

A Linux system can have a lot to suffer from, but it usually suffers only during office hours. Whether in an office environment, a server room or at home, most Linux systems are just idling away during the morning, the evening, the nights and weekends. Using this idle time can be a lot cheaper than buying those machines you'd absolutely need if you want everything done at the same time.

There are three types of delayed execution:

- Waiting a little while and then resuming job execution, using the **sleep** command. Execution time depends on the system time at the moment of submission.

- Running a command at a specified time, using the **at** command. Execution of the job(s) depends on system time, not the time of submission.

- Regularly running a command on a monthly, weekly, daily or hourly basis, using the **cron** facilities.

The following sections discuss each possibility.

4.4.2 The sleep command

The Info page on sleep is probably one of the shortest there is. All **sleep** does is wait. By default the time to wait is expressed in seconds.

So why does it exist? Some practical examples:

Somebody calls you on the phone, you say "Yes I'll be with you in half an hour" but you're about drowned in work as it is and bound to forget your lunch:

(sleep `1800`**; echo** `"Lunch time.."`**) &**

When you can't use the **at** command for some reason, it's five o'clock, you want to go home but there's still work to do and right now somebody is eating system resources:

(sleep `10000`**; myprogram) &**

Make sure there's an auto-logout on your system, and that you log out or lock your desktop/office when submitting this kind of job, or run it in a **screen** session.

When you run a series of printouts of large files, but you want other users to be able to print in between:

lp `lotoftext`**; sleep** `900`**; lp** `hugefile`**; sleep** `900`**; lp** `anotherlargefile`

Printing files is discussed in Chapter 8.

Programmers often use the sleep command to halt script or program execution for a certain time.

4.4.3 The at command

The **at** command executes commands at a given time, using your default shell unless you tell the command otherwise (see the man page).

The options to **at** are rather user-friendly, which is demonstrated in the examples below:

```
steven@home:~> at tomorrow + 2 days
warning: commands will be executed using (in order) a) $SHELL
        b) login shell c) /bin/sh
at> cat reports | mail myboss@mycompany
at> <EOT>
job 1 at 2001-06-16 12:36
```

Typing **Ctrl+D** quits the **at** utility and generates the "EOT" message.

User *steven* does a strange thing here combining two commands; we will study this sort of practice in Chapter 5, Redirecting Input and Output.

```
steven@home:~> at 0237
warning: commands will be executed using (in order) a) $SHELL
        b) login shell c) /bin/sh
at> cd new-programs
at> ./configure; make
at> <EOT>
job 2 at 2001-06-14 02:00
```

The -m option sends mail to the user when the job is done, or explains when a job can't be done. The command **atq** lists jobs; perform this command before submitting jobs in order prevent them from starting at the same time as others. With the **atrm** command you can remove scheduled jobs if you change your mind.

It is a good idea to pick strange execution times, because system jobs are often run at "round" hours, as you can see in Section 4.4.4 the next section. For example, jobs are often run at exactly 1 o'clock in the morning (e.g. system indexing to update a standard locate database), so entering a time of 0100 may easily slow your system down rather than fire it up. To prevent jobs from running all at the same time, you may also use the **batch** command, which queues processes and feeds the work in the queue to the system in an evenly balanced way, preventing excessive bursts of system resource usage. See the Info pages for more information.

4.4.4 Cron and crontab

The cron system is managed by the **cron** daemon. It gets information about which programs and when they should run from the system's and users' crontab entries. Only the root user has access to the system crontabs, while each user should only have access to his own crontabs. On some systems (some) users may not have access to the cron facility.

At system startup the cron daemon searches /var/spool/cron/ for crontab entries which are named after accounts in /etc/passwd, it searches /etc/cron.d/ and it searches /etc/crontab, then uses this information every minute to check if there is something to be done. It executes commands as the user who owns the crontab file and mails any output of commands to the owner.

On systems using Vixie cron, jobs that occur hourly, daily, weekly and monthly are kept in separate directories in /etc to keep an overview, as opposed to the standard UNIX cron function, where all tasks are entered into one big file.

Example of a Vixie crontab file:

```
[root@blob /etc]# more crontab
SHELL=/bin/bash
PATH=/sbin:/bin:/usr/sbin:/usr/bin
MAILTO=root
HOME=/
```

```
# run-parts
# commands to execute every hour
01 * * * * root run-parts /etc/cron.hourly
# commands to execute every day
02 4 * * * root run-parts /etc/cron.daily
# commands to execute every week
22 4 * * 0 root run-parts /etc/cron.weekly
commands to execute every month
42 4 1 * * root run-parts /etc/cron.monthly
```

 Alternative

You could also use the **crontab -l** command to display crontabs.

Some variables are set, and after that there's the actual scheduling, one line per job, starting with 5 time and date fields. The first field contains the minutes (from 0 to 59), the second defines the hour of execution (0-23), the third is day of the month (1-31), then the number of the month (1-12), the last is day of the week (0-7, both 0 and 7 are Sunday). An asterisk in these fields represents the total acceptable range for the field. Lists are allowed; to execute a job from Monday to Friday enter 1-5 in the last field, to execute a job on Monday, Wednesday and Friday enter 1,3,5.

Then comes the user who should run the processes which are listed in the last column. The example above is from a Vixie cron configuration where root runs the program **run-parts** on regular intervals, with the appropriate directories as options. In these directories, the actual jobs to be executed at the scheduled time are stored as shell scripts, like this little script that is run daily to update the database used by the **locate** command:

```
billy@ahost cron.daily]$ cat slocate.cron
#!/bin/sh
renice +19 -p $$ >/dev/null 2>&1
/usr/bin/updatedb -f "nfs,smbfs,ncpfs,proc,devpts" -e \
"/tmp,/var/tmp, /usr/tmp,/afs,/net"
```

Users are supposed to edit their crontabs in a safe way using the **crontab -e** command. This will prevent a user from accidentally opening more than one copy of his/her crontab file. The default editor is **vi** (see Chapter 6, but you can use any text editor, such as **gvim** or **gedit** if you feel more comfortable with a GUI editor.

When you quit, the system will tell you that a new crontab is installed.

This crontab entry reminds *billy* to go to his sports club every Thursday night:

```
billy:~> crontab -l
# DO NOT EDIT THIS FILE - edit the master and reinstall.
# (/tmp/crontab.20264 installed on Sun Jul 20 22:35:14 2003)
# (Cron version -- $Id: chap4.xml,v 1.27 2006/10/26 15:37:52 tille Exp $)
38 16 * * 3 mail -s "sports evening" billy
```

After adding a new scheduled task, the system will tell you that a new crontab is installed. You do not need to restart the **cron** daemon for the changes to take effect. In the example, *billy* added a new line pointing to a backup script:

```
billy:~> crontab -e
45 15 * * 3 mail -s "sports evening" billy
4 4 * * 4,7 /home/billy/bin/backup.sh

<--write and quit-->

crontab: installing new crontab

billy:~>
```

The `backup.sh` script is executed every Thursday and Sunday. See Section 7.2.5 for an introduction to shell scripting. Keep in mind that output of commands, if any, is mailed to the owner of the crontab file. If no mail service is configured, you might find the output of your commands in your local mailbox, `/var/spool/mail/` `<your_username>`, a plain text file.

Who runs my commands?

You don't have to specify the user who should run the commands. They are executed with the user's own permissions by default.

4.5 Summary

Linux is a multi-user, multi-tasking operating system that has a UNIX-like way of handling processes. Execution speed of commands can depend on a thousand tiny things. Among others, we learned a lot of new commands to visualize and handle processes. Here's a list:

Command	Meaning
at	Queue jobs for later execution.
atq	Lists the user's pending jobs.
atrm	Deletes jobs, determined by their job number.
batch	Executes commands when system load level permits.
crontab	Maintain crontab files for individual users.
halt	Stop the system.
init *runlevel*	Process control initialization.
jobs	Lists currently executing jobs.
kill	Terminate a process.

Command	Meaning
mesg	Control write access to your terminal.
netstat	Display network connections, routing tables, interface statistics, masquerade connections and multicast memberships.
nice	Run a program with modified scheduling priority.
pgrep	Display processes.
ps	Report process status.
pstree	Display a tree of processes.
reboot	Stop the system.
renice	Alter priority of running processes.
shutdown	Bring the system down.
sleep	Delay for a specified time.
time	Time a command or report resource usage.
top	Display top CPU processes.
uptime	Show how long the system has been running.
vmstat	Report virtual memory statistics.
w	Show who is logged on and what they are doing.
wall	Send a message to everybody's terminals.
who	Show who is logged on.
write	Send a message to another user.

Table 4.3. New commands in Chapter 4: Processes

4.6 Exercises

These are some exercises that will help you get the feel for processes running on your system.

4.6.1 General

- Run **top** in one terminal while you do the exercises in another.
- Run the **ps** command.
- Read the man pages to find out how to display all your processes.

- Run the command **find /**. What effect does it have on system load? Stop this command.

- In graphical mode, start the **xclock** program in the foreground. Then let it run in the background. Stop the program using the **kill** command.

- Run the **xcalc** directly in the background, so that the prompt of the issuing terminal is released.

- What does **kill -9 -1** do?

- Open two terminals or terminal windows again and use **write** to send a message from one to the other.

- Issue the **dmesg** command. What does it tell?

- How long does it take to execute **ls** in the current directory?

- Based on process entries in /proc, owned by your UID, how would you work to find out which processes these actually represent?

- How long has your system been running?

- Which is your current TTY?

- Name 3 processes that couldn't have had **init** as an initial parent.

- Name 3 commands which use SUID mode. Explain why this is so.

- Name the commands that are generally causing the highest load on your system.

4.6.2 Booting, init etc.

- Can you reboot the system as a normal user? Why is that?

- According to your current run level, name the steps that are taken during shutdown.

- How do you change the system run level? Switch from your default run level to run level 1 and vice versa.

- Make a list of all the services and daemons that are started up when your system has booted.

- Which kernel is currently load at startup?

- Suppose you have to start some exotic server at boot time. Up until now, you logged in after booting the system and started this server manually using a script named deliver_pizza in your home directory. What do you have to do in order to have the service start up automatically in run level 4, which you defined for this purpose only?

4.6.3 Scheduling

- Use **sleep** to create a reminder that your pasta is ready in ten minutes.

- Create an **at** job that copies all files in your home directory to /var/tmp within half an hour. You may want to create a sub-directory in /var/tmp.

- Make a cronjob that does this task every Monday to Friday during lunch.

- Check that it works.

- Make a mistake in the crontab entry, like issuing the nonexistent command **coppy** instead of **cp**. What happens upon execution of the task?

Chapter 5
I/O redirection

This chapter describes more about the powerful UNIX mechanism of redirecting input, output and errors. Topics include:

- Standard input, output and errors

- Redirection operators

- How to use output of one command as input for another

- How to put output of a command in a file for later referrence

- How to append output of multiple commands to a file

- Input redirection

- Handling standard error messages

- Combining redirection of input, output and error streams

- Output filters

5.1 Simple redirections

5.1.1 What are standard input and standard output?

Most Linux commands read input, such as a file or another attribute for the command, and write output. By default, input is being given with the keyboard, and output is displayed on your screen. Your keyboard is your *standard input* (stdin) device, and the screen or a particular terminal window is the *standard output* (stdout) device.

However, since Linux is a flexible system, these default settings don't necessarily have to be applied. The standard output, for example, on a heavily monitored server in a large environment may be a printer.

5.1.2 The redirection operators

5.1.2.1 Output redirection with > and |

Sometimes you will want to put output of a command in a file, or you may want to issue another command on the output of one command. This is known as redirecting output. Redirection is done using either the ">" (greater-than symbol), or using the "|" (pipe) operator which sends the standard output of one command to another command as standard input.

As we saw before, the **cat** command concatenates files and puts them all together to the standard output. By redirecting this output to a file, this file name will be created - or overwritten if it already exists, so take care.

```
nancy:~> cat test1
some words

nancy:~> cat test2
some other words

nancy:~> cat test1 test2 > test3

nancy:~> cat test3
some words
some other words
```

 Don't overwrite!

Be careful not to overwrite existing (important) files when redirecting output. Many shells, including Bash, have a built-in feature to protect you from that risk: **noclobber**. See the Info pages for more information. In Bash, you would want to add the **set -o noclobber** command to your .bashrc configuration file in order to prevent accidental overwriting of files.

Redirecting "nothing" to an existing file is equal to emptying the file:

```
nancy:~> ls -l list
-rw-rw-r--    1 nancy    nancy         117 Apr  2 18:09 list

nancy:~> > list

nancy:~> ls -l list
-rw-rw-r--    1 nancy    nancy           0 Apr  4 12:01 list
```

This process is called *truncating*.

The same redirection to an nonexistent file will create a new empty file with the given name:

```
nancy:~> ls -l newlist
```

```
ls: newlist: No such file or directory

nancy:~> > newlist

nancy:~> ls -l newlist
-rw-rw-r-- 1 nancy    nancy        0 Apr  4 12:05 newlist
```

Chapter 7 gives some more examples on the use of this sort of redirection.

Some examples using piping of commands:

To find a word within some text, display all lines matching "pattern1", and exclude lines also matching "pattern2" from being displayed:

grep *pattern1* **file** | **grep** *-v* *pattern2*

To display output of a directory listing one page at a time:

ls -la | **less**

To find a file in a directory:

ls -l | **grep** *part_of_file_name*

5.1.2.2 Input redirection

In another case, you may want a file to be the input for a command that normally wouldn't accept a file as an option. This redirecting of input is done using the "<" (less-than symbol) operator.

Below is an example of sending a file to somebody, using input redirection.

```
andy:~> mail mike@somewhere.org < to_do
```

If the user *mike* exists on the system, you don't need to type the full address. If you want to reach somebody on the Internet, enter the fully qualified address as an argument to **mail**.

This reads a bit more difficult than the beginner's **cat file** | **mail** *someone*, but it is of course a much more elegant way of using the available tools.

5.1.2.3 Combining redirections

The following example combines input and output redirection. The file text.txt is first checked for spelling mistakes, and the output is redirected to an error log file:

spell < text.txt > error.log

The following command lists all commands that you can issue to examine another file when using **less**:

```
mike:~> less --help | grep -i examine
:e [file]       Examine a new file.
:n         *    Examine the (N-th) next file from the command line.
:p         *    Examine the (N-th) previous file from the command line.
:x         *    Examine the first (or N-th) file from the command line.
```

The -i option is used for case-insensitive searches - remember that UNIX systems are very case-sensitive.

If you want to save output of this command for future reference, redirect the output to a file:

```
mike:~> less --help | grep -i examine > examine-files-in-less

mike:~> cat examine-files-in-less
:e [file]       Examine a new file.
:n         *    Examine the (N-th) next file from the command line.
:p         *    Examine the (N-th) previous file from the command line.
:x         *    Examine the first (or N-th) file from the command line.
```

Output of one command can be piped into another command virtually as many times as you want, just as long as these commands would normally read input from standard input and write output to the standard output. Sometimes they don't, but then there may be special options that instruct these commands to behave according to the standard definitions; so read the documentation (man and Info pages) of the commands you use if you should encounter errors.

Again, make sure you don't use names of existing files that you still need. Redirecting output to existing files will replace the content of those files.

5.1.2.4   The >> operator

Instead of overwriting file data, you can also append text to an existing file using two subsequent greater-than signs:

Example:

```
mike:~> cat wishlist
more money
less work

mike:~> date >> wishlist

mike:~> cat wishlist
more money
less work
Thu Feb 28 20:23:07 CET 2002
```

The **date** command would normally put the last line on the screen; now it is appended to the file wishlist.

5.2   Advanced redirection features

5.2.1 Use of file descriptors

There are three types of I/O, which each have their own identifier, called a file descriptor:

- standard input: 0

- standard output: 1

- standard error: 2

In the following descriptions, if the file descriptor number is omitted, and the first character of the redirection operator is <, the redirection refers to the standard input (file descriptor 0). If the first character of the redirection operator is >, the redirection refers to the standard output (file descriptor 1).

Some practical examples will make this more clear:

ls > dirlist 2>&1

will direct both standard output and standard error to the file `dirlist`, while the command

ls 2>&1 > dirlist

will only direct standard output to `dirlist`. This can be a useful option for programmers.

Things are getting quite complicated here, don't confuse the use of the ampersand here with the use of it in Section 4.1.2.1, where the ampersand is used to run a process in the background. Here, it merely serves as an indication that the number that follows is not a file name, but rather a location that the data stream is pointed to. Also note that the bigger-than sign should not be separated by spaces from the number of the file descriptor. If it would be separated, we would be pointing the output to a file again. The example below demonstrates this:

```
[nancy@asus /var/tmp]$ ls 2> tmp

[nancy@asus /var/tmp]$ ls -l tmp
-rw-rw-r--  1 nancy nancy 0 Sept  7 12:58 tmp

[nancy@asus /var/tmp]$ ls 2 > tmp
ls: 2: No such file or directory
```

The first command that *nancy* executes is correct (eventhough no errors are generated and thus the file to which standard error is redirected is empty). The second command expects that 2 is a file name, which does not exist in this case, so an error is displayed.

All these features are explained in detail in the Bash Info pages.

5.2.2 Examples

5.2.2.1 Analyzing errors

If your process generates a lot of errors, this is a way to thoroughly examine them:

command 2>&1 | less

This is often used when creating new software using the **make** command, such as in:

```
andy:~/newsoft> make all 2>&1 | less
--output ommitted--
```

5.2.2.2 Separating standard output from standard error

Constructs like these are often used by programmers, so that output is displayed in one terminal window, and errors in another. Find out which pseudo terminal you are using issuing the **tty** command first:

```
andy:~/newsoft> make all 2> /dev/pts/7
```

5.2.2.3 Writing to output and files simultaneously

You can use the **tee** command to copy input to standard output and one or more output files in one move. Using the -a option to **tee** results in appending input to the file(s). This command is useful if you want to both see and save output. The > and >> operators do not allow to perform both actions simultaneously.

This tool is usually called on through a pipe (|), as demonstrated in the example below:

```
mireille ~/test> date | tee file1 file2
Thu Jun 10 11:10:34 CEST 2004

mireille ~/test> cat file1
Thu Jun 10 11:10:34 CEST 2004

mireille ~/test> cat file2
Thu Jun 10 11:10:34 CEST 2004

mireille ~/test> uptime | tee -a file2
 11:10:51 up 21 days, 21:21, 57 users,  load average: 0.04, 0.16, 0.26

mireille ~/test> cat file2
Thu Jun 10 11:10:34 CEST 2004
 11:10:51 up 21 days, 21:21, 57 users,  load average: 0.04, 0.16, 0.26
```

5.3 Filters

When a program performs operations on input and writes the result to the standard output, it is called a filter. One of the most common uses of filters is to restructure output. We'll discuss a couple of the most important filters below.

5.3.1 More about grep

As we saw in Section 3.3.3.4, **grep** scans the output line per line, searching for matching patterns. All lines containing the pattern will be printed to standard output. This behavior can be reversed using the -v option.

Some examples: suppose we want to know which files in a certain directory have been modified in February:

```
jenny:~> ls -la | grep Feb
```

The **grep** command, like most commands, is case sensitive. Use the -i option to make no difference between upper and lower case. A lot of GNU extensions are available as well, such as --colour, which is helpful to highlight searchterms in long lines, and --after-context, which prints the number of lines after the last matching line. You can issue a recursive **grep** that searches all subdirectories of encountered directories using the -r option. As usual, options can be combined.

Regular expressions can be used to further detail the exact character matches you want to select out of all the input lines. The best way to start with regular expressions is indeed to read the **grep** documentation. An excellent chapter is included in the **grep** Info page. Since it would lead us too far discussing the ins and outs of regular expressions, it is strongly advised to start here if you want to know more about them.

Play around a bit with **grep**, it will be worth the trouble putting some time in this most basic but very powerful filtering command. The exercises at the end of this chapter will help you to get started, see Section 5.5.

5.3.2 Filtering output

The command **sort** arranges lines in alphabetical order by default:

```
thomas:~> cat people-I-like | sort
Auntie Emmy
Boyfriend
Dad
Grandma
Mum
My boss
```

But there are many more things **sort** can do. Looking at the file size, for instance. With this command, directory content is sorted smallest files first, biggest files last:

ls -la | sort -nk 5

 Old sort syntax

You might obtain the same result with **ls -la | sort +4n**, but this is an old form which does not comply with the current standards.

The **sort** command is also used in combination with the **uniq** program (or **sort -u**) to sort output and filter out double entries:

```
thomas:~> cat itemlist
1
4
2
5
34
567
432
567
34
555

thomas:~> sort itemlist | uniq
1
2
34
4
432
5
555
567
```

5.4 Summary

In this chapter we learned how commands can be linked to each other, and how input from one command can be used as output for another command.

Input/output redirection is a common task on UNIX and Linux machines. This powerful mechanism allows flexible use of the building blocks UNIX is made of.

The most commonly used redirections are **>** and **|**. Refer to Appendix C for an overview of redirection commands and other shell constructs.

Command	Meaning
date	Display time and date information.
set	Configure shell options.

Command	Meaning
sort	Sort lines of text.
uniq	Remove duplicate lines from a sorted file.

Table 5.1. New commands in Chapter 5: I/O redirection

5.5 Exercises

These exercises give more examples on how to combine commands. The main goal is to try and use the **Enter** key as little as possible.

All exercises are done using a normal user ID, so as to generate some errors. While you're at it, don't forget to read those man pages!

- Use the **cut** command on the output of a long directory listing in order to display only the file permissions. Then pipe this output to **sort** and **uniq** to filter out any double lines. Then use the **wc** to count the different permission types in this directory.

- Put the output of **date** in a file. Append the output of **ls** to this file. Send this file to your local mailbox (don't specify anything <@domain>, just the user name will do). When using Bash, you will see a new mail notice upon success.

- List the devices in /dev which are currently used by your UID. Pipe through **less** to view them properly.

- Issue the following commands as a non-privileged user. Determine standard input, output and error for each command.

  - **cat** nonexistentfile

  - **file** /sbin/ifconfig

  - **grep** root /etc/passwd /etc/nofiles > grepresults

  - **/etc/init.d/sshd** start > /var/tmp/output

  - **/etc/init.d/crond** start > /var/tmp/output 2>&1

  - Now check your results by issuing the commands again, now redirecting standardoutput to the file /var/tmp/output and standard error to the file /var/tmp/error.

- How many processes are you currently running?

- How many invisible files are in your home directory?

- Use **locate** to find documentation about the kernel.
- Find out which file contains the following entry:

```
root:x:0:0:root:/root:/bin/bash
```

And this one:

```
system:        root
```

- See what happens upon issuing this command:

  > time; date >> time; cat < time

- What command would you use to check which script in `/etc/init.d` starts a given process?

Chapter 6
Text editors

In this chapter, we will discuss the importance of mastering an editor. We will focus mainly on the Improved **vi** editor.

After finishing this chapter, you will be able to:

- Open and close files in text mode
- Edit files
- Search text
- Undo errors
- Merge files
- Recover lost files
- Find a program or suite for office use

6.1   Text editors

6.1.1 Why should I use an editor?

It is very important to be able to use at least one text mode editor. Knowing how to use an editor on your system is the first step to independence.

We will need to master an editor by the next chapter as we need it to edit files that influence our environment. As an advanced user, you may want to start writing scripts, or books, develop websites or new programs. Mastering an editor will immensely improve your productivity as well as your capabilities.

6.1.2 Which editor should I use?

Our focus is on text editors, which can also be used on systems without a graphical environment and in terminal windows. The additional advantage of mastering a text editor is in using it on remote machines. Since you don't need to transfer the entire graphical environment over the network, working with text editors tremendously improves network speed.

There are, as usual, multiple ways to handle the problem. Let's see what editors are commonly available:

6.1.2.1   Ed

The **ed** editor is line-oriented and used to create, display, modify and otherwise manipulate text files, both interactively and by use in shell scripts.

ed is the original text editor on UNIX machines, and thus widely available. For most purposes, however, it is superceded by full-screen editors such as **emacs** and **vi**, see below.

6.1.2.2   GNU Emacs

Emacs is the extensible, customizable, self-documenting, real-time display editor, known on many UNIX and other systems. The text being edited is visible on the screen and is updated automatically as you type your commands. It is a real-time editor because the display is updated very frequently, usually after each character or pair of characters you type. This minimizes the amount of information you must keep in your head as you edit. Emacs is called advanced because it provides facilities that go beyond simple insertion and deletion: controlling subprocesses; automatic indentation of programs; viewing two or more files at once; editing formatted text; and dealing in terms of characters, words, lines, sentences, paragraphs, and pages, as well as expressions and comments in several different programming languages.

Self-documenting means that at any time you can type a special character, **Ctrl+H**, to find out what your options are. You can also use it to find out what any command does, or to find all the commands that pertain to a topic. *Customizable* means that you can change the definitions of Emacs commands in little ways. For example, if you use a programming language in which comments start with "<**" and end with "**>", you can tell the Emacs comment manipulation commands to use those strings. Another sort of customization is rearrangement of the command set. For example, if you prefer the four basic cursor motion commands (up, down, left and right) on keys in a diamond pattern on the keyboard, you can rebind the keys that way.

Extensible means that you can go beyond simple customization and write entirely new commands, programs in the Lisp language that are run by Emacs's own Lisp interpreter. Emacs is an *online* extensible system, which means that it is divided into many functions that call each other, any of which can be redefined in the middle of an editing session. Almost any part of Emacs can be replaced without making a separate copy of all of Emacs. Most of the editing commands of Emacs are written in

Lisp already; the few exceptions could have been written in Lisp but are written in C for efficiency. Although only a programmer can write an extension, anybody can use it afterward.

When run under the X Window System (started as **xemacs**) Emacs provides its own menus and convenient bindings to mouse buttons. But Emacs can provide many of the benefits of a window system on a text-only terminal. For instance, you can look at or edit several files at once, move text between files, and edit files while running shell commands.

6.1.2.3   Vi(m)

Vim stands for "Vi IMproved". It used to be "Vi IMitation", but there are so many improvements that a name change was appropriate. Vim is a text editor which includes almost all the commands from the UNIX program **vi** and a lot of new ones.

Commands in the **vi** editor are entered using only the keyboard, which has the advantage that you can keep your fingers on the keyboard and your eyes on the screen, rather than moving your arm repeatedly to the mouse. For those who want it, mouse support and a GUI version with scrollbars and menus can be activated.

We will refer to **vi** or **vim** throughout this book for editing files, while you are of course free to use the editor of your choice. However, we recommend to at least get the **vi** basics in the fingers, because it is the standard text editor on almost all UNIX systems, while **emacs** can be an optional package. There may be small differences between different computers and terminals, but the main point is that if you can work with **vi**, you can survive on any UNIX system.

Apart from the **vim** command, the vIm packages may also provide **gvim**, the Gnome version of **vim**. Beginning users might find this easier to use, because the menus offer help when you forgot or don't know how to perform a particular editing task using the standard **vim** commands.

6.2   Using the Vim editor

6.2.1 Two modes

The **vi** editor is a very powerful tool and has a very extensive built-in manual, which you can activate using the **:help** command when the program is started (instead of using **man** or **info**, which don't contain nearly as much information). We will only discuss the very basics here to get you started.

What makes **vi** confusing to the beginner is that it can operate in two modes: command mode and insert mode. The editor always starts in command mode.

Commands move you through the text, search, replace, mark blocks and perform other editing tasks, and some of them switch the editor to insert mode.

This means that each key has not one, but likely two meanings: it can either represent a command for the editor when in command mode, or a character that you want in a text when in insert mode.

 Pronunciation

It's pronounced "vee-eye".

6.2.2 Basic commands

6.2.2.1 Moving through the text

Moving through the text is usually possible with the arrow keys. If not, try:

- **h** to move the cursor to the left
- **l** to move it to the right
- **k** to move up
- **j** to move down

SHIFT-G will put the prompt at the end of the document.

6.2.2.2 Basic operations

These are some popular **vi** commands:

- **n dd** will delete n lines starting from the current cursor position.
- **n dw** will delete n words at the right side of the cursor.
- **x** will delete the character on which the cursor is positioned
- **:n** moves to line n of the file.
- **:w** will save (write) the file
- **:q** will exit the editor.
- **:q!** forces the exit when you want to quit a file containing unsaved changes.
- **:wq** will save and exit
- **:w newfile** will save the text to `newfile`.
- **:wq!** overrides read-only permission (if you have the permission to override permissions, for instance when you are using the *root* account.

- **/astring** will search the string in the file and position the cursor on the first match below its position.

- **/** will perform the same search again, moving the cursor to the next match.

- **:1, $s/word/anotherword/g** will replace word with anotherword throughout the file.

- **yy** will copy a block of text.

- **n p** will paste it n times.

- **:recover** will recover a file after an unexpected interruption.

6.2.2.3 Commands that switch the editor to insert mode

- **a** will append: it moves the cursor one position to the right before switching to insert mode

- **i** will insert

- **o** will insert a blank line under the current cursor position and move the cursor to that line.

Pressing the **Esc** key switches back to command mode. If you're not sure what mode you're in because you use a really old version of **vi** that doesn't display an "INSERT" message, type **Esc** and you'll be sure to return to command mode. It is possible that the system gives a little alert when you are already in command mode when hitting **Esc**, by beeping or giving a visual bell (a flash on the screen). This is normal behavior.

6.2.3 The easy way

Instead of reading the text, which is quite boring, you can use the vimtutor to learn you first Vim commands. This is a thirty minute tutorial that teaches the most basic Vim functionality in eight easy exercises. While you can't learn everything about **vim** in just half an hour, the tutor is designed to describe enough of the commands that you will be able to easily use Vim as an all-purpose editor.

In UNIX and MS Windows, if Vim has been properly installed, you can start this program from the shell or command line, entering the **vimtutor** command. This will make a copy of the tutor file, so that you can edit it without the risk of damaging the original. There are a few translated versions of the tutor. To find out if yours is available, use the two-letter language code. For French this would be **vimtutor fr** (if installed on the system).

6.3 Linux in the office

6.3.1 History

Throughout the last decade the office domain has typically been dominated by MS Office, and, let's face it: the Microsoft Word, Excel and PowerPoint formats are industry standards that you will have to deal with sooner or later.

This monopoly situation of Microsoft proved to be a big disadvantage for getting new users to Linux, so a group of German developers started the StarOffice project, that was, and is still, aimed at making an MS Office clone. Their company, StarDivision, was acquired by Sun Microsystems by the end of the 1990s, just before the 5.2 release. Sun continues development but restricted access to the sources. Nevertheless, development on the original set of sources continues in the Open Source community, which had to rename the project to OpenOffice. OpenOffice is now available for a variety of platforms, including MS Windows, Linux, MacOS and Solaris. There is a screenshot in Section 1.3.2.

Almost simultaneously, a couple of other quite famous projects took off. Also a very common alternative to using MS Office is KOffice, the office suite that used to be popular among SuSE users. Like the original, this clone incorporates an MS Word and Excel compatible program, and much more.

Smaller projects deal with particular programs of the MS example suite, such as Abiword and MS Wordview for compatibility with MS Word documents, and Gnumeric for viewing and creating Excel compatible spreadsheets.

6.3.2 Suites and programs

Current distributions usually come with all the necessary tools. Since these provide excellent guidelines and searchable indexes in the Help menus, we won't discuss them in detail. For references, see you system documentation or the web sites of the projects, such as

- <http://www.openoffice.org>
- <http://www.koffice.org>
- Freshmeat <http://freshmeat.net/> and SourceForge <http://sourceforge.org/> for various other projects.

6.3.3 Remarks

6.3.3.1 General use of office documents

Try to limit the use of office documents for the purposes they were meant for: the office.

An example: it drives most Linux users crazy if you send them a mail that says in the body something like: "Hello, I want to tell you something, see attach", and then the attachement proves to be an MS Word compatible document like: "Hello my friend, how is your new job going and will you have time to have lunch with me tomorrow?" Also a bad idea is the attachment of your signature in such a file, for instance. If you want to sign messages or files, use GPG, the PGP-compatible GNU Privacy Guard or SSL (Secure Socket Layer) certificates.

These users are not annoyed because they are unable to read these documents, or because they are worried that these formats typically generate much larger files, but rather because of the implication that they are using MS Windows, and possibly because of the extra work of starting some additional programs.

6.3.3.2   System and user configuration files

In the next chapter, we start configuring our environment, and this might include editing all kinds of files that determine how a program behave.

Don't edit these files with any office component!

The default file format specification would make the program add several lines of code, defining the format of the file and the fonts used. These lines won't be interpreted in the correct way by the programs depending on them, resulting in errors or a crash of the program reading the file. In some cases, you can save the file as plain text, but you'll run into trouble when making this a habit.

6.3.3.3   But I want a graphical text editor!

If you really insist, try **gedit**, **kedit**, **kwrite** or **xedit**; these programs only do text files, which is what we will be needing. If you plan on doing anything serious, though, stick to a real text mode editor such as **vim** or **emacs**.

An acceptable alternative is **gvim**, the Gnome version of **vim**. You still need to use **vi** commands, but if you are stuck, you can look them up in the menus.

6.4   Summary

In this chapter we learned to use an editor. While it depends on your own individual preference which one you use, it is necessary to at least know how to use one editor.

The **vi** editor is available on every UNIX system.

Most Linux distributions include an office suite and a graphical text editor.

6.5   Exercises

This chapter has only one exercise: start the Vim tutor by entering **vimtutor** in a terminal session, and get started.

You may alternatively start **emacs** and type **Ctrl+H** and then **T** to invoke the self-paced Emacs tutorial.

Practice is the only way!

Chapter 7
Home sweet /home

This chapter is about configuring your environment. Now that we now how to use an editor, we can change all kinds of files to make ourselves feel better at home. After completing this chapter, you will know more about:

- Organizing your environment

- Common shell setup files

- Shell configuration

- Configuring the prompt

- Configuring the graphical environment

- Sound and video applications

- Display and window managers

- How the X client-server system works

- Language and font settings

- Installing new software

- Updating existing packages

7.1 General good housekeeping

7.1.1 Introduction

As we mentioned before, it is easy enough to make a mess of the system. We can't put enough stress on the importance of keeping the place tidy. When you learn this from the start, it will become a good habit that will save you time when programming on a Linux or UNIX system or when confronted with system management tasks. Here are some ways of making life easier on yourself:

- Make a `bin` directory for your program files and scripts.

- Organize non-executable files in appropriate directories, and make as many directories as you like. Examples include separate directories for images, documents, projects, downloaded files, spreadsheets, personal files, and so on.

- Make directories private with the **chmod** *700* **dirname** command.

- Give your files sensible names, such as `Complaint to the prime minister 050302` rather than `letter1`.

7.1.2 Make space

On some systems, the **quota** system may force you to clean up from time to time, or the physical limits of your hard disk may force you to make more space without running any monitoring programs. This section discusses a number of ways, besides using the **rm** command, to reclaim disk space.

Run the **quota** -**v** command to see how much space is left.

7.1.2.1   Emptying files

Sometimes the content of a file doesn't interest you, but you need the file name as a marker (for instance, you just need the timestamp of a file, a reminder that the file was there or should be there some time in the future). Redirecting the output of a null command is how this is done in the Bourne and Bash shells:

```
andy:~> cat wishlist > placeholder

andy:~> ls -la placeholder
-rw-rw-r--    1 andy    andy          200 Jun 12 13:34 placeholder

andy:~> > placeholder

andy:~> ls -la placeholder

-rw-rw-r--    1 andy    andy            0 Jun 12 13:35 placeholder
```

The process of reducing an existing file to a file with the same name that is 0 bytes large is called *truncating*.

For creating a new empty file, the same effect is obtained with the **touch** command. On an existing file, **touch** will only update the timestamp. See the Info pages on **touch** for more details.

To "almost" empty a file, use the **tail** command. Suppose user *andy*'s wishlist becomes rather long because he always adds stuff at the end but never deletes the things he actually gets. Now he only wants to keep the last five items:

```
andy:~> tail -5 wishlist > newlist

andy:~> cat newlist > wishlist

andy:~> rm newlist
```

7.1.2.2   More about log files

Some Linux programs insist on writing all sorts of output in a log file. Usually there are options to only log errors, or to log a minimal amount of information, for example setting the debugging level of the program. But even then, you might not care about the log file. Here are some ways to get rid of them or at least set some limits to their size:

- Try removing the log file when the program is not running, if you are sure that you won't need it again. Some programs may even see, when restarted, that there is no log file and will therefore not log.

- If you remove the log file and the program recreates it, read the documentation for this particular program in search for command options that avoid making log files.

- Try making smaller log files by logging only the information that is relevant to you, or by logging only significant information.

- Try replacing the log file with a symbolic link to /dev/null; if you're lucky the program won't complain. Don't do this with the log files of programs that run at system boot or programs that run from cron (see Chapter 4). These programs might replace the symbolic link with a small file that starts growing again.

7.1.2.3   Mail

Regularly clean out your mailbox, make sub-folders and automatic redirects using **procmail** (see the Info pages) or the filters of your favorite mail reading application. If you have a trash folder, clean it out on a regular basis.

To redirect mail, use the .forward file in your home directory. The Linux mail service looks for this file whenever it has to deliver local mail. The content of the file defines what the mail system should do with your mail. It can contain a single line holding a fully qualified E-mail address. In that case the system will send all your mail to this address. For instance, when renting space for a website, you might want to forward the mail destined for the webmaster to your own account in order not to waste disk space. The webmaster's .forward may look like this:

```
webmaster@www ~/> cat .forward
mike@pandora.be
```

Using mail forwarding is also useful to prevent yourself from having to check several different mailboxes. You can make every address point to a central and easily accessible account.

You can ask your system administrator to define a forward for you in the local mail aliases file, like when an account is being closed but E-mail remains active for a while.

7.1.2.4 Save space with a link

When several users need access to the same file or program, when the original file name is too long or too difficult to remember, use a symbolic link instead of a separate copy for each user or purpose.

Multiple symbolic links may have different names, e.g. a link may be called `monfichier` in one user's directory, and `mylink` in another's. Multiple links (different names) to the same file may also occur in the same directory. This is often done in the `/lib` directory: when issuing the command

ls -l /lib

you will see that this directory is plenty of links pointing to the same files. These are created so that programs searching for one name would not get stuck, so they are pointed to the correct/current name of the libraries they need.

7.1.2.5 Limit file sizes

The shell contains a built-in command to limit file sizes, **ulimit**, which can also be used to display limitations on system resources:

```
cindy:~> ulimit -a
core file size (blocks)     0
data seg size (kbytes)      unlimited
file size (blocks)          unlimited
max locked memory (kbytes)  unlimited
max memory size (kbytes)    unlimited
open files                  1024
pipe size (512 bytes)       8
stack size (kbytes)         8192
cpu time (seconds)          unlimited
max user processes          512
virtual memory (kbytes)     unlimited
```

Cindy is not a developer and doesn't care about core dumps, which contain debugging information on a program. If you do want core dumps, you can set their size using the **ulimit** command. Read the Info pages on **bash** for a detailed explanation.

Core file?

A core file or *core dump* is sometimes generated when things go wrong with a program during its execution. The core file contains a copy of the system's memory, as it was at the time that the error occured.

7.1.2.6 Compressed files

Compressed files are useful because they take less space on your hard disk. Another advantage is that it takes less bandwidth to send a compressed file over your network. A lot of files, such as the man pages, are stored in a compressed format on your system. Yet unpacking these to get a little bit of information and then having to compress them again is rather time-consuming. You don't want to unpack a man page, for instance, read about an option to a command and then compress the man page again. Most people will probably forget to clean up after they found the information they needed.

So we have tools that work on compressed files, by uncompressing them only in memory. The actual compressed file stays on your disk as it is. Most systems support **zgrep**, **zcat**, **bzless** and such to prevent unnecessary decompressing/compressing actions. See your system's binary directory and the Info pages.

See Chapter 9 for more on the actual compressing of files and examples on making archives.

7.2 Your text environment

7.2.1 Environment variables

7.2.1.1 General

We already mentioned a couple of environment variables, such as PATH and HOME. Until now, we only saw examples in which they serve a certain purpose to the shell. But there are many other Linux utilities that need information about you in order to do a good job.

What other information do programs need apart from paths and home directories?

A lot of programs want to know about the kind of terminal you are using; this information is stored in the TERM variable. In text mode, this will be the *linux* terminal emulation, in graphical mode you are likely to use *xterm*. Lots of programs want to know what your favorite editor is, in case they have to start an editor in a subprocess. The shell you are using is stored in the SHELL variable, the operating system type in OS and so on. A list of all variables currently defined for your session can be viewed entering the **printenv** command.

The environment variables are managed by the shell. As opposed to regular shell variables, environment variables are inherited by any program you start, including another shell. New processes are assigned a copy of these variables, which they can read, modify and pass on in turn to their own child processes.

There is nothing special about variable names, except that the common ones are in upper case characters by convention. You may come up with any name you want, although there are standard variables that are important enough to be the same on every Linux system, such as PATH and HOME.

7.2.1.2   Exporting variables

An individual variable's content is usually displayed using the **echo** command, as in these examples:

```
debby:~> echo $PATH
/usr/bin:/usr/sbin:/bin:/sbin:/usr/X11R6/bin:/usr/local/bin

debby:~> echo $MANPATH
/usr/man:/usr/share/man/:/usr/local/man:/usr/X11R6/man
```

If you want to change the content of a variable in a way that is useful to other programs, you have to export the new value from your environment into the environment that runs these programs. A common example is exporting the PATH variable. You may declare it as follows, in order to be able to play with the flight simulator software that is in /opt/FlightGear/bin:

```
debby:~> PATH=$PATH:/opt/FlightGear/bin
```

This instructs the shell to not only search programs in the current path, $PATH, but also in the additional directory /opt/FlightGear/bin.

However, as long as the new value of the PATH variable is not known to the environment, things will still not work:

```
debby:~> runfgfs
bash: runfgfs: command not found
```

Exporting variables is done using the shell built-in command **export**:

```
debby:~> export PATH

debby:~> runfgfs
--flight simulator starts--
```

In Bash, we normally do this in one elegant step:

```
export VARIABLE=value
```

The same technique is used for the MANPATH variable, that tells the **man** command where to look for compressed man pages. If new software is added to the system in new or unusual directories, the documentation for it will probably also be in an unusual directory. If you want to read the man pages for the new software, extend the MANPATH variable:

```
debby:~> export MANPATH=$MANPATH:/opt/FlightGear/man

debby:~> echo $MANPATH
/usr/man:/usr/share/man:/usr/local/man:/usr/X11R6/man:/opt/FlightGear/man
```

You can avoid retyping this command in every window you open by adding it to one of your shell setup files, see Section 7.2.2.

7.2.1.3 Reserved variables

The following table gives an overview of the most common predefined variables:

Variable name	Stored information
DISPLAY	used by the X Window system to identify the display server
DOMAIN	domain name
EDITOR	stores your favorite line editor
HISTSIZE	size of the shell history file in number of lines
HOME	path to your home directory
HOSTNAME	local host name
INPUTRC	location of definition file for input devices such as keyboard
LANG	preferred language
LD_LIBRARY_PATH	paths to search for libraries
LOGNAME	login name
MAIL	location of your incoming mail folder
MANPATH	paths to search for man pages
OS	string describing the operating system
OSTYPE	more information about version etc.
PAGER	used by programs like **man** which need to know what to do in case output is more than one terminal window.
PATH	search paths for commands
PS1	primary prompt

Variable name	Stored information
PS2	secondary prompt
PWD	present working directory
SHELL	current shell
TERM	terminal type
UID	user ID
USER(NAME)	user name
VISUAL	your favorite full-screen editor
XENVIRONMENT	location of your personal settings for X behavior
XFILESEARCHPATH	paths to search for graphical libraries

Table 7.1. Common environment variables

A lot of variables are not only predefined but also preset, using configuration files. We discuss these in the next section.

7.2.2 Shell setup files

When entering the **ls -al** command to get a long listing of all files, including the ones starting with a dot, in your home directory, you will see one or more files starting with a . and ending in *rc*. For the case of **bash**, this is .bashrc. This is the counterpart of the system-wide configuration file /etc/bashrc.

When logging into an interactive login shell, **login** will do the authentication, set the environment and start your shell. In the case of **bash**, the next step is reading the general profile from /etc, if that file exists. **bash** then looks for ~/.bash_profile, ~/.bash_login and ~/.profile, in that order, and reads and executes commands from the first one that exists and is readable. If none exists, /etc/bashrc is applied.

When a login shell exits, **bash** reads and executes commands from the file ~/.bash_logout, if it exists.

This procedure is explained in detail in the **login** and **bash** man pages.

7.2.3 A typical set of setup files

7.2.3.1   /etc/profile example

Let's look at some of these config files. First /etc/profile is read, in which important variables such as PATH, USER and HOSTNAME are set:

```
debby:~> cat /etc/profile
# /etc/profile

# System wide environment and startup programs, for login setup
# Functions and aliases go in /etc/bashrc


# Path manipulation
if [ `id -u` = 0 ] && ! echo $PATH | /bin/grep -q "/sbin" ; then
    PATH=/sbin:$PATH
fi

if [ `id -u` = 0 ] && ! echo $PATH | /bin/grep -q "/usr/sbin" ; then
    PATH=/usr/sbin:$PATH
fi

if [ `id -u` = 0 ] && ! echo $PATH | /bin/grep -q "/usr/local/sbin"
    then
    PATH=/usr/local/sbin:$PATH
fi

if ! echo $PATH | /bin/grep -q "/usr/X11R6/bin" ; then
    PATH="$PATH:/usr/X11R6/bin"
fi
```

These lines check the path to set: if *root* opens a shell (user ID 0), it is checked that /sbin, /usr/sbin and /usr/local/sbin are in the path. If not, they are added. It is checked for everyone that /usr/X11R6/bin is in the path.

```
# No core files by default
ulimit -S -c 0 > /dev/null 2>&1
```

All trash goes to /dev/null if the user doesn't change this setting.

```
USER=`id -un`
LOGNAME=$USER
MAIL="/var/spool/mail/$USER"

HOSTNAME=`/bin/hostname`
HISTSIZE=1000
```

Here general variables are assigned their proper values.

```
if [ -z "$INPUTRC" -a ! -f "$HOME/.inputrc" ]; then
    INPUTRC=/etc/inputrc
fi
```

If the variable INPUTRC is not set, and there is no .inputrc in the user's home directory, then the default input control file is loaded.

```
export PATH USER LOGNAME MAIL HOSTNAME HISTSIZE INPUTRC
```

All variables are exported, so that they are available to other programs requesting information about your environment.

7.2.3.2 The profile.d directory

```
for i in /etc/profile.d/*.sh ; do
    if [ -r $i ]; then
        . $i
    fi
done
unset i
```

All readable shell scripts from the /etc/profile.d directory are read and executed. These do things like enabling *color-ls*, aliasing **vi** to **vim**, setting locales etc. The temporary variable i is unset to prevent it from disturbing shell behavior later on.

7.2.3.3 bash_profile example

Then **bash** looks for a .bash_profile in the user's home directory:

```
debby:~> cat .bash_profile
###################################################################
#                                                                 #
#   .bash_profile file                                            #
#                                                                 #
#   Executed from the bash shell when you log in.                 #
#                                                                 #
###################################################################

source ~/.bashrc
source ~/.bash_login
```

This very straight forward file instructs your shell to first read ~/.bashrc and then ~/.bash_login. You will encounter the **source** built-in shell command regularly when working in a shell environment: it is used to apply configuration changes to the current environment.

7.2.3.4 bash_login example

The ~/.bash_login file defines default file protection by setting the **umask** value, see Section 3.4.2.2. The ~/.bashrc file is used to define a bunch of user-specific aliases and functions and personal environment variables. It first reads /etc/bashrc, which describes the default prompt (PS1) and the default umask value. After that, you can add your own settings. If no ~/.bashrc exists, /etc/bashrc is read by default.

7.2.3.5 /etc/bashrc example

Your /etc/bashrc file might look like this:

```
debby:~> cat /etc/bashrc
# /etc/bashrc
```

```
# System wide functions and aliases
# Environment stuff goes in /etc/profile

# by default, we want this to get set.
# Even for non-interactive, non-login shells.
if [ `id -gn` = `id -un` -a `id -u` -gt 99 ]; then
    umask 002
else
    umask 022
fi
```

These lines set the **umask** value. Then, depending on the type of shell, the prompt is set:

```
# are we an interactive shell?
if [ "$PS1" ]; then
  if [ -x /usr/bin/tput ]; then
    if [ "x`tput kbs`" != "x" ]; then
# We can't do this with "dumb" terminal
      stty erase `tput kbs`
    elif [ -x /usr/bin/wc ]; then
      if [ "`tput kbs|wc -c `" -gt 0 ]; then
# We can't do this with "dumb" terminal
        stty erase `tput kbs`
      fi
    fi
  fi
  case $TERM in
    xterm*)
    if [ -e /etc/sysconfig/bash-prompt-xterm ]; then
        PROMPT_COMMAND=/etc/sysconfig/bash-prompt-xterm
    else
    PROMPT_COMMAND='echo -ne "\033]0;${USER}@${HOSTNAME%%.*}:\
${PWD/$HOME/~}\007"'
    fi
    ;;
    *)
    [ -e /etc/sysconfig/bash-prompt-default ] && PROMPT_COMMAND=\
/etc/sysconfig/bash-prompt-default
        ;;
    esac
    [ "$PS1" = "\\s-\\v\\\$ " ] && PS1="[\u@\h \W]\\$ "

    if [ "x$SHLVL" != "x1" ]; then # We're not a login shell
        for i in /etc/profile.d/*.sh; do
        if [ -x $i ]; then
            . $i
        fi
    done
    fi
fi
```

7.2.3.6   bash_logout example

Upon logout, the commands in ~/.bash_logout are executed, which can for instance clear the terminal, so that you have a clean window upon logging out of a remote session, or upon leaving the system console:

```
debby:~> cat .bash_logout
# ~/.bash_logout

clear
```

Let's take a closer look at how these scripts work in the next section. Keep **info** *bash* close at hand.

7.2.4 The Bash prompt

7.2.4.1   Introduction

The Bash prompt can do much more than displaying such simple information as your user name, the name of your machine and some indication about the present working directory. We can add other information such as the current date and time, number of connected users etc.

Before we begin, however, we will save our current prompt in another environment variable:

```
[jerry@nowhere jerry]$ MYPROMPT=$PS1

[jerry@nowhere jerry]$ echo $MYPROMPT
[\u@\h \W]\$

[jerry@nowhere jerry]$
```

When we change the prompt now, for example by issuing the command PS1="->", we can always get our original prompt back with the command PS1=$MYPROMPT. You will, of course, also get it back when you reconnect, as long as you just fiddle with the prompt on the command line and avoid putting it in a shell configuration file.

7.2.4.2   Some examples

In order to understand these prompts and the escape sequences used, we refer to the Bash Info or man pages.

- **export** PS1="[\t \j]"

  Displays time of day and number of running jobs

- **export PS1=**"*[\d] [\u@\h \w]* :"

  Displays date, user name, host name and current working directory. Note that \W displays only base names of the present working directory.

- **export PS1=**"*{\!}* "

  Displays history number for each command.

- **export PS1=**"*\[\033[1;35m\]\u@\h\[\033[0m\]*"

  Displays user@host in pink.

- **export**
  PS1="*\[\033[1;35m\]\u\[\033[0m\]\[\033[1;34m\]\w\[\033[0m\]*"

  Sets the user name in pink and the present working directory in blue.

- **export PS1=**"*\[\033[1;44m\]$USER is in \w\[\033[0m\]*"

  Prompt for people who have difficulties seeing the difference between the prompt and what they type.

- **export PS1=**"*\[\033[4;34m\]\u@\h \w \[\033[0m\]*"

  Underlined prompt.

- **export PS1=**"*\[\033[7;34m\]\u@\h \w \[\033[0m\]*"

  White characters on a blue background.

- **export PS1=**"*\[\033[3;35m\]\u@\h \w \[\033[0m\]\a*"

  Pink prompt in a lighter font that alerts you when your commands have finished.

- **export PS1=...**

Variables are exported so the subsequently executed commands will also know about the environment. The prompt configuration line that you want is best put in your shell configuration file, ~/.bashrc.

If you want, prompts can execute shell scripts and behave different under different conditions. You can even have the prompt play a tune every time you issue a command, although this gets boring pretty soon. More information can be found in the Bash-Prompt HOWTO <http://www.tldp.org/HOWTO/Bash-Prompt-HOWTO/>.

7.2.5 Shell scripts

7.2.5.1   What are scripts?

A shell script is, as we saw in the shell configuration examples, a text file containing shell commands. When such a file is used as the first non-option argument when invoking Bash, and neither the -c nor -s option is supplied, Bash reads and executes commands from the file, then exits. This mode of operation creates a non-interactive shell. When Bash runs a shell script, it sets the special parameter 0 to the name of the file, rather than the name of the shell, and the positional parameters (everything following the name of the script) are set to the remaining arguments, if any are given. If no additional arguments are supplied, the positional parameters are unset.

A shell script may be made executable by using the **chmod** command to turn on the execute bit. When Bash finds such a file while searching the PATH for a command, it spawns a sub-shell to execute it. In other words, executing

filename *ARGUMENTS*

is equivalent to executing

bash *filename ARGUMENTS*

if "filename" is an executable shell script. This sub-shell reinitializes itself, so that the effect is as if a new shell had been invoked to interpret the script, with the exception that the locations of commands remembered by the parent (see **hash** in the Info pages) are retained by the child.

Most versions of UNIX make this a part of the operating system's command execution mechanism. If the first line of a script begins with the two characters "#!", the remainder of the line specifies an interpreter for the program. Thus, you can specify **bash**, **awk**, **perl** or some other interpreter or shell and write the rest of the script file in that language.

The arguments to the interpreter consist of a single optional argument following the interpreter name on the first line of the script file, followed by the name of the script file, followed by the rest of the arguments. Bash will perform this action on operating systems that do not handle it themselves.

Bash scripts often begin with

```
#! /bin/bash
```

(assuming that Bash has been installed in /bin), since this ensures that Bash will be used to interpret the script, even if it is executed under another shell.

7.2.5.2 Some simple examples

A very simple script consisting of only one command, that says hello to the user executing it:

```
[jerry@nowhere ~] cat hello.sh
#!/bin/bash
echo "Hello $USER"
```

The script actually consists of only one command, **echo**, which uses the *value of* ($) the USER environment variable to print a string customized to the user issuing the command.

Another one-liner, used for displaying connected users:

```
#!/bin/bash
who | cut -d " " -f 1 | sort -u
```

Here is a script consisting of some more lines, that I use to make backup copies of all files in a directory. The script first makes a list of all the files in the current directory and puts it in the variable LIST. Then it sets the name of the copy for each file, and then it copies the file. For each file, a message is printed:

```
tille:~> cat bin/makebackupfiles.sh
#!/bin/bash
# make copies of all files in a directory
LIST=`ls`
for i in $LIST; do
    ORIG=$i
    DEST=$i.old
    cp $ORIG $DEST
    echo "copied $i"
done
```

Just entering a line like **mv * *.old** won't work, as you will notice when trying this on a set of test files. An **echo** command was added in order to display some activity. **echo**'s are generally useful when a script won't work: insert one after each doubted step and you will find the error in no time.

The /etc/rc.d/init.d directory contains loads of examples. Let's look at this script that controls the fictive ICanSeeYou server:

```
#!/bin/sh
# description: ICanSeeYou allows you to see networked people

# process name: ICanSeeYou
# pidfile: /var/run/ICanSeeYou/ICanSeeYou.pid
# config: /etc/ICanSeeYou.cfg

# Source function library.
. /etc/rc.d/init.d/functions
```

```
# See how (with which arguments) we were called.
case "$1" in
    start)
        echo -n "Starting ICanSeeYou: "
        daemon ICanSeeYou
        echo
        touch /var/lock/subsys/ICanSeeYou
        ;;
    stop)
        echo -n "Shutting down ICanSeeYou: "
        killproc ICanSeeYou
        echo
        rm -f /var/lock/subsys/ICanSeeYou
        rm -f /var/run/ICanSeeYou/ICanSeeYou.pid
        ;;
    status)
        status ICanSeeYou
        ;;
    restart)
        $0 stop
        $0 start
        ;;
    *)
        echo "Usage: $0 {start|stop|restart|status}"
        exit 1
esac

exit 0
```

First, with the . command (dot) a set of shell functions, used by almost all shell scripts in /etc/rc.d/init.d, is loaded. Then a **case** command is issued, which defines 4 different ways the script can execute. An example might be **ICanSeeYou** *start*. The decision of which case to apply is made by reading the (first) argument to the script, with the expression *$1*.

When no compliant input is given, the default case, marked with an asterisk, is applied, upon which the script gives an error message. The **case** list is ended with the **esac** statement. In the *start* case the server program is started as a daemon, and a process ID and lock are assigned. In the *stop* case, the server process is traced down and stopped, and the lock and the PID are removed. Options, such as the daemon option, and functions like killproc, are defined in the /etc/rc.d/init.d/ functions file. This setup is specific to the distribution used in this example. The initscripts on your system might use other functions, defined in other files, or none at all.

Upon success, the script returns an exit code of zero to its parent.

This script is a fine example of using functions, which make the script easier to read and the work done faster. Note that they use **sh** instead of **bash**, to make them useful on a wider range of systems. On a Linux system, calling **bash** as **sh** results in the shell running in POSIX-compliant mode.

The **bash** man pages contain more information about combining commands, **for**- and **while**-loops and regular expressions, as well as examples. A comprehensible Bash course for system administrators and power users, with exercises, from the same author as this Introduction to Linux guide, is at <http://tille.xalasys.com/training/bash/>. Detailed description of Bash features and applications is in the reference guide Advanced Bash Scripting <http://tldp.org/LDP/abs/html/index.html>.

7.3 The graphical environment

7.3.1 Introduction

The average user may not care too much about his login settings, but Linux offers a wide variety of flashy window and desktop managers for use under X, the graphical environment. The use and configuration of window managers and desktops is straightforward and may even resemble the standard MS Windows, MacIntosh or UNIX CDE environment, although many Linux users prefer flashier desktops and fancier window managers. We won't discuss the user specific configuration here. Just experiment and read the documentation using the built-in Help functions these managers provide and you will get along fine.

We will, however, take a closer look at the underlying system.

7.3.2 The X Window System

The X Window System is a network-transparent window system which runs on a wide range of computing and graphics machines. X Window System servers run on computers with bitmap displays. The X server distributes user input to and accepts output requests from several client programs through a variety of different interprocess communication channels. Although the most common case is for the client programs to be running on the same machine as the server, clients can be run transparently from other machines (including machines with different architectures and operating systems) as well. We will learn how to do this in Chapter 10 on networking and remote applications.

X supports overlapping hierarchical sub-windows and text and graphics operations, on both monochrome and color displays. The number of X client programs that use the X server is quite large. Some of the programs provided in the core X Consortium distribution include:

- **xterm**: a terminal emulator

- **twm**: a minimalistic window manager

- **xdm**: a display manager

- **xconsole**: a console redirect program

- **bitmap**: a bitmap editor

- **xauth**, **xhost** and **iceauth**: access control programs

- **xset**, **xmodmap** and many others: user preference setting programs

- **xclock**: a clock

- **xlsfonts** and others: a font displayer, utilities for listing information about fonts, windows and displays

- **xfs**: a font server

- ...

We refer again to the man pages of these commands for detailed information. More explanations on available functions can be found in the *Xlib - C language X Interface* manual that comes with your X distribution, the *X Window System Protocol* specification, and the various manuals and documentation of X toolkits. The /usr/share/doc directory contains references to these documents and many others.

Many other utilities, window managers, games, toolkits and gadgets are included as user-contributed software in the X Consortium distribution, or are available using anonymous FTP on the Internet. Good places to start are <http://www.x.org> and <http://www.xfree.org>.

Furthermore, all your graphical applications, such as your browser, your E-mail program, your image viewing programs, sound playing tools and so on, are all clients to your X server. Note that in normal operation, that is in graphical mode, X clients and the X server on Linux run on the same machine.

7.3.2.1 7.3.2.1. Display names

From the user's perspective, every X server has a *display name* in the form of:

hostname:displaynumber.screennumber

This information is used by the application to determine how it should connect to the X server and which screen it should use by default (on displays with multiple monitors):

- *hostname*: The host name specifies the name of the client machine to which the display is physically connected. If the host name is not given, the most efficient way of communicating to a server on the same machine will be used.

- *displaynumber*: The phrase "display" is usually used to refer to a collection of monitors that share a common key board and pointer (mouse, tablet, etc.). Most workstations tend to only have one keyboard, and therefore, only one display. Larger, multi-user systems, however, frequently have several displays so that more than one person can be doing graphics work at once. To avoid confusion, each display on a machine is assigned a *display number* (beginning at 0) when the X server for that display is started. The display number must always be given in a display name.

- *screen number*: Some displays share a single keyboard and pointer among two or more monitors. Since each monitor has its own set of windows, each screen is assigned a *screen number* (beginning at 0) when the X server for that display is started. If the screen number is not given, screen 0 will be used.

On POSIX systems, the default display name is stored in your DISPLAY environment variable. This variable is set automatically by the **xterm** terminal emulator. However, when you log into another machine on a network, you might need to set DISPLAY by hand to point to your display, see Section 10.4.3.2.

More information can be found in the X man pages.

7.3.2.2   Window and desktop managers

The layout of windows on the screen is controlled by special programs called *window managers*. Although many window managers will honor geometry specifications as given, others may choose to ignore them (requiring the user to explicitly draw the window's region on the screen with the pointer, for example).

Since window managers are regular (albeit complex) client programs, a variety of different user interfaces can be built. The X Consortium distribution comes with a window manager named **twm**, but most users prefer something more fancy when system resources permit. Sawfish and Enlightenment are popular examples which allow each user to have a desktop according to mood and style.

A desktop manager makes use of one window manager or another for arranging your graphical desktop in a convenient way, with menubars, drop-down menus, informative messages, a clock, a program manager, a file manager and so on. Among the most popular desktop managers are Gnome and KDE, which both run on almost any Linux distribution and many other UNIX systems.

☞ KDE applications in Gnome/Gnome applications in KDE

You don't need to start your desktop in KDE in order to be able to run KDE applications. If you have the KDE libraries installed (the kdelibs package), you can run these applications from the Gnome menus or start them from a Gnome terminal.

Running Gnome applications in a KDE environment is a bit more tricky, because there is no single set of base-libraries in Gnome. However, the dependencies and thus extra packages you might have to install will become clear when running or installing such an application.

7.3.3 X server configuration

The X distribution that used to come with Linux, *XFree86*, uses the configuration file XF86Config for its initial setup. This file configures your video card and is searched for in a number of locations, although it is usually in /etc/X11.

If you see that the file /etc/X11/XF86Config is present on your system, a full description can be found in the Info or man pages about XF86Config.

Because of licensing issues with XFree86, newer systems usually come with the *X.Org* distribution of the X server and tools. The main configuration file here is xorg.conf, usually also in /etc/X11. The file consists of a number of sections that may occur in any order. The sections contain information about your monitor, your video adaptor, the screen configuration, your keyboard etcetera. As a user, you needn't worry too much about what is in this file, since everything is normally determined at the time the system is installed.

Should you need to change graphical server settings, however, you can run the configuration tools or edit the configuration files that set up the infrastructure to use the XFree86 server. See the man pages for more information; your distribution might have its own tools. Since misconfiguration may result in unreadable garbage in graphical mode, you may want to make a backup copy of the configuration file before attempting to change it, just to be on the safe side.

7.4 Region specific settings

7.4.1 Keyboard setup

Setting the keyboard layout is done using the **loadkeys** command for text consoles. Use your local X configuration tool or edit the *Keyboard* section in XF86Config manually to configure the layout for graphical mode. The XkbdLayout is the one you want to set:

```
XkbLayout       "us"
```

This is the default. Change it to your local settings by replacing the quoted value with any of the names listed in the subdirectories of your keymaps directory. If you can't find the keymaps, try displaying their location on your system issuing the command

locate keymaps

It is possible to combine layout settings, like in this example:

```
Xkblayout       "us,ru"
```

Make a backup of the /etc/X11/XF86Config file before editing it! You will need to use the *root* account to do this.

Log out and reconnect in order to reload X settings.

The Gnome Keyboard Applet enables real-time switching between layouts; no special pemissions are needed for using this program. KDE has a similar tool for switching between keyboard layouts.

7.4.2 Fonts

Use the **setfont** tool to load fonts in text mode. Most systems come with a standard inputrc file which enables combining of characters, such as the French "é" (meta characters). The system admin should then add the line

```
export INPUTRC="/etc/inputrc"
```

to the /etc/bashrc file.

7.4.3 Date and time zone

Setting time information is usually done at installation time. After that, it can be kept up to date using an *NTP* (Network Time Protocol) client. Most Linux systems run **ntpd** by default:

```
debby:~> ps -ef | grep ntpd
ntp       24678      1  0  2002 ?        00:00:33 ntpd -U ntp
```

You can run **ntpdate** manually to set the time, on condition that you can reach a time server. The **ntpd** daemon should not be running when you adjust the time using **ntpdate**. Use a time server as argument to the command:

```
root@box:~# ntpdate 10.2.5.200
26 Oct 14:35:42 ntpdate[20364]: adjust time server 10.2.5.200 offset
 -0.008049 sec
```

See your system manual and the documentation that comes with the NTP package. Most desktop managers include tools to set the system time, providing that you have access to the system administrator's account.

For setting the time zone correct, you can use **tzconfig** or **timezone** commands. Timezone information is usually set during the installation of your machine. Many systems have distribution-specific tools to configure it, see your system documentation.

7.4.4 Language

If you'd rather get your messages from the system in Dutch or French, you may want to set the LANG and LANGUAGE environment variables, thus enabling locale support for the desired language and eventually the fonts related to character conventions in that language.

With most graphical login systems, such as **gdm** or **kdm**, you have the possibility to configure these language settings before logging in.

Note that on most systems, the default tends to be *en_US.UTF-8* these days. This is not a problem, because systems where this is the default, will also come with all the programs supporting this encoding. Thus, **vi** can edit all the files on your system, **cat** won't behave strange and so on.

Trouble starts when you connect to an older system not supporting this font encoding, or when you open a *UTF-8* encoded file on a system supporting only 1-byte character fonts. The **recode** utility might come in handy to convert files from one character set to another. Read the man pages for an overview of features and usage. Another solution might be to temporarily work with another encoding definition, by setting the LANG environment variable:

```
debby:~> acroread /var/tmp/51434s.pdf
Warning: charset "UTF-8" not supported, using "ISO8859-1".
Aborted

debby:~> set | grep UTF
LANG=en_US.UTF-8

debby:~> export LANG=en_US

debby:~> acroread /var/tmp/51434s.pdf
<--new window opens-->
```

Refer to the Mozilla <http://www.mozilla.org/> web site for guidance on how to get Firefox in your language. The OpenOffice.org <http://www.openoffice.org/> web site has information on localization of your OpenOffice.org suite.

7.4.5 Country-specific Information

The list of HOWTOs <http://www.tldp.org/HOWTO/HOWTO-INDEX/howtos. html> contains references to Bangla, Belarusian, Chinese, Esperanto, Finnish,

Francophone, Hebrew, Hellenic, Latvian, Polish, Portugese, Serbian, Slovak, Slovenian, Spanish, Thai and Turkish localization instructions.

7.5 Installing new software

7.5.1 General

Most people are surprised to see that they have a running, usable computer after installing Linux; most distributions contain ample support for video and network cards, monitors and other external devices, so there is usually no need to install extra drivers. Also common tools such as office suites, web browsers, E-mail clients and such are included in the main distributions. Even so, an initial installation might not meet your requirements.

If you just can't find what you need, maybe it is not installed on your system. It may also be that you have the required software, but it does not do what it is supposed to do. Remember that Linux moves fast, and software improves on a daily basis. Don't waste your time troubleshooting problems that might already be resolved.

You can update your system or add packages to it at any time you want. Most software comes in packages. Extra software may be found on your installation CDs or on the Internet. The website of your Linux distribution is a good place to start looking for additional software and contains instructions about how to install it on your type of Linux, see Appendix A. Always read the documentation that comes with new software, and any installation guidelines the package might contain. All software comes with a README file, which you are very strongly advised to read.

7.5.2 Package formats

7.5.2.1 RPM packages

7.5.2.1.1 What is RPM?

RPM, the RedHat Package Manager, is a powerful package manager that you can use to install, update and remove packages. It allows you to search for packages and keeps track of the files that come with each package. A system is built-in so that you can verify the authenticity of packages downloaded from the Internet. Advanced users can build their own packages with RPM.

An RPM package consists of an archive of files and meta-data used to install and erase the archive files. The meta-data includes helper scripts, file attributes, and descriptive information about the package. Packages come in two varieties: binary packages, used to encapsulate software to be installed, and source packages, containing the source code and recipe necessary to produce binary packages.

Many other distributions support RPM packages, among the popular ones RedHat Enterprise Linux, Mandriva (former Mandrake), Fedora Core and SuSE Linux. Apart from the advice for your distribution, you will want to read **man *rpm***.

7.5.2.1.2 RPM examples

Most packages are simply installed with the upgrade option, -U, whether the package is already installed or not. The RPM package contains a complete version of the program, which overwrites existing versions or installs as a new package. The typical usage is as follows:

rpm -Uvh /path/to/rpm-package(s)

The -v option generates more verbose output, and -h makes **rpm** print a progress bar:

```
[root@jupiter tmp]# rpm -Uvh totem-0.99.5-1.fr.i386.rpm
Preparing...                ###########################################
[100%]
   1:totem                  ###########################################
[100%]
[root@jupiter tmp]#
```

New kernel packages, however, are installed with the install option -i, which does not overwrite existing version(s) of the package. That way, you will still be able to boot your system with the old kernel if the new one does not work.

You can also use **rpm** to check whether a package is installed on your system:

```
[david@jupiter ~] rpm -qa | grep vim
vim-minimal-6.1-29
vim-X11-6.1-29
vim-enhanced-6.1-29
vim-common-6.1-29
```

Or you can find out which package contains a certain file or executable:

```
[david@jupiter ~] rpm -qf /etc/profile
setup-2.5.25-1

[david@jupiter ~] which cat
cat is /bin/cat

[david@jupiter ~] rpm -qf /bin/cat
coreutils-4.5.3-19
```

Note that you need not have access to administrative privileges in order to use **rpm** to query the RPM database. You only need to be *root* when adding, modifying or deleting packages.

Below is one last example, demonstrating how to uninstall a package using **rpm**:

```
[root@jupiter root]# rpm -e totem
[root@jupiter root]#
```

Note that uninstalling is not that verbose by default, it is normal that you don't see much happening. When in doubt, use **rpm -qa** again to verify that the package has been removed.

RPM can do much more than the couple of basic functions we discussed in this introduction; the RPM HOWTO <http://www.tldp.org/HOWTO/RPM-HOWTO/index.html> contains further references.

7.5.2.2   DEB (.deb) packages

7.5.2.2.1 What are Debian packages?

This package format is the default on Debian GNU/Linux, where **dselect**, and, nowadays more common, **aptitude**, is the standard tool for managing the packages. It is used to select packages that you want to install or upgrade, but it will also run during the installation of a Debian system and help you to define the access method to use, to list available packages and to configure packages.

The Debian web site <http://debian.org/> contains all information you need, including a "dselect Documentation for Beginners".

According to the latest news, the Debian package format is becoming more and more popular. At the time of this writing, 5 of the top-10 distributions use it. Also **apt-get** (see Section 7.5.3.2 is becoming extremely popular, also on non-DEB systems.

7.5.2.2.2 Examples with DEB tools

Checking whether a package is installed is done using the **dpkg** command. For instance, if you want to know which version of the Gallery software is installed on your machine:

```
nghtwsh@gorefest:~$ dpkg -l *gallery*
Desired=Unknown/Install/Remove/Purge/Hold
| Status=Not/Installed/Config-files/Unpacked/Failed-config/Half-installed
|/ Err?=(none)/Hold/Reinst-required/X=both-problems (Status,Err:
uppercase=bad)
||/ Name           Version         Description
+++-==============-==============-
=============================================
ii  gallery        1.5-1sarge2     a web-based photo album written in php
```

The "ii" prefix means the package is installed. Should you see "un" as a prefix, that means that the package is known in the list that your computer keeps, but that it is not installed.

Searching which package a file belongs to is done using the -S to **dpkg**:

```
nghtwsh@gorefest:~$ dpkg -S /bin/cat
coreutils: /bin/cat
```

More information can be found in the Info pages for **dpkg**.

7.5.2.3   Source packages

The largest part of Linux programs is Free/Open Source, so source packages are available for these programs. Source files are needed for compiling your own program version. Sources for a program can be downloaded from its web site, often as a compressed tarball (`program-version.tar.gz` or similar). For RPM-based distributions, the source is often provided in the `program-version.src.rpm`. Debian, and most distributions based on it, provide themselves the adapted source which can be obtained using **apt-get** *source*.

Specific requirements, dependencies and installation instructions are provided in the README file. You will probably need a C compiler, **gcc**. This GNU C compiler is included in most Linux systems and is ported to many other platforms.

7.5.3 Automating package management and updates

7.5.3.1   General remarks

The first thing you do after installing a new system is applying updates; this applies to all operating systems and Linux is not different.

The updates for most Linux systems can usually be found on a nearby site mirroring your distribution. Lists of sites offering this service can be found at your distribution's web site, see Appendix A.

Updates should be applied regularly, daily if possible - but every couple of weeks would be a reasonable start. You really should try to have the most recent version of your distribution, since Linux changes constantly. As we said before, new features, improvements and bug fixes are supplied at a steady rhythm, and sometimes important security problems are addressed.

The good news is that most Linux distributions provide tools so that you don't have to upgrade tens of packages daily by hand. The following sections give an overview of *package manager managers*. There is much more to this subject, even regular updates of source packages is manageable automatically; we only list the most commonly known systems. Always refer to the documentation for your specific distribution for advised procedures.

7.5.3.2 APT

The Advanced Package Tool is a management system for software packages. The command line tool for handling packages is **apt-get**, which comes with an excellent man page describing how to install and update packages and how to upgrade singular packages or your entire distribution. APT has its roots in the Debian GNU/Linux distribution, where it is the default manager for the Debian packages. APT has been ported to work with RPM packages as well. The main advantage of APT is that it is free and flexible to use. It will allow you to set up systems similar to the distribution specific (and in some cases commercial) ones listed in the next sections.

Generally, when first using **apt-get**, you will need to get an index of the available packages. This is done using the command

apt-get *update*

After that, you can use **apt-get** to upgrade your system:

apt-get *upgrade*

Do this often, it's an easy way to keep your system up-to-date and thus safe.

Apart from this general usage, **apt-get** is also very fast for installing individual packages. This is how it works:

```
[david@jupiter ~] su - -c "apt-get install xsnow"
Password:
Reading Package Lists... Done
Building Dependency Tree... Done
The following NEW packages will be installed:
  xsnow
0 packages upgraded, 1 newly installed, 0 removed and 3 not upgraded.
Need to get 33.6kB of archives.
After unpacking 104kB of additional disk space will be used.
Get:1 http://ayo.freshrpms.net redhat/9/i386/os xsnow 1.42-10 [33.6kB]
Fetched 33.6kB in 0s (106kB/s)
Executing RPM (-Uvh)...
Preparing...                ###########################################
[100%]
   1:xsnow                   ###########################################
[100%]
```

Note the -c option to the **su** command, which indicates to the root shell to only execute this command, and then return to the user's environment. This way, you cannot forget to quit the root account.

If there are any dependencies on other packages, **apt-get** will download and install these supporting packages.

More information can be found in the APT HOWTO <http://www.debian.org/doc/user-manuals#apt-howto>.

7.5.3.3   Systems using RPM packages

Update Agent, which originally only supported RedHat RPM packages, is now ported to a wider set of software, including non-RedHat repositories. This tool provides a complete system for updating the RPM packages on a RedHat or Fedora Core system. On the command line, type **up2date** to update your system. On the desktop, by default a small icon is activated, telleng you whether or not there are updates available for your system.

Yellowdog's Updater Modified (**yum**) is another tool that recently became more popular. It is an interactive but automated update program for installing, updating or removing RPM packages on a system. It is the tool of choice on Fedora systems.

On SuSE Linux, everything is done with YaST, Yet another Setup Tool, which supports a wide variety of system administration tasks, among which updating RPM packages. Starting from SuSE Linux 7.1 you can also upgrade using a web interface and YOU, Yast Online Update.

Mandrake Linux and Mandriva provide so-called URPMI tools, a set of wrapper programs that make installing new software easier for the user. These tools combine with RPMDrake and MandrakeUpdate to provide everything needed for smooth install and uninstall of software packages. MandrakeOnline offers an extended range of services and can automatically notify administrators when updates are available for your particular Mandrake system. See **man urpmi**, among others, for more info.

Also the KDE and Gnome desktop suites have their own (graphical) versions of package managers.

7.5.4 Upgrading your kernel

Most Linux installations are fine if you periodically upgrade your distribution. The upgrade procedure will install a new kernel when needed and make all necessary changes to your system. You should only compile or install a new kernel manually if you need kernel features that are not supported by the default kernel included in your Linux distribution.

Whether compiling your own optimized kernel or using a pre-compiled kernel package, install it in co-existence with the old kernel until you are sure that everything works according to plan.

Then create a dual boot system that will allow you to choose which kernel to boot by updating your boot loader configuration file `grub.conf`. This is a simple example:

```
# grub.conf generated by anaconda
#
# Note that you do not have to rerun grub after making config changes.
```

```
# NOTICE:   You have a /boot partition.  This means that
#           all kernel and initrd paths are relative to /boot/, e.g.
#           root (hd0,0)
#           kernel /vmlinuz-version ro root=/dev/hde8
#           initrd /initrd-version.img
#boot=/dev/hde
default=0
timeout=10
splashimage=(hd0,0)/grub/splash.xpm.gz
title Red Hat Linux new (2.4.9-31)
    root (hd0,0)
    kernel /vmlinuz-2.4.9-31 ro root=/dev/hde8
    initrd /initrd-2.4.9-31.img
title old-kernel
        root (hd0,0)
        kernel /vmlinuz-2.4.9-21 ro root=/dev/hde8
        initrd /initrd-2.4.9-21.img
```

After the new kernel has proven to work, you may remove the lines for the old one from the GRUB config file, although it is best to wait a couple of days just to be sure.

7.5.5 Installing extra packages from the installation CDs

7.5.5.1 Mounting a CD

This is basically done in the same way as installing packages manually, except that you have to append the file system of the CD to your machine's file system to make it accessible. On most systems, this will be done automatically upon insertion of a CD in the drive because the **automount** daemon is started up at boot time. If your CD is not made available automatically, issue the **mount** command in a terminal window. Depending on your actual system configuration, a line similar to this one will usually do the trick:

mount /dev/cdrom /mnt/cdrom

On some systems, only *root* can mount removable media; this depends on the configuration.

For automation purposes, the CD drive usually has an entry in /etc/fstab, which lists the file systems and their mount points, that make up your file system tree. This is such a line:

```
[david@jupiter ~] grep cdrom /etc/fstab
/dev/cdrom  /mnt/cdrom  iso9660     noauto,owner,ro 0 0
```

This indicates that the system will understand the command **mount /mnt/cdrom**. The noauto option means that on this system, CDs are not mounted at boot time.

You may even try to right click on the CD icon on your desktop to mount the CD if your file manager doesn't do it for you. You can check whether it worked issuing the **mount** command with no arguments:

```
[david@jupiter ~] mount | grep cdrom
/dev/cdrom on /mnt/cdrom type iso9660 (ro,nosuid,nodev)
```

7.5.5.2 Using the CD

After mounting the CD, you can change directories, usually to the mount point /mnt/cdrom, where you can access the content of the CD-ROM. Use the same commands for dealing with files and directories as you would use for files on the hard disk.

7.5.5.3 Ejecting the CD

In order to get the CD out of the drive after you've finished using it, the file system on the CD should be unused. Even being in one of the subdirectories of the mount point, /mnt/cdrom in our example, will be considered as "using the file system", so you should get out of there. Do this for instance by typing **cd** with no arguments, which will put you back in your home directory. After that, you can either use the command

umount /mnt/cdrom

or

eject *cdrom*

 Blocked drives

NEVER force the drive. The trick with the paperclip is a bad idea, because this will eventually expunge the CD, but your system will think the CD is still there because normal procedures were not followed. Chances are likely that you will have to reboot to get the system back in a consistent state.

If you keep getting "device busy" messages, check first that all shell sessions have left the CD file system and that no graphical applications are using it anymore. When in doubt, use the **lsof** tool to trace down the process(es) still using the CD resource.

7.6 Summary

When everything has its place, that means already half the work is done.

While keeping order is important, it is equally important to feel at home in your environment, whether text or graphical. The text environment is controlled through the shell setup files. The graphical environment is primarily dependent on the X server configuration, on which a number of other applications are built, such as window and desktop managers and graphical applications, each with their own config files. You should read the system and program specific documentation to find out about how to configure them.

Regional settings such as keyboard setup, installing appropriate fonts and language support are best done at installation time.

Software is managed either automatically or manually using a package system.

The following commands were introduced in this chapter:

Command	Meaning
aptitude	Manage packages Debian-style.
automount	automatically include newly inserted file systems.
dpkg	Debian package manager.
dselect	Manage packages Debian-style.
loadkeys	Load keyboard configuration.
lsof	Identify processes.
mount	Include a new file system into the existing file system tree.
ntpdate	Set the system time and date using a time server.
quota	Display information about allowed disk space usage.
recode	Convert files to another character set.
rpm	Manage RPM packages.
setfont	Choose a font.
timezone	Set the timezone.
tzconfig	Set the timezone.
ulimit	Set or display resource limits.
up2date	Manage RPM packages.
urpmi	Manage RPM packages.
yum	Manage RPM packages.

Table 7.2. commands in Chapter 7: Making yourself at home

7.7 Exercises

7.7.1 Shell environment

- Print out your environment settings. Which variable may be used to store the CPU type of your machine?

- Make a script that can say something on the lines of "hello, world." Give it appropriate permissions so it can be run. Test your script.

- Create a directory in your home directory and move the script to the new directory. Permanently add this new directory to your search path. Test that the script can be executed without giving a path to its actual location.

- Create subdirectories in your home directory to store various files, for instance a directory music to keep audio files, a directory documents for your notes, and so on. And use them!

- Create a personalized prompt.

- Display limits on resource usage. Can you change them?

- Try to read compressed man pages without decompressing them first.

- Make an alias **lll** which actually executes **ls -la**.

- Why does the command **tail testfile > testfile** not work?

- Mount a data CD, such as your Linux installation CD, and have a look around. Don't forget to unmount when you don't need it anymore.

- The script from Section 7.2.5.2 is not perfect. It generates errors for files that are directories. Adapt the script so that it only selects plain files for copying. Use **find** to make the selection. Do not forget to make the script executable before you try to run it.

7.7.2 Graphical environment

- Try all the mouse buttons in different regions (terminal, background, task bar).

- Explore the menus.

- Customize your terminal window.

- Use the mouse buttons to copy and paste text from one terminal to another.

- Find out how to configure your window manager; try different workspaces (virtual screens).

- Add an applet, such as a load monitor, to the task bar.

- Apply a different theme.

- Enable the so-called *sloppy* focus - this is when a window is activated by just moving the mouse over it, so that you do not need to click the window in order to be able to use it.

- Switch to a different window manager.

- Log out and select a different session type, like KDE if you were using Gnome before. Repeat the previous steps.

Chapter 8
Printers and printing

In this chapter we will learn more about printers and printing files. After reading this part, you will be able to:

- Format documents
- Preview documents before sending them to the printer
- Choose a good printer that works with your Linux system
- Print files and check on printer status
- Troubleshoot printing problems
- Find necessary documentation to install a printer

8.1   Printing files

8.1.1 Command line printing

8.1.1.1   Getting the file to the printer

Printing from within an application is very easy, selecting the Print option from the menu.

From the command line, use the **lp** or **lpr** command.

lp `file(s)`

lpr `file(s)`

These commands can read from a pipe, so you can print the output of commands using

command | lp

There are many options available to tune the page layout, the number of copies, the printer that you want to print to if you have more than one available, paper size, one-side or double-sided printing if your printer supports this feature, margins and so on. Read the man pages for a complete overview.

8.1.1.2 Status of your print jobs

Once the file is accepted in the print queue, an identification number for the print job is assigned:

```
davy:~> lp /etc/profile
request id is blob-253 (1 file(s))
```

To view (query) the print queue, use the **lpq** or **lpstat** command. When entered without arguments, it displays the contents of the default print queue.

```
davy:~> lpq
blob is ready and printing
Rank     Owner   Job File(s)      Total Size
active   davy       253 profile     1024 bytes
davy:~> lpstat
blob-253      davy      1024    Tue 25 Jul 2006 10:20_01 AM CEST
```

8.1.1.3 Status of your printer

Which is the default printer on a system that has access to multiple printers?

lpstat -d

```
davy:~> lpstat -d
system default destination: blob
```

What is the status of my printer(s)?

lpstat -p

```
davy:~> lpstat -p
printer blob now printing blob-253. enabled since Jan 01 18:01
```

8.1.1.4 Removing jobs from the print queue

If you don't like what you see from the status commands, use **lprm** or **cancel** to delete jobs.

```
davy:~> lprm 253
```

In the graphical environment, you may see a popup window telling you that the job has been canceled.

In larger environments, **lpc** may be used to control multiple printers. See the Info or man pages on each command.

There are many GUI print tools used as a front-end to **lp**, and most graphical applications have a print function that uses **lp**. See the built-in Help functions and program specific documentation for more.

Why are there two commands for every task related to printing?

Printing on UNIX and alikes has a long history. There used to be two rather different approaches: the BSD-style printing and the SystemV-style printing. For compatibility, Linux with CUPS supports the commands from both styles. Also note that **lp** does not behave exactly like **lpr**, **lpq** has somewhat different options than **lpstat** and **lprm** is almost, but not quite, like **cancel**. Which one you use is not important, just pick the commands that you are comfortable with, or that you may know from previous experiences with UNIX-like systems.

8.1.2 Formatting

8.1.2.1 Tools and languages

If we want to get something sensible out of the printer, files should be formatted first. Apart from an abundance of formatting software, Linux comes with the basic UNIX formatting tools and languages.

Modern Linux systems support direct printing, without any formatting by the user, of a range of file types: text, PDF, PostScript and several image formats like PNG, JPEG, BMP and GIF.

For those file formats that do need formatting, Linux comes with a lot of formatting tools, such as the **pdf2ps**, **fax2ps** and **a2ps** commands, that convert other formats to PostScript. These commands can create files that can then be used on other systems that don't have all the conversion tools installed.

Apart from these command line tools there are a lot of graphical word processing programs. Several complete office suites are available, many are free. These do the formatting automatically upon submission of a print job. Just to name a few: OpenOffice.org, KOffice, AbiWord, WordPerfect, etc.

The following are common languages in a printing context:

- **groff**: GNU version of the UNIX **roff** command. It is a front-end to the groff document formatting system. Normally it runs the **troff** command and a post-processor appropriate for the selected device. It allows generation of PostScript files.

- TeX and the macro package LaTeX: one of the most widely used markup languages on UNIX systems. Usually invoked as **tex**, it formats files and outputs a corresponding device-independent representation of the typeset document.

  Technical works are *still* frequently written in LaTeX because of its support for mathematic formulas, although efforts are being made at W3C

<http://www.w3.org/> (the World Wide Web Consortium) to include this feature in other applications.

- SGML and XML: Free parsers are available for UNIX and Linux. XML is the next generation SGML, it forms the basis for DocBook XML, a document system (this book is written in XML, for instance).

☞ Printing documentation

The man pages contain pre-formatted **troff** data which has to be formatted before it can roll out of your printer. Printing is done using the `-t` option to the **man** command:

```
man -t command > man-command.ps
```

Then print the PostScript file. If a default print destination is configured for your system/account, you can just issue the command **man -t command** to send the formatted page to the printer directly.

8.1.2.2   Previewing formatted files

Anything that you can send to the printer can normally be sent to the screen as well. Depending on the file format, you can use one of these commands:

- PostScript files: with the **gv** (GhostView) command.

- TeX dvi files: with **xdvi**, or with KDE's **kdvi**.

- PDF files: **xpdf**, **kpdf**, **gpdf** or Adobe's viewer, **acroread**, which is also available for free but is not free software. Adobe's reader supports PDF 1.6, the others only support PDF versions up to 1.5. The version of a PDF file can be determined using the **file** command.

- From within applications, such as Firefox or OpenOffice, you can usually select Print Preview from one of the menus.

8.2   The server side

8.2.1 General

Until a couple of years ago, the choice for Linux users was simple: everyone ran the same old LPD from BSD's Net-2 code. Then LPRng became more popular, but nowadays most modern Linux distributions use CUPS <http://www.cups.org/>, the Common UNIX Printing System. CUPS is an implementation of the Internet Printing Protocol (IPP), an HTTP-like RFC standard replacement protocol for the venerable (and clunky) LPD protocol. CUPS is distributed under the GNU Public License. CUPS is also the default print system on MacOS X.

8.2.2 Graphical printer configuration

Most distributions come with a GUI for configuring networked and local (parallel port or USB) printers. They let you choose the printer type from a list and allow easy testing. You don't have to bother about syntax and location of configuration files. Check your system documentation before you attempt installing your printer.

CUPS can also be configured using a web interface that runs on port 631 on your computer. To check if this feature is enabled, try browsing to localhost:631/help or localhost:631/.

8.2.3 Buying a printer for Linux

As more and more printer vendors make drivers for CUPS available, CUPS will allow easy connection with almost any printer that you can plug into a serial, parallel, or USB port, plus any printer on the network. CUPS will ensure a uniform presentation to you and your applications of all different types of printers.

Printers that only come with a Win9x driver could be problematic if they have no other support. Check with <http://linuxprinting.org/> when in doubt.

In the past, your best choice would have been a printer with native PostScript support in the firmware, since nearly all UNIX or Linux software producing printable output, produces it in PostScript, the publishing industry's printer control language of choice. PostScript printers are usually a bit more expensive, but it is a device-independent, open programming language and you're always 100% sure that they will work. These days, however, the importance of this rule of thumb is dwindling.

8.3 Print problems

In this section, we will discuss what you can do as a user when something goes wrong. We won't discuss any problems that have to do with the daemon-part of the printing service, as that is a task for system administrators.

8.3.1 Wrong file

If you print the wrong file, the job may be canceled using the command **lprm** *jobID*, where jobID is in the form *printername-printjobnumber* (get it from information displayed by **lpq** or **lpstat**). This will work when other jobs are waiting to be printed in this printer's queue. However, you have to be really quick if you are the only one using this printer, since jobs are usually spooled and send to the printer in only seconds. Once they arrive on the printer, it is too late to remove jobs using Linux tools.

What you can try in those cases, or in cases where the wrong print driver is configured and only rubbish comes out of the printer, is power off the printer. However, that might not be the best course of action, as you might cause paper jams and other irregularities.

8.3.2 My print hasn't come out

Use the **lpq** command and see if you can spot your job:

```
elly:~> lpq
Printer: lp@blob
 Queue: 2 printable jobs
 Server: pid 29998 active
 Unspooler: pid 29999 active
 Status: waiting for subserver to exit at 09:43:20.699
 Rank    Owner/ID            Class Job Files          Size Time
 1       elly@blob+997         A   997 (STDIN)          129 09:42:54
 2       elly@blob+22          A    22 /etc/profile      917 09:43:20
```

Lots of printers have web interfaces these days, which can display status information by typing the printer's IP address in your web browser:

Figure 8.1. Printer Status through web interface

CUPS web interface versus printer web interface

Note that this is not the CUPS web interface and only works for printers supporting this feature. Check the documentation of your printer.

If your job ID is not there and not on the printer, contact your system administrator. If your job ID is listed in the output, check that the printer is currently printing. If so, just wait, your job will get done in due time.

If the printer is not printing, check that it has paper, check the physical connections to both electricity and data network. If that's okay, the printer may need restarting. Ask your system admin for advice.

In the case of a network printer, try printing from another host. If the printer is reachable from your own host (see Chapter 10 for the **ping** utility), you may try to put the formatted file on it, like `file.ps` in case of a PostScript printer, using an FTP client. If that works, your print system is misconfigured. If it doesn't work, maybe the printer doesn't understand the format you are feeding it.

The GNU/Linux Printing site <http://www.linuxprinting.org/> contains more tips and tricks.

8.4 Summary

The Linux print service comes with a set of printing tools based on the standard UNIX LPD tools, whether it be the SystemV or BSD implementation. Below is a list of print-related commands.

Command	Meaning
lpr or **lp**	Print file
lpq or **lpstat**	Query print queue
lprm or **cancel**	Remove print job
acroread	PDF viewer
groff	Formatting tool
gv	PostScript viewer
printconf	Configure printers
xdvi	DVI viewer
xpdf	PDF viewer
***2ps**	Convert file to PostScript

Table 8.1. New commands in Chapter 8: Printing

8.5 Exercises

Configuring and testing printers involves being in the possession of one, and having access to the *root* account. If so, you may try:

- Installing the printer using the GUI on your system.

- Printing a test page using the GUI.

- Printing a test page using the **lp** command.

- Print from within an application, for example Mozilla or OpenOffice, by choosing File->Print from the menu.

- Disconnect the printer from the network or the local machine/print-server. What happens when you try to print something?

The following exercises can be done without printer or root access.

- Try to make PostScript files from different source files, (e.g. HTML, PDF, man pages). Test the results with the **gv** viewer.

- Check that the print daemon is running.

- Print the files anyway. What happens?

- Make a PostScript file using Mozilla. Test it with **gv**.

- Convert it to PDF format. Test with **xpdf**.

- How would you go about printing a GIF file from the command line?

- Use **a2ps** to print the /etc/profile file to an output file. Test again with **gv**. What happens if you don't specify an output file?

Chapter 9
Fundamental Backup Techniques

Accidents will happen sooner or later. In this chapter, we'll discuss how to get data to a safe place using other hosts, floppy disks, CD-ROMs and tapes. We will also discuss the most popular compressing and archiving commands.

Upon completion of this chapter, you will know how to:

- Make, query and unpack file archives
- Handle floppy disks and make a boot disk for your system
- Write CD-ROMs
- Make incremental backups
- Create Java archives
- Find documentation to use other backup devices and programs
- Encrypt your data

9.1   Introduction

Although Linux is one of the safest operating systems in existence, and even if it is designed to keep on going, data can get lost. Data loss is most often the consequence of user errors, but occasionally a system fault, such as a power or disk failure, is the cause, so it's always a good idea to keep an extra copy of sensitive and/or important data.

9.1.1 Preparing your data

9.1.1.1   Archiving with tar

In most cases, we will first collect all the data to back up in a single archive file, which we will compress later on. The process of archiving involves concatenating all listed files and taking out unnecessary blanks. In Linux, this is commonly done with the **tar** command. **tar** was originally designed to archive data on tapes, but it can also make archives, known as *tarballs*.

tar has many options, the most important ones are cited below:

- `-v`: verbose

- `-t`: test, shows content of a tarball

- `-x`: extract archive

- `-c`: create archive

- `-f archivedevice`: use `archivedevice` as source/destination for the tarball, the device defaults to the first tape device (usually `/dev/st0` or something similar)

- `-j`: filter through **bzip2**, see Section 9.1.1.2

It is common to leave out the dash-prefix with **tar** options, as you can see from the examples below.

Use GNU tar for compatibility

The archives made with a proprietary **tar** version on one system, may be incompatible with **tar** on another proprietary system. This may cause much headaches, such as if the archive needs to be recovered on a system that doesn't exist anymore. Use the GNU **tar** version on all systems to prevent your system admin from bursting into tears. Linux always uses GNU tar. When working on other UNIX machines, enter **tar --help** to find out which version you are using. Contact your system admin if you don't see the word GNU somewhere.

In the example below, an archive is created and unpacked.

```
gaby:~> ls images/
me+tux.jpg  nimf.jpg

gaby:~> tar cvf images-in-a-dir.tar images/
images/
images/nimf.jpg
images/me+tux.jpg

gaby:~> cd images

gaby:~/images> tar cvf images-without-a-dir.tar *.jpg
me+tux.jpg
nimf.jpg

gaby:~/images> cd
```

```
gaby:~> ls */*.tar
images/images-without-a-dir.tar

gaby:~> ls *.tar
images-in-a-dir.tar

gaby:~> tar xvf images-in-a-dir.tar
images/
images/nimf.jpg
images/me+tux.jpg

gaby:~> tar tvf images/images-without-dir.tar
-rw-r--r-- gaby/gaby   42888 1999-06-30 20:52:25 me+tux.jpg
-rw-r--r-- gaby/gaby    7578 2000-01-26 12:58:46 nimf.jpg

gaby:~> tar xvf images/images-without-a-dir.tar
me+tux.jpg
nimf.jpg

gaby:~> ls *.jpg
me+tux.jpg  nimf.jpg
```

This example also illustrates the difference between a tarred directory and a bunch of tarred files. It is advisable to only compress directories, so files don't get spread all over when unpacking the tarball (which may be on another system, where you may not know which files were already there and which are the ones from the archive).

When a tape drive is connected to your machine and configured by your system administrator, the file names ending in .tar are replaced with the tape device name, for example:

tar cvf /dev/tape mail/

The directory mail and all the files it contains are compressed into a file that is written on the tape immediately. A content listing is displayed because we used the verbose option.

9.1.1.2   Incremental backups with tar

The **tar** tool supports the creation of incremental backups, using the -N option. With this option, you can specify a date, and **tar** will check modification time of all specified files against this date. If files are changed more recent than date, they will be included in the backup. The example below uses the timestamp on a previous archive as the date value. First, the initial archive is created and the timestamp on the initial backup file is shown. Then a new file is created, upon which we take a new backup, containing only this new file:

```
jimmy:~> tar cvpf /var/tmp/javaproggies.tar java/*.java
java/btw.java
```

```
java/error.java
java/hello.java
java/income2.java
java/income.java
java/inputdevice.java
java/input.java
java/master.java
java/method1.java
java/mood.java
java/moodywaitress.java
java/test3.java
java/TestOne.java
java/TestTwo.java
java/Vehicle.java

jimmy:~> ls -l /var/tmp/javaproggies.tar
-rw-rw-r-- 1 jimmy    jimmy   10240 Jan 21 11:58 /var/tmp/javaproggies.tar

jimmy:~> touch java/newprog.java

jimmy:~> tar -N /var/tmp/javaproggies.tar \
-cvp /var/tmp/incremental1-javaproggies.tar java/*.java 2> /dev/null
java/newprog.java

jimmy:~> cd /var/tmp/

jimmy:~> tar xvf incremental1-javaproggies.tar
java/newprog.java
```

Standard errors are redirected to /dev/null. If you don't do this, **tar** will print a message for each unchanged file, telling you it won't be dumped.

This way of working has the disadvantage that it looks at timestamps on files. Say that you download an archive into the directory containing your backups, and the archive contains files that have been created two years ago. When checking the timestamps of those files against the timestamp on the initial archive, the new files will actually seem old to **tar**, and will not be included in an incremental backup made using the -N option.

A better choice would be the -g option, which will create a list of files to backup. When making incremental backups, files are checked against this list. This is how it works:

```
jimmy:~> tar cvpf work-20030121.tar -g snapshot-20030121 work/
work/
work/file1
work/file2
work/file3

jimmy:~> file snapshot-20030121
snapshot-20030121: ASCII text
```

The next day, user *jimmy* works on `file3` a bit more, and creates `file4`. At the end of the day, he makes a new backup:

```
jimmy:~> tar cvpf work-20030122.tar -g snapshot-20030121 work/
work/
work/file3
work/file4
```

These are some very simple examples, but you could also use this kind of command in a cronjob (see Section 4.4.4), which specifies for instance a snapshot file for the weekly backup and one for the daily backup. Snapshot files should be replaced when taking full backups, in that case.

More information can be found in the **tar** documentation.

The real stuff

As you could probably notice, **tar** is OK when we are talking about a simple directory, a set of files that belongs together. There are tools that are easier to manage, however, when you want to archive entire partitions or disks or larger projects. We just explain about **tar** here because it is a very popular tool for distributing archives. It will happen quite often that you need to install a software that comes in a so-called "compressed tarball". See Section 9.3 for an easier way to perform regular backups.

9.1.1.3 Compressing and unpacking with gzip or bzip2

Data, including tarballs, can be compressed using zip tools. The **gzip** command will add the suffix .gz to the file name and remove the original file.

```
jimmy:~> ls -la | grep tar
-rw-rw-r-- 1 jimmy   jimmy      61440 Jun  6 14:08 images-without-dir.tar

jimmy:~> gzip images-without-dir.tar

jimmy:~> ls -la images-without-dir.tar.gz
-rw-rw-r-- 1 jimmy   jimmy      50562 Jun  6 14:08 images-without-dir.tar.gz
```

Uncompress gzipped files with the -d option.

bzip2 works in a similar way, but uses an improved compression algorithm, thus creating smaller files. See the **bzip2** info pages for more.

Linux software packages are often distributed in a gzipped tarball. The sensible thing to do after unpacking that kind of archives is find the README and read it. It will generally contain guidelines to installing the package.

The GNU **tar** command is aware of gzipped files. Use the command `tar zxvf file.tar.gz`

for unzipping and untarring `.tar.gz` or `.tgz` files. Use

`tar jxvf file.tar.bz2`

for unpacking **tar** archives that were compressed with **bzip2**.

9.1.1.4   Java archives

The GNU project provides us with the **jar** tool for creating Java archives. It is a Java application that combines multiple files into a single JAR archive file. While also being a general purpose archiving and compression tool, based on ZIP and the ZLIB compression format, **jar** was mainly designed to facilitate the packing of Java code, applets and/or applications in a single file. When combined in a single archive, the components of a Java application, can be downloaded much faster.

Unlike **tar**, **jar** compresses by default, independent from other tools - because it is basically the Java version of **zip**. In addition, it allows individual entries in an archive to be signed by the author, so that origins can be authenticated.

The syntax is almost identical as for the **tar** command, we refer to **info** `jar` for specific differences.

tar, jar and symbolic links

One noteworthy feature not really mentioned in the standard documentation is that **jar** will follow symbolic links. Data to which these links are pointing will be included in the archive. The default in **tar** is to only backup the symbolic link, but this behavior can be changed using the `-h` to **tar**.

9.1.1.5   Transporting your data

Saving copies of your data on another host is a simple but accurate way of making backups. See Chapter 10 for more information on **scp**, **ftp** and more.

In the next section we'll discuss local backup devices.

9.2   Moving your data to a backup device

9.2.1 Making a copy on a floppy disk

9.2.1.1   Formatting the floppy

On most Linux systems, users have access to the floppy disk device. The name of the device may vary depending on the size and number of floppy drives, contact your system admin if you are unsure. On some systems, there will likely be a link

/dev/floppy pointing to the right device, probably /dev/fd0 (the auto-detecting floppy device) or /dev/fd0H1440 (set for 1,44MB floppies).

fdformat is the low-level floppy disk formatting tool. It has the device name of the floppy disk as an option. **fdformat** will display an error when the floppy is write-protected.

```
emma:~> fdformat /dev/fd0H1440
Double-sided, 80 tracks, 18 sec/track. Total capacity 1440 kB.
Formatting ... done
Verifying ... done
emma:~>
```

The **mformat** command (from the mtools package) is used to create DOS-compatible floppies which can then be accessed using the **mcopy**, **mdir** and other m-commands.

Graphical tools are also available.

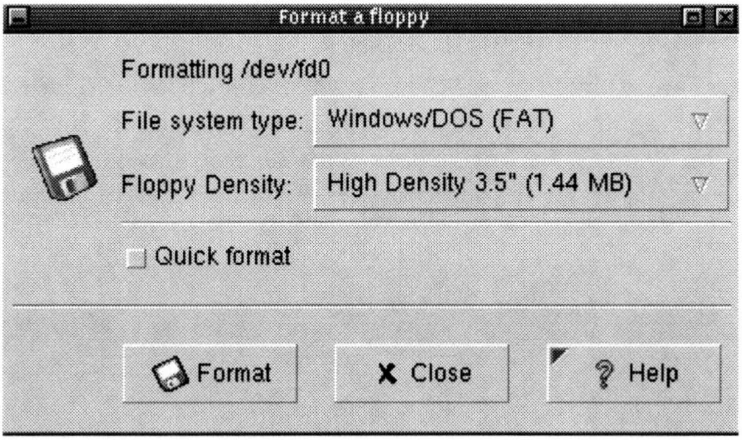

Figure 9.1. Floppy formatter

After the floppy is formatted, it can be mounted into the file system and accessed as a normal, be it small, directory, usually via the /mnt/floppy entry.

Should you need it, install the **mkbootdisk** utility, which makes a floppy from which the current system can boot.

9.2.1.2 Using the dd command to dump data

The **dd** command can be used to put data on a disk, or get it off again, depending on the given input and output devices. An example:

```
gaby:~> dd if=images-without-dir.tar.gz of=/dev/fd0H1440
98+1 records in
98+1 records out
```

```
gaby~> dd if=/dev/fd0H1440 of=/var/tmp/images.tar.gz
2880+0 records in
2880+0 records out

gaby:~> ls /var/tmp/images*
/var/tmp/images.tar.gz
```

Note that the dumping is done on an unmounted device. Floppies created using this method will not be mountable in the file system, but it is of course the way to go for creating boot or rescue disks. For more information on the possibilities of **dd**, read the man pages.

This tool is part of the GNU *coreutils* package.

 Dumping disks

The **dd** command can also be used to make a raw dump of an entire hard disk.

9.2.2 Making a copy with a CD-writer

On some systems users are allowed to use the CD-writer device. Your data will need to be formatted first. Use the **mkisofs** command to do this in the directory containing the files you want to backup. Check with **df** that enough disk space is available, because a new file about the same size as the entire current directory will be created:

```
[rose@blob recordables] df -h .
Filesystem              Size  Used Avail Use% Mounted on
/dev/hde5               19G   15G  3.2G  82% /home

[rose@blob recordables] du -h -s .
325M     .

[rose@blob recordables] mkisofs -J -r -o cd.iso .
<--snap-->
making a lot of conversions
<--/snap-->
98.95% done, estimate finish Fri Apr  5 13:54:25 2002
Total translation table size: 0
Total rockridge attributes bytes: 35971
Total directory bytes: 94208
Path table size(bytes): 452
Max brk space used 37e84
166768 extents written (325 Mb)
```

The -J and -r options are used to make the CD-ROM mountable on different systems, see the man pages for more. After that, the CD can be created using the **cdrecord** tool with appropriate options:

```
[rose@blob recordables] cdrecord -dev 0,0,0 -speed=8 cd.iso
Cdrecord 1.10 (i686-pc-linux-gnu) (C) 1995-2001 Joerg Schilling
```

```
scsidev: '0,0,0'
scsibus: 0 target: 0 lun: 0
Linux sg driver version: 3.1.20
Using libscg version 'schily-0.5'
Device type     : Removable CD-ROM
Version         : 0
Response Format: 1
Vendor_info     : 'HP        '
Identification : 'CD-Writer+ 8100 '
Revision        : '1.0g'
Device seems to be: Generic mmc CD-RW.
Using generic SCSI-3/mmc CD-R driver (mmc_cdr).
Driver flags    : SWABAUDIO
Starting to write CD/DVD at speed 4 in write mode for single session.
Last chance to quit, starting real write in 0 seconds.
Operation starts.
```

Depending on your CD-writer, you now have the time to smoke^H^H^H^H^H eat a healthy piece of fruit and/or get a cup of coffee. Upon finishing the job, you will get a confirmation message:

```
Track 01: Total bytes read/written: 341540864/341540864
         (166768 sectors).
```

There are some graphical tools available to make it easier on you. One of the popular ones is **xcdroast**, which is freely available from the X-CD-Roast web site <http://www.xcdroast.org/> and is included on most systems and in the GNU directory. Both the KDE and Gnome desktop managers have facilities to make your own CDs.

9.2.3 Backups on/from jazz drives, USB devices and such

These devices are usually mounted into the file system. After the mount procedure, they are accessed as normal directories, so you can use the standard commands for manipulating files.

In the example below, images are copied from a USB camera to the hard disk:

```
robin:~> mount /mnt/camera

robin:~> mount | grep camera
/dev/sda1 on /mnt/camera type vfat (rw,nosuid,nodev)
```

If the camera is the only USB storage device that you ever connect to your system, this is safe. But keep in mind that USB devices are assigned entries in /dev as they are connected to the system. Thus, if you first connect a USB stick to your system, it will be on the /dev/sda entry, and if you connect your camera after that, it will be assigned to /dev/sdb - provided that you do not have any SCSI disks, which are also on /dev/sd*. On newer systems, since kernel 2.6, a hotplug system called HAL (Hardware Abstraction Layer) ensures that users don't have to deal with this burden. If you want to check where your device is, type **dmesg** after inserting it.

You can now copy the files:

```
robin:~> cp -R /mnt/camera/* images/

robin:~> umount /mnt/camera
```

Likewise, a jazz drive may be mounted on /mnt/jazz.

Appropriate lines should be added in /etc/modules.conf and /etc/fstab to make this work. Refer to specific hardware HOWTOs for more information. On systems with a 2.6.x kernel or higher, you may also want to check the man pages for **modprobe** and modprobe.conf.

9.2.4 Backing up data using a tape device

This is done using **tar** (see above). The **mt** tool is used for controlling the magnetic tape device, like /dev/st0. Entire books have been written about tape backup, therefore, refer to our reading-list in Appendix B for more information. Keep in mind that databases might need other backup procedures because of their architecture.

The appropriate backup commands are usually put in one of the *cron* directories in order to have them executed on a regular basis. In larger environments, the freely available Amanda backup suite or a commercial solution may be implemented to back up multiple machines. Working with tapes, however, is a system administration task beyond the scope of this document.

9.2.5 Tools from your distribution

Most Linux distributions offer their own tools for making your life easy. A short overview:

- SuSE: YaST now includes expanded backup and restore modules.

- RedHat: the File Roller tool provides visual management of (compressed) archives. They seem to be in favour of the X-CD-Roast tool for moving backups to an external device.

- Mandrake: X-CD-Roast.

- Most distributions come with the BSD **dump** and **restore** utilities for making backups of *ext2* and *ext3* file systems. This tool can write to a variety of devices and literally dumps the file(s) or file system bit per bit onto the specified device. Like **dd**, this allows for backing up special file types such as the ones in /dev.

9.3   Using rsync

9.3.1 Introduction

The **rsync** program is a fast and flexible tool for remote backup. It is common on UNIX and UNIX-like systems, easy to configure and use in scripts. While the *r* in **rsync** stands for "remote", you do not need to take this all too literally. Your "remote" device might just as well be a USB storage device or another partition on your hard disk, you do not need to have two separated machines.

9.3.2 An example: rsync to a USB storage device

As discussed in Section 3.1.2.3, we will first have to mount the device. Possibly, this should be done as *root*:

```
root@theserver# mkdir /mnt/usbstore
```

```
root@theserver# mount -t vfat /dev/sda1 /mnt/usbstore
```

 Userfriendly

> More and more distributions give access to removable devices for non-prilileged users and mount USB devices, CD-ROMs and such automatically.

Note that this guideline requires USB support to be installed on your system. See the USB Guide <http://www.linux-usb.org/USB-guide/> for help if this does not work. Check with **dmesg** that /dev/sda1 is indeed the device to mount.

Then you can start the actual backup, for instance of the /home/karl directory:

```
karl@theserver:~> rsync -avg /home/karl /mnt/usbstore
```

As usual, refer to the man pages for more.

9.4   Encryption

9.4.1 General remarks

9.4.1.1   Why should you encrypt data?

Encryption is synonym to secrecy. In the context of backups, encryption can be very useful, for instance if you need to leave your backed up data in a place where you can not control access, such as the server of your provider.

Apart from that, encryption can be applied to E-mails as well: normally, mail is not encrypted and it is often sent in the open over the netwerk or the Internet. If your message contains sensitive information, better encrypt it.

9.4.1.2   GNU Privacy Guard

On Linux systems you will find GnuPG, the GNU Privacy Guard, which is a suite of programs that are compatible with the PGP (Pretty Good Privacy) tools that are commercially available.

In this guide we will only discuss the very simple usage of the encryption tools and show what you will need in order to generate an encryption key and use it to encrypt data for yourself, which you can then safely store in a public place. More advanced usage directions can be found in the man pages of the various commands.

9.4.2 Generate a key

Before you can start encrypting your data, you need to create a pair of keys. The pair consists of a private and a public key. You can send the public key to correspondents, who can use it to encrypt data for you, which you decrypt with your private key. You always keep the private key, never share it with somebody else, or they will be able to decrypt data that is only destined for you. Just to make sure that no accidents happen, the private key is protected with a password. The key pair is created using this command:

```
willy@ubuntu:~$ gpg --key-gen
gpg (GnuPG) 1.4.2.2; Copyright (C) 2005 Free Software Foundation, Inc.
This program comes with ABSOLUTELY NO WARRANTY.
This is free software, and you are welcome to redistribute it
under certain conditions.  See the file COPYING for details.

gpg: directory `/home/willy.gnupg' created
gpg: new configuration file `/home/willy/.gnupg/gpg.conf' created
gpg: WARNING: options in `/home/willy/.gnupg/gpg.conf' are not yet
 active during this run
gpg: keyring `/home/willy/.gnupg/secring.gpg' created
gpg: keyring `/home/willy/.gnupg/pubring.gpg' created
Please select what kind of key you want:
    (1) DSA and Elgamal (default)
    (2) DSA (sign only)
    (5) RSA (sign only)
Your selection? 1
DSA keypair will have 1024 bits.
ELG-E keys may be between 1024 and 4096 bits long.
What keysize do you want? (2048) 4096
Requested keysize is 4096 bits
Please specify how long the key should be valid.
        0 = key does not expire
      <n>  = key expires in n days
      <n>w = key expires in n weeks
      <n>m = key expires in n month
      <n>y = key expires in n years
Key is valid for? (0) 0
Key does not expire at all
```

```
Is this correct? (y/N) y

You need a user ID to identify your key; the software constructs the
user ID from the Real Name, Comment and Email Address in this form:
    "Heinrich Heine (Der Dichter) <heinrichh@duesseldorf.de>"

Real name: Willy De Wandel
Email address: wdw@mvg.vl
Comment: Willem
You selected this USER-ID:
    "Willy De Wandel (Willem) <wdw@mvg.vl>"

Change (N)ame, (C)omment, (E)mail or (O)kay/(Q)uit? O
You need a Passphrase to protect your secret key.

Passphrase:
```

Now enetr your password. This can be a phrase, the longer, the better, the only condition is that you should be able to remember it at all times. For verification, you need to enter the same phrase again.

Now the key pair is generated by a program that spawns random numbers and that is, among other factors, fed with the activity data of the system. So it is a good idea to start some programs now, to move the mouse cursor or to type some random characters in a terminal window. That way, the chances to generate a number that contains lots of different digits will be much bigger and the key will be more difficult to crack.

9.4.3 About your key

When your key has been created, you will get a message about the *fingerprint*. This is a sequence of 40 hexadecimal numbers, which is so long that it is very, very hard to generate the same key twice, on any computer. You can be rather sure that this is a unique sequence. The short form of this key consists of your name, followed by the last 8 hexadecimal numbers.

You can get information about your key as follows:

```
willy@ubuntu:~$ gpg --list-keys
/home/willy/.gnupg/pubring.gpg
--------------------------------
pub    1024D/BF5C3DBB 2006-08-08
uid                   Willy De Wandel (Willem) <wdw@mvg.vl>
sub    4096g/A3449CF7 2006-08-08
```

The *key ID* of this key is "BF5C3DBB". You can send your key ID and your name to a *key server*, so that other people can get this info about you and use it to encrypt data for you. Alternatively, you can send your public key directly to the people who need it. The public part of your key is the long series of numbers that you see when using the --export option to the **gpg** command:

```
gpg --export -a
```

However, as far is this guide is concerned, we assume that you only need your key in order to encrypt and decrypt data for yourself. Read the **gpg** man pages if you want to know more.

9.4.4 Encrypt data

Now you can encrypt a `.tar` archive or a compressed archive, prior to saving it to a backup medium or transporting it to the backup server. Use the **gpg** command like this:

```
gpg -e -r (part of) uid archive
```

The `-e` option tells **gpg** to encrypt, the `-r` option indicates who to encrypt for. Keep in mind that only only the user name(s) following this `-r` option will be able to decrypt the data again. An example:

```
willy@ubuntu:~$ gpg -e -r Willy /var/tmp/home-willy-20060808.tar
```

9.4.5 Decrypting files

Using the `-d` option, you can decrypt files that have been encrypted for you. The data will scroll over your screen, but an encrypted copy will remain on disk. So for file formats other than plain text, you will want to save the decrypted data, so that you can view them with the appropriate program. This is done using the `-o` option to the **gpg** command:

```
willy@ubuntu:~$ gpg -d -o /var/tmp/home-willy-decrypt.tar
/var/tmp/home-willy-20060808.tar.gpg

You need a passphrase to unlock the secret key for
user: "Willy De Wandel (Willem) <wdw@mvg.vl>"
4096 ELG-E key, ID A3449CF7, created 2006-08-08 (main key ID BF5C3DBB)

gpg: encrypted with 4096-bit ELG-E key, ID A3449CF7, created 2006-08-08
      "Willy De Wandel (Willem) <wdw@mvg.vl>"
```

⚠ No password = no data

If you can not remember your password, the data is lost. Not even the system administrator will be able to decrypt the data. That is why a copy of important keys is sometimes kept in a sealed vault in a bank.

9.5 Summary

Here's a list of the commands involving file backup:

Command	Meaning
bzip2	A block-sorting file compressor.
cdrecord	Record audio or data Compact Disks from a master.
dd	Convert and copy a file
fdformat	Low-level formats a floppy disk.
gpg	Encrypt and decrypt data.
gzip	Compress or expand files.
mcopy	Copy MSDOS files to/from UNIX.
mdir	Display an MSDOS directory.
mformat	Add an MSDOS file system to a low-level formatted floppy disk.
mkbootdisk	Creates a stand-alone boot floppy for the running system.
mount	Mount a file system (integrate it with the current file system by connecting it to a mount point).
tar	Tape archiving utility, also used for making archives on disk instead of on tape.
umount	Unmount file systems.

Table 9.1. New commands in Chapter 9: Backup

9.6 Exercises

- Make a backup copy of your home directory in /var/tmp using the **tar** command. Then further compress the file using **gzip** or **bzip2**. Make it a clean tarred file, one that doesn't make a mess when unpacking.

- Format a floppy and put some files from your home directory on it. Switch floppies with another trainee and recover his/her floppy in your home directory.

- DOS format the floppy. Use the *mtools* to put and delete files on it.

- What happens to an unformatted floppy when you want to mount it into the file system?

- If you have any USB storage, try to put a file on it.

- Using **rsync**, make a copy of your home directory to another local or remote file system.

- When leaving files on a network server, it's best to encrypt them. Make a tar archive of your home directory and encrypt it.

Chapter 10
Networking

When it comes to networking, Linux is your operating system of choice, not only because networking is tightly integrated with the OS itself and a wide variety of free tools and applications are available, but for the robustness under heavy loads that can only be achieved after years of debugging and testing in an Open Source project.

Bookshelves full of information have been written about Linux and networking, but we will try to give an overview in this chapter. After completing this, you will know more about

- Supported networking protocols

- Network configuration files

- Commands for configuring and probing the network

- Daemons and client programs enabling different network applications

- File sharing and printing

- Remote execution of commands and applications

- Basic network interconnection

- Secure execution of remote applications

- Firewalls and intrusion detection

10.1 Networking Overview

10.1.1   The OSI Model

A protocol is, simply put, a set of rules for communication.

In order to get data over the network, for instance an E-mail from your computer to some computer at the other end of the world, lots of different hard- and software needs to work together.

All these pieces of hardware and the different software programs speak different languages. Imagine your E-mail program: it is able to talk to the computer operating system, through a specific protocol, but it is not able to talk to the computer hardware. We need a special program in the operating system that performs this function. In turn, the computer needs to be able to communicate with the telephone line or other Internet hookup method. And behind the scenes, network connection hardware needs to be able to communicate in order to pass your E-mail from one appliance to the other, all the way to the destination computer.

All these different types of communication protocols are classified in 7 layers, which are known as the *Open Systems Interconnection Reference Model*, the *OSI Model* for short. For easy understanding, this model is reduced to a 4-layer protocol description, as described in the table below:

Layer name	Layer Protocols
Application layer	HTTP, DNS, SMTP, POP, ...
Transport layer	TCP, UDP
Network layer	IP, IPv6
Network access layer	PPP, PPPoE, Ethernet

Table 10.1. The simplified OSI Model

Each layer can only use the functionality of the layer below; each layer can only export functionality to the layer above. In other words: layers communicate only with adjacent layers. Let's take the example of your E-mail message again: you enter it through the application layer. In your computer, it travels down the transport and network layer. Your computer puts it on the network through the network access layer. That is also the layer that will move the message around the world. At the destination, the receiving computer will accept the message through it's own network layer, and will display it to the recepient using the transport and application layer.

It's really much more complicated

The above and following sections are included because you will come across some networking terms sooner or later; they will give you some starting points, should you want to find out about the details.

10.1.2   Some popular networking protocols

Linux supports many different networking protocols. We list only the most important:

10.1.2.1 TCP/IP

The *Transport Control Protocol* and the *Internet Protocol* are the two most popular ways of communicating on the Internet. A lot of applications, such as your browser and E-mail program, are built on top of this protocol suite.

Very simply put, IP provides a solution for sending packets of information from one machine to another, while TCP ensures that the packets are arranged in streams, so that packets from different applications don't get mixed up, and that the packets are sent and received in the correct order.

A good starting point for learning more about TCP and IP is in the following documents:

- **man 7 *ip***: Describes the IPv4 protocol implementation on Linux (version 4 currently being the most wide-spread edition of the IP protocol).

- **man 7 *tcp***: Implementation of the TCP protocol.

- RFC793, RFC1122, RFC2001 for TCP, and RFC791, RFC1122 and RFC1112 for IP.

The Request For Comments <http://www.ietf.org/rtf/> documents contain the descriptions of networking standards, protocols, applications and implementation. These documents are managed by the Internet Engineering Task Force, an international community concerned with the smooth operation of the Internet and the evolution and development of the Internet architecture.

Your ISP usually has an RFC archive available, or you can browse the RFCs via <http://www.ietf.org/rfc.html>.

10.1.2.2 TCP/IPv6

Nobody expected the Internet to grow as fast as it does. IP proved to have quite some disadvantages when a really large number of computers is in a network, the most important being the availability of unique addresses to assign to each machine participating. Thus, IP version 6 was deviced to meet the needs of today's Internet.

Unfortunately, not all applications and services support IPv6, yet. A migration is currently being set in motion in many environments that can benefit from an upgrade to IPv6. For some applications, the old protocol is still used, for applications that have been reworked the new version is already active. So when checking your network configuration, sometimes it might be a bit confusing since all kinds of measures can be taken to hide one protocol from the other so as the two don't mix up connections.

More information can be found in the following documents:

- **man 7** *ipv6*: the Linux IPv6 protocol implementation.
- RFC1883 describing the IPv6 protocol.

10.1.2.3 PPP, SLIP, PLIP, PPPOE

The Linux kernel has built-in support for PPP (Point-to-Point-Protocol), SLIP (Serial Line IP), PLIP (Parallel Line IP) and PPPP Over EThernet. PPP is the most popular way individual users access their ISP (Internet Service Provider), although in densely populated areas it is often being replaced by PPPOE, the protocol used for ADSL (Asymmetric Digital Subscriber Line) connections.

Most Linux distributions provide easy-to-use tools for setting up an Internet connection. The only thing you basically need is a username and password to connect to your Internet Service Provider (ISP), and a telephone number in the case of PPP. These data are entered in the graphical configuration tool, which will likely also allow for starting and stopping the connection to your provider.

10.1.2.4 ISDN

The Linux kernel has built-in ISDN capabilities. Isdn4linux controls ISDN PC cards and can emulate a modem with the Hayes command set ("AT" commands). The possibilities range from simply using a terminal program to full connection to the Internet.

Check your system documentation.

10.1.2.5 AppleTalk

Appletalk is the name of Apple's internetworking stack. It allows a peer-to-peer network model which provides basic functionality such as file and printer sharing. Each machine can simultaneously act as a client and a server, and the software and hardware necessary are included with every Apple computer.

Linux provides full AppleTalk networking. Netatalk is a kernel-level implementation of the AppleTalk Protocol Suite, originally for BSD-derived systems. It includes support for routing AppleTalk, serving UNIX and AFS file systems using AppleShare and serving UNIX printers and accessing AppleTalk printers.

10.1.2.6 SMB/NMB

For compatibility with MS Windows environments, the Samba suite, including support for the NMB and SMB protocols, can be installed on any UNIX-like system. The Server Message Block protocol (also called Session Message Block, NetBIOS or

LanManager protocol) is used on MS Windows 3.11, NT, 95/98, 2K and XP to share disks and printers.

The basic functions of the Samba suite are: sharing Linux drives with Windows machines, accessing SMB shares from Linux machines, sharing Linux printers with Windows machines and sharing Windows printers with Linux machines.

Most Linux distributions provide a *samba* package, which does most of the server setup and starts up **smbd**, the Samba server, and **nmbd**, the netbios name server, at boot time by default. Samba can be configured graphically, via a web interface or via the command line and text configuration files. The daemons make a Linux machine appear as an MS Windows host in an MS Windows My Network Places/Network Neighbourhood window; a share from a Linux machine will be indistinguishable from a share on any other host in an MS Windows environment.

More information can be found at the following locations:

- **man smb.conf**: describes the format of the main Samba configuration file.

- The Samba Project Documentation <http://www.samba.org/> (or check your local samba.org mirror) contains an easy to read installation and testing guide, which also explains how to configure your Samba server as a Primary Domain Controller. All the man pages are also available here.

10.1.2.7 Miscellaneous protocols

Linux also has support for Amateur Radio, WAN internetworking (X25, Frame Relay, ATM), InfraRed and other wireless connections, but since these protocols usually require special hardware, we won't discuss them in this document.

10.2 Network configuration and information

10.2.1   Configuration of network interfaces

All the big, userfriendly Linux distributions come with various graphical tools, allowing for easy setup of the computer in a local network, for connecting it to an Internet Service Provider or for wireless access. These tools can be started up from the command line or from a menu:

- Ubuntu configuration is done selecting System->Administration->Networking.

- RedHat Linux comes with **redhat-config-network**, which has both a graphical and a text mode interface.

- Suse's YAST or YAST2 is an all-in-one configuration tool.

- Mandrake/Mandriva comes with a Network and Internet Configuration Wizard, which is preferably started up from Mandrake's Control Center.

- On Gnome systems: **gnome-network-preferences**.

- On KDE systems: **knetworkconf**.

Your system documentation provides plenty of advice and information about availability and use of tools.

Information that you will need to provide:

- For connecting to the local network, for instance with your home computers, or at work: hostname, domainname and IP address. If you want to set up your own network, best do some more reading first. At work, this information is likely to be given to your computer automatically when you boot it up. When in doubt, it is better not to specify any information than making it up.

- For connecting to the Internet: username and password for your ISP, telephone number when using a modem. Your ISP usually automatically assigns you an IP address and all the other things necessary for your Internet applications to work.

10.2.2   Network configuration files

The graphical helper tools edit a specific set of network configuration files, using a couple of basic commands. The exact names of the configuration files and their location in the file system is largely dependent on your Linux distribution and version. However, a couple of network configuration files are common on all UNIX systems:

10.2.2.1 /etc/hosts

The /etc/hosts file always contains the *localhost* IP address, 127.0.0.1, which is used for interprocess communication. Never remove this line! Sometimes contains addresses of additional hosts, which can be contacted without using an external naming service such as DNS (the Domain Name Server).

A sample hosts file for a small home network:

```
# Do not remove the following line, or various programs
# that require network functionality will fail.
127.0.0.1       localhost.localdomain   localhost
192.168.52.10   tux.mylan.com       tux
192.168.52.11   winxp.mylan.com     winxp
```

Read more in **man hosts**.

10.2.2.2 /etc/resolv.conf

The /etc/resolv.conf file configures access to a DNS server, see Section 10.3.7. This file contains your domain name and the name server(s) to contact:

```
search mylan.com
nameserver 193.134.20.4
```

Read more in the resolv.conf man page.

10.2.2.3 /etc/nsswitch.conf

The /etc/nsswitch.conf file defines the order in which to contact different name services. For Internet use, it is important that *dns* shows up in the "hosts" line:

```
[bob@tux ~] grep hosts /etc/nsswitch.conf
hosts:   files dns
```

This instructs your computer to look up hostnames and IP addresses first in the /etc/hosts file, and to contact the DNS server if a given host does not occur in the local hosts file. Other possible name services to contact are LDAP, NIS and NIS+.

More in **man nsswitch.conf**.

10.2.3   Network configuration commands

10.2.3.1 The ip command

The distribution-specific scripts and graphical tools are front-ends to **ip** (or **ifconfig** and **route** on older systems) to display and configure the kernel's networking configuration.

The **ip** command is used for assigning IP addresses to interfaces, for setting up routes to the Internet and to other networks, for displaying TCP/IP configurations etcetera.

The following commands show IP address and routing information:

```
benny@home benny> ip addr show
1: lo: <LOOPBACK,UP> mtu 16436 qdisc noqueue
    link/loopback 00:00:00:00:00:00 brd 00:00:00:00:00:00
    inet 127.0.0.1/8 brd 127.255.255.255 scope host lo
    inet6 ::1/128 scope host
2: eth0: <BROADCAST,MULTICAST,UP> mtu 1500 qdisc pfifo_fast qlen 100
    link/ether 00:50:bf:7e:54:9a brd ff:ff:ff:ff:ff:ff
    inet 192.168.42.15/24 brd 192.168.42.255 scope global eth0
    inet6 fe80::250:bfff:fe7e:549a/10 scope link

benny@home benny> ip route show
192.168.42.0/24 dev eth0   scope link
127.0.0.0/8 dev lo   scope link
default via 192.168.42.1 dev eth0
```

Things to note:

- two network interfaces, even on a system that has only one network interface card: "lo" is the local loop, used for internal network communication; "eth0" is a common name for a *real* interface. Do not ever change the local loop configuration, or your machine will start mallfunctioning! Wireless interfaces are usually defined as "wlan0"; modem interfaces as "ppp0", but there might be other names as well.

- IP addresses, marked with "inet": the local loop always has 127.0.0.1, the physical interface can have any other combination.

- The hardware address of your interface, which might be required as part of the authentication procedure to connect to a network, is marked with "ether". The local loop has 6 pairs of all zeros, the physical loop has 6 pairs of hexadecimal characters, of which the first 3 pairs are vendor-specific.

10.2.3.2 The ifconfig command

While **ip** is the most novel way to configure a Linux system, **ifconfig** is still very popular. Use it without option for displaying network interface information:

```
els@asus:~$ /sbin/ifconfig
eth0      Link encap:Ethernet  HWaddr 00:50:70:31:2C:14
          inet addr:60.138.67.31  Bcast:66.255.255.255  Mask:255.255.255.192
          inet6 addr: fe80::250:70ff:fe31:2c14/64 Scope:Link
          UP BROADCAST RUNNING MULTICAST  MTU:1500  Metric:1
          RX packets:31977764 errors:0 dropped:0 overruns:0 frame:0
          TX packets:51896866 errors:0 dropped:0 overruns:0 carrier:0
          collisions:802207 txqueuelen:1000
          RX bytes:2806974916 (2.6 GiB)  TX bytes:2874632613 (2.6 GiB)
          Interrupt:11 Base address:0xec00
lo        Link encap:Local Loopback
          inet addr:127.0.0.1  Mask:255.0.0.0
          inet6 addr: ::1/128 Scope:Host
          UP LOOPBACK RUNNING  MTU:16436  Metric:1
          RX packets:765762 errors:0 dropped:0 overruns:0 frame:0
          TX packets:765762 errors:0 dropped:0 overruns:0 carrier:0
          collisions:0 txqueuelen:0
          RX bytes:624214573 (595.2 MiB)  TX bytes:624214573 (595.2 MiB)
```

Here, too, we note the most important aspects of the interface configuration:

- The IP address is marked with "inet addr".

- The hardware address follows the "HWaddr" tag.

Both **ifconfig** and **ip** display more detailed configuration information and a number of statistics about each interface and, maybe most important, whether it is "UP" and "RUNNING".

10.2.3.3 PCMCIA commands

On your laptop which you usually connect to the company network using the onboard Ethernet connection, but which you are now to configure for dial-in at home or in a hotel, you might need to activate the PCMCIA card. This is done using the **cardctl** control utility, or the **pccardctl** on newer distributions.

A usage example:

cardctl *insert*

Now the card can be configured, either using the graphical or the command line interface. Prior to taking the card out, use this command:

cardctl *eject*

However, a good distribution should provide PCMCIA support in the network configuration tools, preventing users from having to execute PCMCIA commands manually.

10.2.3.4 More information

Further discussion of network configuration is out of the scope of this document. Your primary source for extra information is the man pages for the services you want to set up. Additional reading:

- The Modem-HOWTO <http://www.tldp.org/HOWTO/Modem-HOWTO. html>: Help with selecting, connecting, configuring, trouble-shooting, and understanding analog modems for a PC.

- LDP HOWTO Index, section 4.4 <http://www.tldp.org/HOWTO/HOWTO-INDEX/networking.html#NETGENERAL>: categorized list of HOWTOs about general networking, protocols, dial-up, DNS, VPNs, bridging, routinfg, security and more.

- Most systems have a version of the ip-cref file (locate it using the **locate** command); the PS format of this file is viewable with for instance **gv**.

10.2.4 Network interface names

On a Linux machine, the device name *lo* or the *local loop* is linked with the internal 127.0.0.1 address. The computer will have a hard time making your applications work if this device is not present; it is always there, even on computers which are not networked.

The first ethernet device, *eth0* in the case of a standard network interface card, points to your local LAN IP address. Normal client machines only have one network interface card. Routers, connecting networks together, have one network device for each network they serve.

If you use a modem to connect to the Internet, your network device will probably be named *ppp0*.

There are many more names, for instance for Virtual Private Network interfaces (VPNs), and multiple interfaces can be active simultaneously, so that the output of the **ifconfig** or **ip** commands might become quite extensive when no options are used. Even multiple interfaces of the same type can be active. In that case, they are numbered sequentially: the first will get the number 0, the second will get a suffix of 1, the third will get 2, and so on. This is the case on many application servers, on machines which have a failover configuration, on routers, firewalls and many more.

10.2.5   Checking the host configuration with netstat

Apart from the **ip** command for displaying the network configuration, there's the common **netstat** command which has a lot of options and is generally useful on any UNIX system.

Routing information can be displayed with the -nr option to the **netstat** command:

```
bob:~> netstat -nr
Kernel IP routing table
Destination  Gateway       Genmask        Flags MSS Window irtt Iface
192.168.42.0 0.0.0.0       255.255.255.0 U      40  0         0 eth0
127.0.0.0    0.0.0.0       255.0.0.0     U      40  0         0 lo
0.0.0.0      192.168.42.1  0.0.0.0       UG     40  0         0 eth0
```

This is a typical client machine in an IP network. It only has one network device, *eth0*. The *lo* interface is the local loop.

The modern way

The novel way to get this info from your system is by using the **ip** command:

ip *route show*

When this machine tries to contact a host that is on another network than its own, indicated by the line starting with 0.0.0.0, it will send the connection requests to the machine (router) with IP address 192.168.42.1, and it will use its primary interface, eth0, to do this.

Hosts that are on the same network, the line starting with 192.168.42.0, will also be contacted through the primary network interface, but no router is necessary, the data are just put on the network.

Machines can have much more complicated routing tables than this one, with lots of different "Destination-Gateway" pairs to connect to different networks. If you have the occasion to connect to an application server, for instance at work, it is most educating to check the routing information.

10.2.6   Other hosts

An impressive amount of tools is focused on network management and remote administration of Linux machines. Your local Linux software mirror will offer plenty of those. It would lead us too far to discuss them in this document, so please refer to the program-specific documentation.

We will only discuss some common UNIX/Linux text tools in this section.

10.2.6.1 The host command

To display information on hosts or domains, use the **host** command:

```
[emmy@pc10 emmy]$ host www.eunet.be
www.eunet.be. has address 193.74.208.177

[emmy@pc10 emmy]$ host -t any eunet.be
eunet.be. SOA dns.eunet.be. hostmaster.Belgium.EU.net.
  2002021300 28800 7200 604800 86400
eunet.be. mail is handled by 50 pophost.eunet.be.
eunet.be. name server ns.EU.net.
eunet.be. name server dns.eunet.be.
```

Similar information can be displayed using the **dig** command, which gives additional information about how records are stored in the name server.

10.2.6.2 The ping command

To check if a host is alive, use **ping**. If your system is configured to send more than one packet, interrupt **ping** with the **Ctrl+C** key combination:

```
[emmy@pc10 emmy]$ ping a.host.be
PING a.host.be (1.2.8.3) from 80.20.84.26: 56(84) bytes of data.
64 bytes from a.host.be(1.2.8.3):icmp_seq=0 ttl=244 time=99.977msec
--- a.host.be ping statistics ---
1 packets transmitted, 1 packets received, 0% packet loss
round-trip min/avg/max/mdev = 99.977/99.977/99.977/0.000 ms
```

10.2.6.3 The traceroute command

To check the route that packets follow to a network host, use the **traceroute** command:

```
[emmy@pc10 emmy]$ /usr/sbin/traceroute www.eunet.be
traceroute to www.eunet.be(193.74.208.177),30 hops max,38b packets
```

```
1 blob (10.0.0.1)
       0.297ms  0.257ms  0.174ms
2 adsl-65.myprovider.be (217.136.111.1)
       12.120ms 13.058ms 13.009ms
3 194.78.255.177 (194.78.255.177)
       13.845ms 14.308ms 12.756ms
4 gigabitethernet2-2.intl2.gam.brussels.skynet.be (195.238.2.226)
       13.123ms 13.164ms 12.527ms
5 pecbru2.car.belbone.be (194.78.255.118)
       16.336ms 13.889ms 13.028ms
6 ser-2-1-110-ias-be-vil-ar01.kpnbelgium.be (194.119.224.9)
       14.602ms 15.546ms 15.959ms
7 unknown-195-207-939.eunet.be (195.207.93.49)
       16.514ms 17.661ms 18.889ms
8 S0-1-0.Leuven.Belgium.EU.net (195.207.129.1)
       22.714ms 19.193ms 18.432ms
9 dukat.Belgium.EU.net (193.74.208.178) 22.758ms * 25.263ms
```

On some systems, **traceroute** has been renamed to **tracepath**.

10.2.6.4 The whois command

Specific domain name information can be queried using the **whois** command, as is explained by many **whois** servers, like the one below:

```
[emmy@pc10 emmy]$ whois cnn.com
[whois.crsnic.net]

Whois Server Version 1.3

    $<--snap server message-->

  Domain Name: CNN.COM
  Registrar: NETWORK SOLUTIONS, INC.
  Whois Server: whois.networksolutions.com
  Referral URL: http://www.networksolutions.com
  Name Server: TWDNS-01.NS.AOL.COM
  Name Server: TWDNS-02.NS.AOL.COM
  Name Server: TWDNS-03.NS.AOL.COM
  Name Server: TWDNS-04.NS.AOL.COM
  Updated Date: 12-mar-2002
>>> Last update of whois database: Fri, 5 Apr 2002 05:04:55 EST <<<

The Registry database contains ONLY .COM, .NET, .ORG, .EDU domains
and Registrars.

[whois.networksolutions.com]

        $<--snap server message-->

Registrant:
Turner Broadcasting (CNN-DOM)
   1 CNN Center
   Atlanta, GA 30303
```

```
Domain Name: CNN.COM

Administrative Contact:
     $<--snap contactinfo-->
Technical Contact:
     $<--snap contactinfo-->
Billing Contact:
  $<--snap contactinfo-->
Record last updated on 12-Mar-2002.
Record expires on 23-Sep-2009.
Record created on 22-Sep-1993.
Database last updated on 4-Apr-2002 20:10:00 EST.

Domain servers in listed order:

TWDNS-01.NS.AOL.COM        149.174.213.151
TWDNS-02.NS.AOL.COM        152.163.239.216
TWDNS-03.NS.AOL.COM        205.188.146.88
TWDNS-04.NS.AOL.COM        64.12.147.120
```

For other domain names than .com, .net, .org and .edu, you might need to specify the whois server, such as this one for .be domains:

whois *domain.be@whois.dns.be*

10.3 Internet/Intranet applications

The Linux system is a great platform for offering networking services. In this section, we will try to give an overview of most common network servers and applications.

10.3.1 Server types

10.3.1.1 Standalone server

Offering a service to users can be approached in two ways. A daemon or service can run in standalone mode, or it can be dependent on another service to be activated.

Network services that are heavily and/or continuously used, usually run in the standalone mode: they are independent program daemons that are always running. They are most likely started up at system boot time, and they wait for requests on the specific connection points or ports for which they are set up to listen. When a request comes, it is processed, and the listening continues until the next request. A web server is a typical example: you want it to be available 24 hours a day, and if it is too busy it should create more listening instances to serve simultaneous users. Other examples are the large software archives such as Sourceforge <http://sourceforge.net/> or your Tucows mirror <http://tucows.com/>, which must handle thousands of FTP requests per day.

An example of a standalone network service on your home computer might be the **named** (name daemon), a caching name server. Standalone services have their own processes running, you can check any time using **ps**:

```
bob:~> ps auxw | grep named
named    908  0.0  1.0 14876 5108 ?    S  Mar14  0:07 named -u named
```

However, there are some services that you can use on your PC, even if there is no server process running for that services. Examples could be the FTP service, the secure copy service or the finger service. Those services have the Internet Daemon (**inetd**) listening in their place.

10.3.1.2 (x)inetd

On your home PC, things are usually a bit calmer. You may have a small network, for instance, and you may have to transfer files from one PC to another from time to time, using FTP or Samba (for connectivity with MS Windows machines). In those cases, starting all the services which you only need occasionally and having them run all the time would be a waste of resources. So in smaller setups, you will find the necessary daemons dependent on a central program, that listen on all the ports of the services for which it is responsible.

This super-server, the Internet services daemon, is started up at system initialization time. There are two common implementations: **inetd** and **xinetd** (the extended Internet services daemon). One or the other is usually running on every Linux system:

```
bob:~> ps -ef | grep inet
root   926    1 0 Mar14 ?   00:00:00 xinetd-ipv6 -stayalive -reuse \
-pidfile /var/run/xinetd.pid
```

The services for which the Internet daemon is responsible, are listed in its configuration file, /etc/inetd.conf, for **inetd**, and in the directory /etc/xinetd.d for **xinetd**. Commonly managed services include file share and print services, SSH, FTP, telnet, the Samba configuration daemon, talk and time services.

As soon as a connection request is received, the central server will start an instance of the required server. Thus, in the example below, when user *bob* starts an FTP session to the local host, an FTP daemon is running as long as the session is active:

```
bob:~> ps auxw | grep ftp
bob     793  0.1  0.2  3960 1076 pts/6   S   16:44   0:00 ncftp localhost
ftp     794  0.7  0.5  5588 2608 ?       SN  16:44   0:00 ftpd:
localhost.localdomain: anonymous/bob@his.server.com: IDLE
```

Of course, the same happens when you open connections to remote hosts: either a daemon answers directly, or a remote **(x)inetd** starts the service you need and stops it when you quit.

10.3.2 Mail

10.3.2.1 Servers

Sendmail is the standard mail server program or Mail Transport Agent for UNIX platforms. It is robust, scalable, and when properly configured with appropriate hardware, handles thousands of users without blinking. More information about how to configure Sendmail is included with the sendmail and sendmail-cf packages, you may want to read the README and README.cf files in /usr/share/doc/ sendmail. The **man *sendmail*** and **man *aliases*** are also useful.

Qmail is another mail server, gaining popularity because it claims to be more secure than Sendmail. While Sendmail is a monolithic program, Qmail consists of smaller interacting program parts that can be better secured. Postfix is another mail server which is gaining popularity.

These servers handle mailing lists, filtering, virus scanning and much more. Free and commercial scanners are available for use with Linux. Examples of mailing list software are Mailman, Listserv, Majordomo and EZmlm. See the web page of your favorite virus scanner for information on Linux client and server support. Amavis and Spamassassin are free implementations of a virus scanner and a spam scanner.

10.3.2.2 Remote mail servers

The most popular protocols to access mail remotely are *POP3* and *IMAP4*. IMAP and POP both allow offline operation, remote access to new mail and they both rely on an SMTP server to send mail.

While POP is a simple protocol, easy to implement and supported by almost any mail client, IMAP is to be preferred because:

- It can manipulate persistent message status flags.
- It can store as well as fetch mail messages.
- It can access and manage multiple mailboxes.
- It supports concurrent updates and shared mailboxes.
- It is also suitable for accessing Usenet messages and other documents.
- IMAP works both on-line and off-line.
- it is optimized for on-line performance, especially over low-speed links.

10.3.2.3 Mail user-agents

There are plenty of both text and graphical E-mail clients, we'll just name a few of the common ones. Pick your favorite.

The UNIX **mail** command has been around for years, even before networking existed. It is a simple interface to send messages and small files to other users, who can then save the message, redirect it, reply to it and such.

While it is not commonly used as a client anymore, the **mail** program is still useful, for example to mail the output of a command to somebody:

mail <future.employer@whereIwant2work.com> < cv.txt

The **elm** mail reader is a much needed improvement to **mail**, and so is **pine** (Pine Is Not ELM). The **mutt** mail reader is even more recent and offers features like threading.

For those users who prefer a graphical interface to their mail (and a tennis elbow or a mouse arm), there are hundreds of options. The most popular for new users are Mozilla Mail/Thunderbird, which has easy anti-spam configuring options, and Evolution, the MS Outlook clone. Kmail is popular among KDE users.

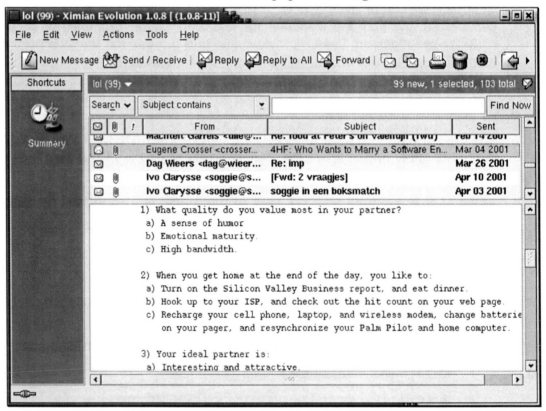

Figure 10.1. Evolution mail and news reader

There are also tens of web mail applications available, such as Squirrelmail, Yahoo! mail, gmail from Google and Hotmail.

An overview is available via the Linux Mail User HOWTO < http://www.tldp.org/HOWTO/Mail-User-HOWTO/index.html>.

Most Linux distributions include **fetchmail**, a mail-retrieval and forwarding utility. It fetches mail from remote mail servers (POP, IMAP and some others) and forwards it to your local delivery system. You can then handle the retrieved mail using normal mail clients. It can be run in daemon mode to repeatedly poll one or more systems at a specified interval. Information and usage examples can be found in the Info pages; the directory `/usr/share/doc/fetchmail[-<version>]` contains a full list of features and a FAQ for beginners.

The **procmail** filter can be used for filtering incoming mail, to create mailing lists, to pre-process mail, to selectively forward mail and more. The accompanying **formail** program, among others, enables generation of auto-replies and splitting up mailboxes. Procmail has been around for years on UNIX and Linux machines and is a very robust system, designed to work even in the worst circumstances. More information may be found in the `/usr/share/doc/procmail[-<version>]` directory and in the man pages.

10.3.3   Web

10.3.3.1 The Apache Web Server

Apache is by far the most popular web server, used on more than half of all Internet web servers. Most Linux distributions include Apache. Apache's advantages include its modular design, SSL support, stability and speed. Given the appropriate hardware and configuration it can support the highest loads.

On Linux systems, the server configuration is usually done in the `/etc/httpd` directory. The most important configuration file is `httpd.conf`; it is rather self-explanatory. Should you need help, you can find it in the **httpd** man page or on the Apache website <http://www.apache.org/>.

10.3.3.2 Web browsers

A number of web browsers, both free and commercial, exist for the Linux platform. Netscape Navigator as the only decent option has long been a thing of the past, as Mozilla/Firefox offers a competitive alternative running on many other operating systems, like MS Windows and MacOS X as well.

Amaya is the W3C browser. Opera is a commercial browser, compact and fast. Many desktop managers offer web browsing features in their file manager, like **nautilus**.

Among the popular text based browsers are **lynx** and **links**. You may need to define proxy servers in your shell, by setting the appropriate variables. Text browsers are fast and handy when no graphical environment is available, such as when used in scripts.

10.3.3.3 Proxy servers

10.3.3.3.1 What is a proxy server?

Companies and organizations often want their users to use a proxy server. Especially in environments with lots of users, a proxy server can enable faster downloads of web pages. The proxy server stores web pages. When a user asks for a web page that has already been requested previously, the proxy server will give that page to the user directly, so that s/he does not need to get it from the Internet, which would take longer. Of course, measures can be taken so that the proxy server does a quick check and always serves the most recent version of a page. In some environments, usage of the proxy server is compulsory, in other environments you may have the choice whether or not to use it.

10.3.3.3.2 Proxy configuration

If you have the proxy server name and port, it should be rather obvious to feed that information into your browser. However, many (command line) applications depend on the variables `http_proxy` and `ftp_proxy` for correct functioning. For your convenience, you might want to add a line like the following to your `~/.bashrc`:

export http_proxy=*http://username:password@proxy_server_name:port_number*

For instance:

export http_proxy=*http://willy:Appelsi3ntj3@proxy:80*

If you do not need to give a username and password, simply leave out everything before the "@" sign, this sign included.

10.3.4   File Transfer Protocol

10.3.4.1 FTP servers

On a Linux system, an FTP server is typically run from **xinetd**, using the WU-ftpd server, although the FTP server may be configured as a stand-alone server on systems with heavy FTP traffic. See the exercises.

Other FTP servers include among others vsftpd, Ncftpd and Proftpd.

Most Linux distributions contain the anonftp package, which sets up an anonymous FTP server tree and accompanying configuration files.

10.3.4.2 FTP clients

Most Linux distributions include **ncftp**, an improved version of the common UNIX **ftp** command, which you may also know from the Windows command line. The **ncftp** program offers extra features such as a nicer and more comprehensible user interface, file name completion, append and resume functions, bookmarking, session management and more:

```
thomas:~> ncftp blob
NcFTP 3.0.3 (April 15, 2001) by Mike Gleason (ncftp@ncftp.com).
Connecting to blob...
blob.some.net FTP server (Version wu-2.6.1-20) ready.
Logging in...
Guest login ok, access restrictions apply.
Logged in to blob.
ncftp / > help
Commands may be abbreviated.  'help showall' shows hidden and
unsupported commands.
'help <command>' gives a brief description of <command>.

ascii      cat       help      lpage     open      quote     site
bgget      cd        jobs      lpwd      page      rename    type
bgput      chmod     lcd       lrename   pdir      rhelp     umask
bgstart    close     lchmod    lrm       pls       rm        version
binary     debug     lls       lrmdir    put       rmdir
bookmark   dir       lmkdir    ls        pwd       set
bookmarks  get       lookup    mkdir     quit      show
ncftp / >
```

Excellent help with lot of examples can be found in the man pages. And again, a number of GUI applications are available.

FTP is insecure!

Don't use the File Transfer Protocol for non-anonymous login unless you know what you are doing. Your user name and password might be captured by malevolent fellow network users! Use secure FTP instead; the **sftp** program comes with the Secure SHell suite, see Section 10.4.4.4.

10.3.5   Chatting and conferencing

Various clients and systems are available in each distribution, replacing the old-style IRC text-based chat. A short and incomplete list of the most popular programs:

- **gaim**: multi-protocol instant messaging client for Linux, Windows and Mac, compatible with MSN Messenger, ICQ, IRC and much more; see the Info pages or the Gaim site <http://gaim.sourceforge.net/> for more.

- **xchat**: IRC client for the X window system:

The home page is at SourceForge <http://sourceforge.net/projects/xchat/>.

- aMSN: an MSN clone.

- **Konversation, kopete, KVIrc** and many other K-tools from the KDE suite.

- **gnomemeeting**: videoconferencing program for UNIX (now Ekiga).

- **jabber**: Open Source Instant Messenging platform, compatible with ICQ, AIM, Yahoo, MSN, IRC, SMTP and much more.

- **psi**: jabber client, see the PSI Jabber Client Homepage <http://psi.affinix. com/>.

- **skype**: program for making telephone-like calls over the Internet to other Skype users, see <http://www.skype.com> for more info. Skype is free but not open.

- Gizmo: a free (but not open) phone for your computer, see <http://www. gizmoproject.com>.

10.3.6   News services

Running a Usenet server involves a lot of expertise and fine-tuning, so refer to the INN homepage <http://www.isc.org/> for more information.

There are a couple of interesting newsgroups in the *comp.** hierarchy, which can be accessed using a variety of text and graphical clients. A lot of mail clients support newsgroup browsing as well, check your program or see your local Open Source software mirror for text clients such as **tin, slrnn** and **mutt**, or download Mozilla or one of a number of other graphical clients.

Deja.com <http://deja.com/> keeps a searchable archive of all newsgroups, powered by Google. This is a very powerful instrument for getting help: chances are very high that somebody has encountered your problem, found a solution and posted it in one of the newsgroups.

10.3.7   The Domain Name System

All these applications need DNS services to match IP addresses to host names and vice versa. A DNS server does not know all the IP addresses in the world, but networks with other DNS servers which it can query to find an unknown address. Most UNIX systems can run **named**, which is part of the BIND (Berkeley Internet Name Domain) package distributed by the Internet Software Consortium. It can run as a stand-alone caching *nameserver*, which is often done on Linux systems in order to speed up network access.

Your main client configuration file is `/etc/resolv.conf`, which determines the order in which Domain Name Servers are contacted:

```
search somewhere.org
nameserver 192.168.42.1
nameserver 193.74.208.137
```

More information can be found in the Info pages on **named**, in the `/usr/share/doc/bind[-<version>]` files and on the Bind project <http://www.isc.org/products/BIND> homepage. The DNS HOWTO <http://www.tldp.org/HOWTO/DNS-HOWTO.html> covers the use of BIND as a DNS server.

10.3.8   DHCP

DHCP is the Dynamic Host Configuration Protocol, which is gradually replacing good old **bootp** in larger environments. It is used to control vital networking parameters such as IP addresses and name servers of hosts. DHCP is backward compatible with **bootp**. For configuring the server, you will need to read the HOWTO.

DHCP client machines will usually be configured using a GUI that configures the **dhcpcd**, the DHCP client daemon. Check your system documentation if you need to configure your machine as a DHCP client.

10.3.9   Authentication services

10.3.9.1 Traditional

Traditionally, users are authenticated locally, using the information stored in `/etc/passwd` and `/etc/shadow` on each system. But even when using a network service for authenticating, the local files will always be present to configure system accounts for administrative use, such as the root account, the daemon accounts and often accounts for additional programs and purposes.

These files are often the first candidates for being examined by hackers, so make sure the permissions and ownerships are strictly set as should be:

```
bob:~> ls -l /etc/passwd /etc/shadow
-rw-r--r--    1 root     root          1803 Mar 10 13:08 /etc/passwd
-r--------    1 root     root          1116 Mar 10 13:08 /etc/shadow
```

10.3.9.2 PAM

Linux can use PAM, the Pluggable Authentication Module, a flexible method of UNIX authentication. Advantages of PAM:

- A common authentication scheme that can be used with a wide variety of applications.

- PAM can be implemented with various applications without having to recompile the applications to specifically support PAM.

- Great flexibility and control over authentication for the administrator and application developer.

- Application developers do not need to develop their program to use a particular authentication scheme. Instead, they can focus purely on the details of their program.

The directory `/etc/pam.d` contains the PAM configuration files (used to be `/etc/pam.conf`). Each application or service has its own file. Each line in the file has four elements:

- *Module*:

    - `auth`: provides the actual authentication (perhaps asking for and checking a password) and sets credentials, such as group membership or Kerberos tickets.

    - `account`: checks to make sure that access is allowed for the user (the account has not expired, the user is allowed to log in at this time of day, and so on).

    - `password`: used to set passwords.

    - `session`: used after a user has been authenticated. This module performs additional tasks which are needed to allow access (for example, mounting the user's home directory or making their mailbox available).

The order in which modules are stacked, so that multiple modules can be used, is very important.

- *Control Flags*: tell PAM which actions to take upon failure or success. Values can be `required`, `requisite`, `sufficient` or `optional`.

- *Module Path*: path to the pluggable module to be used, usually in `/lib/security`.

- *Arguments*: information for the modules

Shadow password files are automatically detected by PAM.

More information can be found in the **pam** man pages or at the Linux-PAM project homepage.

10.3.9.3 LDAP

The Lightweight Directory Access Protocol is a client-server system for accessing global or local directory services over a network. On Linux, the OpenLDAP implementation is used. It includes **slapd**, a stand-alone server; **slurpd**, a stand-alone LDAP replication server; libraries implementing the LDAP protocol and a series of utilities, tools and sample clients.

The main benefit of using LDAP is the consolidation of certain types of information within your organization. For example, all of the different lists of users within your organization can be merged into one LDAP directory. This directory can be queried by any LDAP-enabled applications that need this information. It can also be accessed by users who need directory information.

Other LDAP or X.500 Lite benefits include its ease of implementation (compared to X.500) and its well-defined Application Programming Interface (API), which means that the number of LDAP-enabled applications and LDAP gateways should increase in the future.

On the negative side, if you want to use LDAP, you will need LDAP-enabled applications or the ability to use LDAP gateways. While LDAP usage should only increase, currently there are not very many LDAP-enabled applications available for Linux. Also, while LDAP does support some access control, it does not possess as many security features as X.500.

Since LDAP is an open and configurable protocol, it can be used to store almost any type of information relating to a particular organizational structure. Common examples are mail address lookups, central authentication in combination with PAM, telephone directories and machine configuration databases.

See your system specific information and the man pages for related commands such as **ldapmodify** and **ldapsearch** for details. More information can be found in the LDAP Linux HOWTO <http://www.tldp.org/HOWTO/LDAP-HOWTO.html>, which discusses installation, configuration, running and maintenance of an LDAP server on Linux. The author of this Introduction to Linux document also wrote an LDAP Operations HOWTO <http://tille.xalasys.com/training/ldap/>, describing the basics everyone should know about when dealing with LDAP management, operations and integration of services.

10.4 Remote execution of applications

10.4.1   Introduction

There are a couple of different ways to execute commands or run programs on a remote machine and have the output, be it text or graphics, sent to your workstation. The connections can be secure or insecure. While it is of course advised to use secure connections instead of transporting your password over the network unencrypted, we will discuss some practical applications of the older (unsafe) mechanisms, as they are still useful in a modern networked environment, such as for troubleshooting or running exotic programs.

10.4.2   Rsh, rlogin and telnet

The **rlogin** and **rsh** commands for remote login and remote execution of commands are inherited from UNIX. While seldom used because they are blatantly insecure, they still come with almost every Linux distribution for backward compatibility with UNIX programs.

Telnet, on the other hand, is still commonly used, often by system and network administrators. Telnet is one of the most powerful tools for remote access to files and remote administration, allowing connections from anywhere on the Internet. Combined with an X server, remote graphical applications can be displayed locally. There is no difference between working on the local machine and using the remote machine.

Because the entire connection is unencrypted, allowing **telnet** connections involves taking high security risks. For normal remote execution of programs, Secure SHell or **ssh** is advised. We will discuss the secure method later in this section.

However, **telnet** is still used in many cases. Below are some examples in which a mail server and a web server are tested for replies:

Checking that a mail server works:

```
[jimmy@blob ~] telnet mailserver 25
Trying 192.168.42.1...
Connected to mailserver.
Escape character is '^]'.
220 m1.some.net ESMTP Sendmail 8.11.6/8.11.6; 200302281626
ehlo some.net
250-m1.some.net Hello blob.some.net [10.0.0.1], pleased to meet you
250-ENHANCEDSTATUSCODES
250-8BITMIME
250-SIZE
250-DSN
250-ONEX
250-ETRN
```

```
250-XUSR
250 HELP
mail from: jimmy@some.net
250 2.1.0 jimmy@some.net... Sender ok
rcpt to: davy@some.net
250 2.1.5 davy@some.net... Recipient ok
data
354 Enter mail, end with "." on a line by itself
test
.
250 2.0.0 g2MA1R619237 Message accepted for delivery
quit
221 2.0.0 m1.some.net closing connection
Connection closed by foreign host.
```

Checking that a web server answers to basic requests:

```
[jimmy@blob ~] telnet www.some.net 80
Trying 64.39.151.23...
Connected to www.some.net.
Escape character is '^]'.
HEAD / ;HTTP/1.1

HTTP/1.1 200 OK
Date: Fri, 22 Mar 2002 10:05:14 GMT
Server: Apache/1.3.22 (UNIX) (Red-Hat/Linux)
 mod_ssl/2.8.5 OpenSSL/0.9.6
 DAV/1.0.2 PHP/4.0.6 mod_perl/1.24_01
Last-Modified: Fri, 04 Jan 2002 08:21:00 GMT
ETag: "70061-68-3c3565ec"
Accept-Ranges: bytes
Content-Length: 104
Connection: close
Content-Type: text/html

Connection closed by foreign host.

[jimmy@blob ~]
```

This is perfectly safe, because you never have to give a username and/or password for getting the data you want, so nobody can snoop that important information off the cable.

10.4.3   The X Window System

10.4.3.1 X features

As we already explained in Chapter 7 (see Section 7.3.3), the X Window system comes with an X server which serves graphics to clients that need a display.

It is important to realize the distinction between the X server and the X client application(s). The X server controls the display directly and is responsible for all input and output via keyboard, mouse and display. The X client, on the other hand, does not access the input and output devices directly. It communicates with the X server which handles input and output. It is the X client which does the real work, like computing values, running applications and so forth. The X server only opens windows to handle input and output for the specified client.

In normal operation (graphical mode), every Linux workstation is an X server to itself, even if it only runs client applications. All the applications you are running (for example, Gimp, a terminal window, your browser, your office application, your CD playing tool, and so on) are clients to your X server. Server and client are running on the same machine in this case.

This client/server nature of the X system makes it an ideal environment for remote execution of applications and programs. Because the process is actually being executed on the remote machine, very little CPU power is needed on the local host. Such machines, purely acting as servers for X, are called X terminals and were once very popular. More information may be found in the Remote X applications mini-HOWTO <http://www.tldp.org/HOWTO/Remote-X-Apps.html >.

10.4.3.2 Telnet and X

If you would want to use **telnet** to display graphical applications running on a remote machine, you first need to give the remote machine access to your display (to your X server!) using the **xhost** command, by typing a command similar to the one below in a terminal window on your local machine:

```
davy:~> xhost +remote.machine.com
```

After that, connect to the remote host and tell it to display graphics on the local machine by setting the environment variable DISPLAY:

```
[davy@remote ~] export DISPLAY="local.host.com:0.0"
```

After completing this step, any application started in this terminal window will be displayed on your local desktop, using remote resources for computing, but your local graphical resources (your X server) for displaying the application.

This procedure assumes that you have some sort of X server (XFree86, X.org, Exceed, Cygwin) already set up on the machine where you want to display images. The architecture and operating system of the client machine are not important as long as they allow you to run an X server on it.

Mind that displaying a terminal window from the remote machine is also considered to be a display of an image.

10.4.4 The SSH suite

10.4.4.1 Introduction

Most UNIX and Linux systems now run Secure SHell in order to leave out the security risks that came with **telnet**. Most Linux systems will run a version of OpenSSH, an Open Source implementation of the SSH protocol, providing secure encrypted communications between untrusted hosts over an untrusted network. In the standard setup X connections are automatically forwarded, but arbitrary TCP/IP ports may also be forwarded using a secure channel.

The **ssh** client connects and logs into the specified host name. The user must provide his identity to the remote machine as specified in the sshd_config file, which can usually be found in /etc/ssh. The configuration file is rather self-explanatory and by defaults enables most common features. Should you need help, you can find it in the **sshd** man pages.

When the user's identity has been accepted by the server, the server either executes the given command, or logs into the machine and gives the user a normal shell on the remote machine. All communication with the remote command or shell will be automatically encrypted.

The session terminates when the command or shell on the remote machine exits and all X11 and TCP/IP connections have been closed.

When connecting to a host for the first time, using any of the programs that are included in the SSH collection, you need to establish the authenticity of that host and acknowledge that you want to connect:

```
lenny ~> ssh blob
The authenticity of host 'blob (10.0.0.1)' can't be established.
RSA fingerprint is 18:30:50:46:ac:98:3c:93:1a:56:35:09:8d:97:e3:1d.
Are you sure you want to continue connecting (yes/no)? yes
Warning: Permanently added 'blob,192.168.30.2' (RSA) to the list of
known hosts.
Last login: Sat Dec 28 13:29:19 2002 from octarine
This space for rent.

lenny is in ~
```

It is important that you type "yes", in three characters, not just "y". This edits your ~/.ssh/known_hosts file, see Section 10.4.4.3.

If you just want to check something on a remote machine and then get your prompt back on the local host, you can give the commands that you want to execute remotely as arguments to **ssh**:

```
lenny ~> ssh blob who
jenny@blob's password:
```

```
root      tty2          Jul 24 07:19
lena      tty3          Jul 23 22:24
lena      0:        Jul 25 22:03

lenny ~> uname -n
magrat.example.com
```

10.4.4.2 X11 and TCP forwarding

If the X11Forwarding entry is set to *yes* on the target machine and the user is using X applications, the DISPLAY environment variable is set, the connection to the X11 display is automatically forwarded to the remote side in such a way that any X11 programs started from the shell will go through the encrypted channel, and the connection to the real X server will be made from the local machine. The user should not manually set DISPLAY. Forwarding of X11 connections can be configured on the command line or in the **sshd** configuration file.

The value for DISPLAY set by **ssh** will point to the server machine, but with a display number greater than zero. This is normal, and happens because **ssh** creates a *proxy* X server on the server machine (that runs the X client application) for forwarding the connections over the encrypted channel.

This is all done automatically, so when you type in the name of a graphical application, it is displayed on your local machine and not on the remote host. We use **xclock** in the example, since it is a small program which is generally installed and ideal for testing:

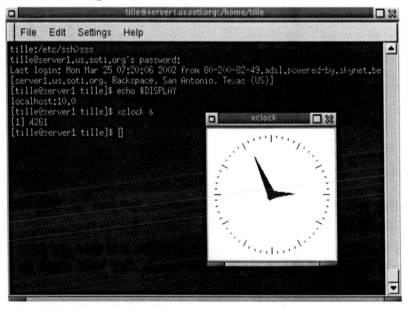

Figure 10.2. SSH X11 forwarding

SSH will also automatically set up Xauthority data on the server machine. For this purpose, it will generate a random authorization cookie, store it in Xauthority on the server, and verify that any forwarded connections carry this cookie and replace it by the real cookie when the connection is opened. The real authentication cookie is never sent to the server machine (and no cookies are sent in the plain).

Forwarding of arbitrary TCP/IP connections over the secure channel can be specified either on the command line or in a configuration file.

The X server

This procedure assumes that you have a running X server on the client where you want to display the application from the remote host. The client may be of different architecture and operating system than the remote host, as long as it can run an X server, such as Cygwin (which implements an X.org server for MS Windows clients and others) or Exceed, it should be possible to set up a remote connection with any Linux or UNIX machine.

10.4.4.3 Server authentication

The **ssh** client/server system automatically maintains and checks a database containing identifications for all hosts it has ever been used with. Host keys are stored in $HOME/.ssh/known_hosts in the user's home directory. Additionally, the file /etc/ssh/ssh_known_hosts is automatically checked for known hosts. Any new hosts are automatically added to the user's file. If a host's identification ever changes, **ssh** warns about this and disables password authentication to prevent a Trojan horse from getting the user's password. Another purpose of this mechanism is to prevent man-in-the-middle attacks which could otherwise be used to circumvent the encryption. In environments where high security is needed, **sshd** can even be configured to prevent logins to machines whose host keys have changed or are unknown.

10.4.4.4 Secure remote copying

The SSH suite provides **scp** as a secure alternative to the **rcp** command that used to be popular when only **rsh** existed. **scp** uses **ssh** for data transfer, uses the same authentication and provides the same security as **ssh**. Unlike **rcp**, **scp** will ask for passwords or passphrases if they are needed for authentication:

```
lenny /var/tmp> scp Schedule.sdc.gz blob:/var/tmp/
lenny@blob's password:
Schedule.sdc.gz  100% |****************************| 100 KB 00:00

lenny /var/tmp>
```

Any file name may contain a host and user specification to indicate that the file is to be copied to/from that host. Copies between two remote hosts are permitted. See the Info pages for more information.

If you would rather use an FTP-like interface, use **sftp**:

```
lenny /var/tmp> sftp blob
Connecting to blob...
lenny@blob's password:

sftp> cd /var/tmp

sftp> get Sch*
Fetching /var/tmp/Schedule.sdc.gz to Schedule.sdc.gz

sftp> bye

lenny /var/tmp>
```

Secure copy or FTP GUIs

Don't feel comfortable with the command line yet? Try Konqueror's capabilities for secure remote copy, or install Putty.

10.4.4.5 Authentication keys

The **ssh-keygen** command generates, manages and converts authentication keys for **ssh**. It can create RSA keys for use by SSH protocol version 1 and RSA or DSA keys for use by SSH protocol version 2.

Normally each user wishing to use SSH with RSA or DSA authentication runs this once to create the authentication key in $HOME/.ssh/identity, id_dsa or id_rsa. Additionally, the system administrator may use this to generate host keys for the system.

Normally this program generates the key and asks for a file in which to store the private key. The public key is stored in a file with the same name but *.pub* appended. The program also asks for a passphrase. The passphrase may be empty to indicate no passphrase (host keys must have an empty passphrase), or it may be a string of arbitrary length.

There is no way to recover a lost passphrase. If the passphrase is lost or forgotten, a new key must be generated and copied to the corresponding public keys.

We will study SSH keys in the exercises. All information can be found in the man or Info pages.

10.4.5 VNC

VNC or Virtual Network Computing is in fact a remote display system which allows viewing a desktop environment not only on the local machine on which it is running, but from anywhere on the Internet and from a wide variety of machines and architectures, including MS Windows and several UNIX distributions. You could, for example, run MS Word on a Windows NT machine and display the output on your Linux desktop. VNC provides servers as well as clients, so the opposite also works and it may thus be used to display Linux programs on Windows clients. VNC is probably the easiest way to have X connections on a PC. The following features make VNC different from a normal X server or commercial implementations:

- No state is stored at the viewer side: you can leave your desk and resume from another machine, continuing where you left. When you are running a PC X server, and the PC crashes or is restarted, all remote applications that you were running will die. With VNC, they keep on running.

- It is small and simple, no installation needed, can be run from a floppy if needed.

- Platform independent with the Java client, runs on virtually everything that supports X.

- Sharable: one desktop may be displayed on multiple viewers.

- Free.

More information can be found in the VNC client man pages (**man vncviewer**) or on the VNC website <http://www.realvnc.com/>.

10.4.6 The rdesktop protocol

In order to ease management of MS Windows hosts, recent Linux distributions support the Remote Desktop Protocol (RDP), which is implemented in the **rdesktop** client. The protocol is used in a number of Microsoft products, including Windows NT Terminal Server, Windows 2000 Server, Windows XP and Windows 2003 Server.

Surprise your friends (or management) with the fullscreen mode, multiple types of keyboard layouts and single application mode, just like the real thing. The **man rdesktop** manual provides more information. The project's homepage is at <http://www.rdesktop.org/>.

10.4.7 Cygwin

Cygwin <http://www.cygwin.com/> provides substantial UNIX functionality on MS Windows systems. Apart from providing UNIX command line tools and graphical applications, it can also be used to display a Linux desktop on an MS Windows machine, using remote X. From a Cygwin Bash shell, type the command

/usr/X11R6/bin/XWin.exe `-query your_linux_machine_name_or_IP`

The connection is by default denied. You need to change the X Display Manager (XDM) configuration and possibly the X Font Server (XFS) configuration to enable this type of connection, where you get a login screen on the remote machine. Depending on your desktop manager (Gnome, KDE, other), you might have to change some configurations there, too.

If you do not need to display the entire desktop, you can use SSH in Cygwin, just like explained in Section 10.4.4. without all the fuss of editing configuration files.

10.5 Security

10.5.1   Introduction

As soon as a computer is connected to the network, all kinds of abuse becomes possible, be it a UNIX-based or any other system. Admittedly, mountains of papers have been spilled on this subject and it would lead us too far to discuss the subject of security in detail. There are, however, a couple of fairly logical things even a novice user can do to obtain a very secure system, because most break-ins are the result of ignorant or careless users.

Maybe you are asking yourself if this all applies to you, using your computer at home or working at your office on a desktop in a fairly protected environment. The questions you should be asking yourself, however, are more on the lines of:

- Do you want to be in control of your own system?
- Do you want to (unwittingly) participate in criminal activities?
- Do you want your equipment to be used by someone else?
- Do you want to take risks on losing your Internet connection?
- Do you want to rebuild your system every time it has been hacked?
- Do you want to risk personal or other data loss?

Presuming you don't, we will quickly list the steps you can take to secure your machine. Extended information can be found in the Linux Security HOWTO <http://www.tldp.org/HOWTO/Security-HOWTO.html>.

10.5.2   Services

The goal is to run as few services as possible. If the number of ports that are open for the outside world are kept to a minimum, this is all the better to keep an overview. If services can't be turned off for the local network, try to at least disable them for outside connections.

A rule of thumb is that if you don't recognize a particular service, you probably won't need it anyway. Also keep in mind that some services are not really meant to be used over the Internet. Don't rely on what *should* be running, check which services are listening on what TCP ports using the **netstat** command:

```
[elly@mars ~] netstat -l | grep tcp
tcp     0       0 *:32769                   *:*       LISTEN
tcp     0       0 *:32771                   *:*       LISTEN
tcp     0       0 *:printer                 *:*       LISTEN
tcp     0       0 *:kerberos_master         *:*       LISTEN
tcp     0       0 *:sunrpc                  *:*       LISTEN
tcp     0       0 *:6001                    *:*       LISTEN
tcp     0       0 *:785                     *:*       LISTEN
tcp     0       0 localhost.localdom:smtp   *:*       LISTEN
tcp     0       0 *:ftp                     *:*       LISTEN
tcp     0       0 *:ssh                     *:*       LISTEN
tcp     0       0 ::1:x11-ssh-offset        *:*       LISTEN
```

Things to avoid:

- **exec**, **rlogin** and **rsh**, and **telnet** just to be on the safe side.

- X11 on server machines.

- No lp if no printer is physically attached.

- No MS Windows hosts in the network, no Samba required.

- Don't allow FTP unless an FTP server is required.

- Don't allow NFS and NIS over the Internet, disable all related services on a stand-alone installation.

- Don't run an MTA if you're not actually on a mail server.

- ...

Stop running services using the **chkconfig** command, the initscripts or by editing the **(x)inetd** configuration files.

10.5.3   Update regularly

Its ability to adapt quickly in an ever changing environment is what makes Linux thrive. But it also creates a possibility that security updates have been released even while you are installing a brand new version, so the first thing you should do (and this goes for about any OS you can think of) after installing is getting the updates as soon as possible. After that, update *all* the packages you use regularly.

Some updates may require new configuration files, and old files may be replaced. Check the documentation, and ensure that everything runs normal after updating.

Most Linux distributions provide mailing list services for security update announcements, and tools for applying updates to the system. General Linux only security issues are reported among others at Linuxsecurity.com <http://linuxsecurity.com/>.

Updating is an ongoing process, so it should be an almost daily habit.

10.5.4   Firewalls and access policies

10.5.4.1 What is a firewall?

In the previous section we already mentioned firewall capabilities in Linux. While firewall administration is one of the tasks of your network admin, you should know a couple of things about firewalls.

Firewall is a vague term that can mean anything that acts as a protective barrier between us and the outside world, generally the Internet. A firewall can be a dedicated system or a specific application that provides this functionality. Or it can be a combination of components, including various combinations of hardware and software. Firewalls are built from "rules" that are used to define what is allowed to enter and/or exit a given system or network.

After disabling unnecessary services, we now want to restrict accepted services as to allow only the minimum required connections. A fine example is working from home: only the specific connection between your office and your home should be allowed, connections from other machines on the Internet should be blocked.

10.5.4.2 Packet filters

The first line of defense is a *packet filter*, which can look inside IP packets and make decisions based on the content. Most common is the Netfilter package, providing the **iptables** command, a next generation packet filter for Linux.

One of the most noteworthy enhancements in the newer kernels is the *stateful inspection* feature, which not only tells what is inside a packet, but also detects if a packet belongs or is related to a new or existing connection.

The Shoreline Firewall or Shorewall for short is a front-end for the standard firewall functionality in Linux.

More information can be found at the Netfilter/iptables project page <http://www.netfilter.org/>.

10.5.4.3 TCP wrappers

TCP wrapping provides much the same results as the packet filters, but works differently. The wrapper actually accepts the connection attempt, then examines configuration files and decides whether to accept or reject the connection request. It controls connections at the application level rather than at the network level.

TCP wrappers are typically used with **xinetd** to provide host name and IP-address-based access control. In addition, these tools include logging and utilization management capabilities that are easy to configure.

The advantages of TCP wrappers are that the connecting client is unaware that wrappers are used, and that they operate separately from the applications they protect.

The host based access is controlled in the `hosts.allow` and `hosts.deny` files. More information can be found in the TCP wrapper documentation files in `/usr/share/doc/tcp_wrappers[-<version>/]` or `/usr/share/doc/tcp` and in the man pages for the host based access control files, which contain examples.

10.5.4.4 Proxies

Proxies can perform various duties, not all of which have much to do with security. But the fact that they are an intermediary make proxies a good place to enforce access control policies, limit direct connections through a firewall, and control how the network behind the proxy looks to the Internet.

Usually in combination with a packet filter, but sometimes all by themselves, proxies provide an extra level of control. More information can be found in the Firewall HOWTO <http://www.tldp.org/HOWTO/Firewall-HOWTO.html> or on the Squid website.

10.5.4.5 Access to individual applications

Some servers may have their own access control features. Common examples include Samba, X Window, Bind, Apache and CUPS. For every service you want to offer check which configuration files apply.

10.5.4.6 Log files

If anything, the UNIX way of logging all kinds of activities into all kinds of files confirms that "it is doing something." Of course, log files should be checked regularly, manually or automatically. Firewalls and other means of access control tend to create huge amounts of log files, so the trick is to try and only log abnormal activities.

10.5.5   Intrusion detection

Intrusion Detection Systems are designed to catch what might have gotten past the firewall. They can either be designed to catch an active break-in attempt in progress, or to detect a successful break-in after the fact. In the latter case, it is too late to prevent any damage, but at least we have early awareness of a problem. There are two basic types of IDS: those protecting networks, and those protecting individual hosts.

For host based IDS, this is done with utilities that monitor the file system for changes. System files that have changed in some way, but should not change, are a dead give-away that something is amiss. Anyone who gets in and gets root access will presumably make changes to the system somewhere. This is usually the very first thing done, either so he can get back in through a backdoor, or to launch an attack against someone else, in which case, he has to change or add files to the system. Some systems come with the **tripwire** monitoring system, which is documented at the Tripwire Open Source Project website <http://www.tripwire.org/>.

Network intrusion detection is handled by a system that sees all the traffic that passes the firewall (not by portscanners, which advertise usable ports). Snort <http://www.snort.org/> is an Open Source example of such a program. Whitehats.com features an open Intrusion detection database, arachNIDS <http://www.whitehats.com/>.

10.5.6   More tips

Some general things you should keep in mind:

- Do not allow root logins. UNIX developers came up with the **su** over two decades ago for extra security.

- Direct root access is always dangerous and susceptible to human errors, be it by allowing root login or by using the **su -** command. Rather than using **su**, it is even better to use **sudo** to only execute the command that you need extra permissions for, and to return afterwards to your own environment.

- Take passwords seriously. Use shadow passwords. Change your passwords regularly.

- Try to always use SSH or SSL. Avoid **telnet**, FTP and E-mail clients and other client programs which send unencrypted passwords over the network. Security is not only about securing your computer, it is also about securing your passwords.

- Limit resources using **quota** and/or **ulimit**.

- The mail for root should be delivered to, or at least read by, an actual person.

- The SANS institute <http://www.sans.org/> has more tips and tricks, sorted per distribution, with mailing list service.

- Check the origin of new software, get it from a trusted place/site. Verify new packages before installing.

- When using a non-permanent Internet connection, shut it down as soon as you don't need it anymore.

- Run private services on odd ports instead of the ones expected by possible hackers.

- Know your system. After a while, you can almost feel when something is happening.

10.5.7   Have I been hacked?

How can you tell? This is a checklist of suspicious events:

- Mysterious open ports, strange processes.

- System utilities (common commands) behaving strange.

- Login problems.

- Unexplained bandwidth usage.

- Damaged or missing log files, syslog daemon behaving strange.

- Interfaces in unusual modes.

- Unexpectedly modified configuration files.

- Strange entries in shell history files.

- Unidentified temporary files.

10.5.8   Recovering from intrusion

In short, stay calm. Then take the following actions in this order:

- Disconnect the machine from the network.

- Try to find out as much as you can about how your security was breached.

- Backup important non-system data. If possible, check these data against existing backups, made before the system was compromised, to ensure data integrity.

- Re-install the system.

- Use new passwords.
- Restore from system and data backups.
- Apply all available updates.
- Re-examine the system: block off unnecessary services, check firewall rules and other access policies.
- Reconnect.

10.6 Summary

Linux and networking go hand in hand. The Linux kernel has support for all common and most uncommon network protocols. The standard UNIX networking tools are provided in each distribution. Next to those, most distributions offer tools for easy network installation and management.

Linux is well known as a stable platform for running various Internet services, the amount of Internet software is endless. Like UNIX, Linux can be just as well used and administered from a remote location, using one of several solutions for remote execution of programs.

We briefly touched the subject of security. Linux is an ideal firewall system, light and cheap, but can be used in several other network functions such as routers and proxy servers.

Increasing network security is mainly done by applying frequent updates and common sense.

Here is an overview of network related commands:

Command	Meaning
ftp	Transfer files to another host (insecure).
host	Get information about networked hosts.
ifconfig	Display IP address information.
ip	Display IP address information.
netstat	Display routing information and network statistics.
ping	Send answer requests to other hosts.
rdesktop	Display and MS Windows desktop on your Linux system.
route	Show routing information.
scp	Secure copy files to and from other hosts.

Command	Meaning
sftp	Secure FTP files to and from other hosts.
ssh	Make an encrypted connection to another host.
ssh-keygen	Generate authentication keys for Secure SHell.
telnet	Make an insecure connection to another hosts.
tracepath/traceroute	Print the route that packets follow to another host.
whois	Get information about a domain name.
xclock	X Window clock application, handy for testing remote display.
xhost	X Window access control tool.

Table 10.2. New commands in Chapter 10: Networking

10.7 Exercises

10.7.1   General networking

- Display network information for your workstation: IP address, routes, name servers.

- Suppose no DNS is available. What would you do to reach your neighbour's machine without typing the IP address all the time?

- How would you permanently store proxy information for a text mode browser such as **links**?

- Which name servers handle the redhat.com domain?

- Send an E-mail to your local account. Try two different ways to send and read it. How can you check that it really arrived?

- Does your machine accept anonymous FTP connections? How do you use the **ncftp** program to authenticate with your user name and password?

- Does your machine run a web server? If not, make it do so. Check the log files!

10.7.2   Remote connections

- From your local workstation, display a graphical application, such as **xclock** on your neighbour's screen. The necessary accounts will have to be set up. Use a secure connection!

- Set up SSH keys so you can connect to your neighbour's machine without having to enter a password.

- Make a backup copy of your home directory in /var/tmp on your neighbour's "backup server," using **scp**. Archive and compress before starting the data transfer! Connect to the remote host using **ssh**, unpack the backup, and put one file back on the original machine using **sftp**.

10.7.3   Security

- Make a list of open (listening) ports on your machine.

- Supposing you want to run a web server. Which services would you deactivate? How would you do that?

- Install available updates.

- How can you see who connected to your system?

- Make a repetitive job that reminds you to change your password every month, and preferably the *root* password as well.

Chapter 11
Sound and Video

This chapter addresses the following tasks (briefly, as the field of sound and video is very wide):

- Sound card configuration
- Playing CDs, copying CDs,
- Playing music files
- Volume control
- Video and television
- Recording sound

11.1 Audio Basics

11.1.1   Installation

Most likely, your system is already installed with audio drivers and the configuration was done at installation time. Likewise, should you ever need to replace your audio hardware, most systems provide tools that allow easy setup and configuration of the device. Most currently available plug-and-play sound cards should be recognized automatically. If you can hear the samples that are played during configuration, just click OK and everything will be set up for you.

If your card is not detected automatically, you may be presented with a list of sound cards and/or of sound card properties from which to choose. After that, you will have to provide the correct I/O port, IRQ and DMA settings. Information about these settings can be found in your sound card documentation. If you are on a dual boot system with MS Windows, this information can be found in the Windows Control Panel as well.

If automatic sound card detection fails

If your soundcard is not supported by default, you will need to apply other techniques. These are described in the Linux Sound HOWTO <http://www.tldp.org/HOWTO/Sound-HOWTO/index.html>.

11.1.2   Drivers and Architecture

There are generally two types of sound architecture: the older Open Sound System or OSS, which works with every UNIX-like system, and the newer Advanced Linux Sound Architecture or ALSA, that has better support for Linux, as the name indicates. ALSA also has more features and allows for faster driver development. We will focus here on the ALSA system.

Today, almost all mainstream audio chipsets are supported. Only some high-end professional solutions and some cards developed by manufacturers refusing to document their chipset specifications are unsupported. An overview of supported devices can be found on the ALSA site at <http://www.alsa-project.org/alsa-doc/index.php?vendor=All#matrix>.

Configuring systems installed with ALSA is done using the **alsaconf** tool. Additionally, distributions usually provide their own tools for configuring the sound card; these tools might even integrate the old and the new way of handling sound devices.

11.2 Sound and video playing

11.2.1   CD playing and copying

The *cdp* package comes with most distributions and provides **cdp** or **cdplay**, a text-based CD player. Desktop managers usually include a graphical tool, such as the **gnome-cd** player in Gnome, that can be started from a menu.

Be sure to understand the difference between an audio CD and a data CD. You do not have to mount an audio CD into the file system in order to listen to it. This is because the data on such a CD are not Linux file system data; they are accessed and sent to the audio output channel directly, using a CD player program. If your CD is a data CD containing .mp3 files, you will first need to mount it into the file system, and then use one of the programs that we discuss below in order to play the music. How to mount CDs into the file system is explained in Section 7.5.5.

The **cdparanoia** tool from the package with the same name reads audio directly as data from the CD, without analog conversions, and writes data to a file or pipe in different formats, of which .wav is probably the most popular. Various tools for conversion to other formats, formats, such as .mp3, come with most distributions or are downloadable as separate packages. The GNU project provides several CD playing, ripping and encoding tools, database managers; see the Free Software Directory, Audio section <http://www.gnu.org/directory/audio/> for detailed information.

Audio-CD creation is eased, among many others, with the **kaudiocreator** tool from the KDE suite. It comes with clear information from the KDE Help Center.

CD burning is covered in general in Section 9.2.2.

11.2.2 Playing music files

11.2.2.1 mp3 files

The popular .mp3 format is widely supported on Linux machines. Most distributions include multiple programs that can play these files. Among many other applications, XMMS, which is presented in the screenshot below, is one of the most wide-spread, partially because it has the same look and feel as the Windows tool.

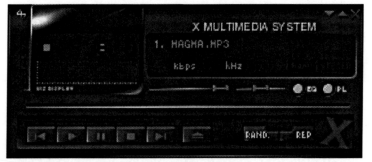

Figure 11.1. XMMS mp3 player

Also very popular for playing music are AmaroK, a KDE application that is steadily gaining popularity, and MPlayer, which can also play movies.

Restrictions

Some distributions don't allow you to play MP3's without modifying your configuration, this is due to license restrictions on the MP3 tools. You might need to install extra software to be able to play your music.

In text mode, you can use the **mplayer** command:

```
[tille@octarine ~]$ mplayer /opt/mp3/oriental/*.mp3
MPlayer 1.0pre7-RPM-3.4.2 (C) 2000-2005 MPlayer Team
CPU: Advanced Micro Devices Duron Spitfire (Family: 6, Stepping: 1)
Detected cache-line size is 64 bytes
```

```
CPUflags:  MMX: 1 MMX2: 1 3DNow: 1 3DNow2: 1 SSE: 0 SSE2: 0
Playing /opt/oldopt/mp3/oriental/Mazika_Diana-Krozon_Super-Star_Ensani-Ma-
Bansak.mp3.
Cache fill:  1.17% (98304 bytes)    Audio file detected.
Clip info:
Title: Ensani-Ma-Bansak.mp3
Artist: Diana-Krozon
Album: Super-Star
Year:
Comment:
Genre: Unknown
==============================================================================
Opening audio decoder: [mp3lib] MPEG layer-2, layer-3
mpg123: Can't rewind stream by 450 bits!
AUDIO: 44100 Hz, 2 ch, s16le, 160.0 kbit/11.34% (ratio: 20000->176400)
Selected audio codec: [mp3] afm:mp3lib (mp3lib MPEG layer-2, layer-3)
==============================================================================
Checking audio filter chain for 44100Hz/2ch/s16le -> 44100Hz/2ch/s16le...
AF_pre: 44100Hz/2ch/s16le
AO: [oss] 44100Hz 2ch s16le (2 bps)
Building audio filter chain for 44100Hz/2ch/s16le -> 44100Hz/2ch/s16le...
Video: no video
Starting playback...
A: 227.8 (03:23:.1) 1.8% 12%
```

11.2.2.2 Other formats

It would lead us too far to discuss all possible audio formats and ways to play them. An (incomplete) overview of other common sound playing and manipulating software:

- Ogg Vorbis: Free audio format: see the GNU audio directory <http://www.gnu.org/directory/audio/ogg/> for tools - they might be included in your distribution as well. The format was developed because MP3 is patented.

- Real audio and video: **realplay** from RealNetworks <http://real.com/>.

- SoX or Sound eXchange: actually a sound converter, comes with th e **play** program. Plays .wav, . ogg and various other formats, including raw binary formats.

- Playmidi: a MIDI player, see the GNU directory.

- AlsaPlayer: from the Advanced Linux Sound Architecture project, see the AlsaPlayer web site <http://www.alsaplayer.org/>.

- **mplayer**: plays just about anything, including mp3 files. More info on the MPlayerHQ website <http://www.mplayerhq.hu/>.

- **hxplay**: supports RealAudio and RealVideo, mp3, mp4 audio, Flash, wav and more, see HelixDNA <http://www.helixdna.com/> (not all components of this software are completely free).

- **rhythmbox**: based on the GStreamer framework, can play everything supported in GStreamer, which claims to be able to play everything, see the Rhythmbox <http://www.rhythmbox.org/> and GStreamer <http://gstreamer.freedesktop.org/> sites.

Check your system documentation and man pages for particular tools and detailed explanations on how to use them.

I don't have these applications on my system!

A lot of the tools and applications discussed in the above sections are optional software. It is possible that such applications are not installed on your system by default, but that you can find them in your distribution as additional packages. It might also very well be that the application that you are looking for is not in your distribution at all. In that case, you need to download it from the application's web site.

11.2.2.3 Volume control

aumix and **alsamixer** are two common text tools for adjusting audio controls. Use the arrow keys to toggle settings. The **alsamixer** has a graphical interface when started from the Gnome menu or as **gnome-alsamixer** from the command line. The **kmix** tool does the same in KDE.

Regardless of how you choose to listen to music or other sounds, remember that there may be other people who may not be interested in hearing you or your computer. Try to be courteous, especially in office environments. Use a quality headset, rather than the ones with the small ear pieces. This is better for your ears and causes less distraction for your colleagues.

11.2.3   Recording

Various tools are again available that allow you to record voice and music. For recording voice you can use **arecord** on the command line:

```
alexey@russia:~> arecord /var/tmp/myvoice.wav
Recording WAVE '/var/tmp/myvoice.wav' : Unsigned 8 bit, Rate 8000 Hz, Mono
Aborted by signal Interrups...
```

"Interrupt" means that the application has caught a **Ctrl+C**. Play the sample using the simple **play** command.

This is a good test that you can execute prior to testing applications that need voice input, like Voice over IP (VoIP). Keep in mind that the microphone input should be activated. If you don't hear your own voice, check your sound settings. It often happens that the microphone is muted or on verry low volume. This can be easily adjusted using **alsamixer** or your distribution-specific graphical interface to the sound system.

In KDE you can start the **krec** utility, Gnome provides the **gnome-sound-recorder**.

11.3 Video playing, streams and television watching

Various players are available:

- **xine**: a free video player
- **ogle**: DVD player.
- **okle**: KDE version of **ogle**
- **mplayer**: Movie Player for Linux
- **totem**: plays both audio and video files, audio CDs, VCD and DVD.
- **realplay**: from RealNetworks.
- **hxplay**: a Real alternative, see HelixDNA <http://helixcommunity.org/>.
- **kaffeine**: media player for KDE3.

Most likely, you will find one of these in your graphical menus.

Keep in mind that all codecs necessary for viewing different types of video might not be on your system by default. You can get a long way downloading W32codecs and libdvdcss.

The LDP <http://www.tldp.org/> released a document that is very appropriate for this section. It is entitled DVD Playback HOWTO <http://www.tldp.org/HOWTO/DVD-Playback-HOWTO/index.html> and describes the different tools available for viewing movies on a system that has a DVD drive. It is a fine addition to the DVD HOWTO <http://www.tldp.org/HOWTO/DVD-HOWTO.html> that explains installation of the drive.

For watching TV there is choice of the following tools, among many others for watching and capturing TV, video and other streams:

- **tvtime**: great program with station management, interaction with teletext, film mode and much more.
- **zapping**: Gnome-specific TV viewer.
- **xawtv**: X11 TV viewer.

11.4 Internet Telephony

11.4.1   What is it?

Internet telephony, or more common, Voice over IP (VoIP) or digital telephony allows parties to exchange voice data flows over the network. The big difference is that the data flows over a general purpose network, the Internet, contrary to conventional telephony, that uses a dedicated network of voice transmission lines. The two networks can be connected, however, under special circumstances, but for now this is certainly not a standard. In other words: it is very likely that you will not be able to call people who are using a conventional telephone. If it is possible at all, it is likely that you will need to pay for a subscription.

While there are currently various applications available for free download, both free and proprietary, there are some major drawbacks to telephony over the Internet. Most noticably, the system is unreliable, it can be slow or there can be a lot of noise on the connection, and it can thus certainly not be used to replace conventional telephony - think about emergency calls. While some providers take their precautions, there is no guarantee that you can reach the party that you want to call.

Most applications currently do not use encryption, so be aware that it is potentially easy for someone to eavesdrop on your conversations. If security is a concern for you, read the documentation that comes with your VoIP client. Additionally, if you are using a firewall, it should be configured to allow incoming connections from anywhere, so using VoIP also includes taking risks on the level of site security.

11.4.2   What do you need?

11.4.2.1 Server Side

First of all, you need a provider offering the service. This service might integrate traditional telephony and it might or might not be free. Among others are SIPphone <http://www.sipphone.com/>, Vonage <http://www.vonage.com/>, Lingo <http://www.lingo.com/>, AOL TotalTalk <http://www.totaltalk.com/> and many locally accessible providers offering the so-called "full phone service". Internet phone service only is offered by Skype <http://www.skype.com/>, SIP Broker <http://www.sipbroker.com/>, Google <http://www.google.com/talk/> and many others.

If you want to set up a server of your own, you might want to look into Asterisk <http://www.asterisk.org/>.

11.4.2.2 Client Side

On the client side, the applications that you can use depend on your network configuration. If you have a direct Internet connection, there won't be any problems, provided that you know on what server you can connect, and usually that you also have a username and password to authenticate to the service.

If you are behind a firewall that does Network Address Translation (NAT), however, some services might not work, as they will only see the IP address of the firewall and not the address of your computer, which might well be unroutable over the Internet, for instance when you are in a company network and your IP address starts with 10., 192.168. or another non-routable subnet prefix. This depends on the protocol that is used by the application.

Also, available bandwidth might be a blocking factor: some applications are optimized for low bandwidth consumption, while others might require high bandwidth connections. This depends on the codec that is used by the application.

Among the most common applications are the Skype client, which has an interface that reminds of instant messaging, and X-Lite <http://www.counterpath.com/>, the free version of the XTen softphone, which looks like a mobile telephone. However, while these programs are available for free download and very popular, they are not free as in free speech: they use proprietary protocols and/or are only available in binary packages, not in source format.

Free *and open* VoIP clients are for instance Gizmo <http://www.gizmoproject. com/>, Linphone <http://www.linphone.org/>, GnomeMeeting <http://www. gnomemeeting.org/> and KPhone <http://www.wirlab.net/kphone/>.

 Client hardware

While your computer, especially if it is a laptop PC, might have a built-in microphone, the result will be far better if you connect a headset. If you have the choice, opt for a USB headset, as it functions independently from existing audio hardware. Use **alsamixer** to configure input and output sound levels to your taste.

VoIP applications are definitely a booming market. Volunteers try to document the current status at <http://www.voip-info.org/>.

11.5 Summary

The GNU/Linux platform is fully multi-media enabled. A wide variety of devices like sound cards, tv-cards, headsets, microphones, CD and DVD players is supported. The list of applications is sheer endless, that is why we needed to shorten the list of new commands below and limit ourselves to general audio commands.

Command	Meaning
alsaconf	Configure the ALSA sound system.
alsamixer	Tune output levels of ALSA driver.
arecord	Record a sound sample.
aumix	Audio mixer tool.
cdp	Play an audio CD.
cdparanoia	Rip an audio CD.
cdplay	Play an audio CD.
gnome-alsamixer	Gnome ALSA front-end.
gnome-cd	Gnome front-end for playing audio CDs.
gnome-sound-recorder	Gnome front-end for recording sound samples.
kaudiocreator	KDE front-end for creating audio CDs.
kmix	KDE front-end for sound settings.
krec	KDE front-end for recording sound samples.
mplayer	Multi-media player.
play	Command line tool for playing sound samples.

Table 11.1. New commands in Chapter 11: Audio

11.6 Exercises

1. From the Gnome or KDE menu, open your sound configuration panel. Make sure audio boxes or headset are connected to your system and find an output level that is comfortable for you. Make sure, when your system is ALSA-compatible, that you use the appropriate panel.

2. If you have a microphone, try recording a sample of your own voice. Make sure the input volume is not too high, as this will result in high-pitched tones when you communicate with others, or in transfering background noise to the other party. On the command line, you might even try to use **arecord** and **aplay** for recording and playing sound.

3. Locate sound files on your system and try to play them.

4. Insert an audio CD and try to play it.

5. Find a chat partner and configure a VoIP program. (You might need to install one first.)

6. Can you listen to Internet radio?

7. If you have a DVD player and a movie on a DVD disk, try to play it.

Appendix A
Where to go from here?

This document gives an overview of useful books and sites.

A.1 Useful Books

A.1.1 General Linux

- "Linux in a Nutshell" by Ellen Siever, Jessica P. Hackman, Stephen Spainhour, Stephen Figgins, O'Reilly UK, ISBN 0596000251

- "Running Linux" by Matt Welsh, Matthias Kalle Dalheimer, Lar Kaufman, O'Reilly UK, ISBN 156592469X

- "Linux Unleashed" by Tim Parker, Bill Ball, David Pitts, Sams, ISBN 0672316889

- "When You Can't Find Your System Administrator" by Linda Mui, O'Reilly UK, ISBN 1565921046

- When you actually buy a distribution, it will contain a very decent user manual.

A.1.2 Editors

- "Learning the Vi Editor" by Linda Lamb and Arnold Robbins, O'Reilly UK, ISBN 1565924266

- "GNU Emacs Manual" by Richard M.Stallman, iUniverse.Com Inc., ISBN 0595100333

- "Learning GNU Emacs" by Debra Cameron, Bill Rosenblatt and Eric Raymond, O'Reilly UK, ISBN 1565921526

- "Perl Cookbook" by Tom Christiansen and Nathan Torkington, O'Reilly UK, ISBN 1565922433

A.1.3 Shells

- "Unix Shell Programming" by Stephen G.Kochan and Patrick H.Wood, Sams Publishing, ISBN 067248448X

- "Learning the Bash Shell" by Cameron Newham and Bill Rosenblatt, O'Reilly UK, ISBN 1565923472

- "The Complete Linux Shell Programming Training Course" by Ellie Quigley and Scott Hawkins, Prentice Hall PTR, ISBN 0130406767

- "Linux and Unix Shell Programming" by David Tansley, Addison Wesley Publishing Company, ISBN 0201674726

- "Unix C Shell Field Guide" by Gail and Paul Anderson, Prentice Hall, ISBN 013937468X

A.1.4 X Window

- "Gnome User's Guide" by the Gnome Community, iUniverse.Com Inc., ISBN 0595132251

- "KDE Bible" by Dave Nash, Hungry Minds Inc., ISBN 0764546929

- "The Concise Guide to XFree86 for Linux" by Aron HSiao, Que, ISBN 0789721821

- "The New XFree86" by Bill Ball, Prima Publishing, ISBN 0761531521

- "Beginning GTK+ and Gnome" by Peter Wright, Wrox Press, ISBN 1861003811

- "KDE 2.0 Development" by David Sweet and Matthias Ettrich, Sams Publishing, ISBN 0672318911

- "GTK+/Gnome Application Development" by Havoc Pennington, New Riders Publishing, ISBN 0735700788

A.1.5 Networking

- "TCP/IP Illustrated, Volume I: The Protocols" by W. Richard Stevens, Addison-Wesley Professional Computing Series, ISBN 0-201-63346-9

- "DNS and BIND" by Paul Albitz, Cricket Liu, Mike Loukides and Deborah Russell, O'Reilly & Associates, ISBN 0596001584

- "The Concise Guide to DNS and BIND" by Nicolai Langfeldt, Que, ISBN 0789722739

- "Implementing LDAP" by Mark Wilcox, Wrox Press, ISBN 1861002211

- "Understanding and deploying LDAP directory services" by Tim Howes and co., Sams, ISBN 0672323168

- "Sendmail" by Brian Costales and Eric Allman, O'Reilly UK, ISBN 1565922220

- "Removing the Spam : Email Processing and Filtering" by Geoff Mulligan, Addison Wesley Publishing Company, ISBN 0201379570

- "Managing IMAP" by Dianna & Kevin Mullet, O'Reilly UK, ISBN 059600012X

A.2 Useful sites

A.2.1 General information

- The Linux documentation project: <http://www.tldp.org/> all docs, manpages, HOWTOs, FAQs

- LinuxQuestions.org <http://www.linuxquestions.org/>: forum, downloads, docs and much more

- Google for Linux <http://www.google.com/linux>: the specialized search engine

- Google Groups <http://groups.google.com/>: an archive of all newsgroup postings, including the comp.os.linux hierarchy

- Slashdot <http://slashdot.org/>: daily news

- O'Reilly <http://www.oreilly.com/>: books on Linux System and Network administration, Perl, Java, ...

- POSIX <http://www.posix.com/posix.html>: the standard

- Linux HQ <http://www.linuxhq.com/>: Maintains a complete database of source, patches and documentation for various versions of the Linux kernel.

A.2.2 Architecture Specific References

- AlphaLinux <http://www.alphalinux.org/>: Linux on Alpha architecture (e.g. Digital Workstation)

- Linux-MIPS <http://www.linux-mips.org/>: Linux on MIPS (e.g. SGI Indy)

- Linux on the Road <http://tldp.org/LDP/Mobile-Guide/html/index.html>: Specific guidelines for installing and running Linux on laptops, PDAs, mobile phones and so on. Configuration files for various models.

- MkLinux <http://www.mklinux.org/>: Linux on Apple

A.2.3 Distributions

- The Fedora Project <http://fedora.redhat.com/>: RedHat-sponsored community effort OS.

- Mandriva <http://www.mandriva.com/>

- Ubuntu <http://www.ubuntu.com/>

- Debian <http://www.debian.org/>

- TurboLinux <http://www.turbolinux.com/>

- Slackware <http://www.slackware.com/>

- SuSE <http://www.suse.de/>

- LinuxISO.org <http://www.linuxiso.org/>: CD images for all distributions.

- Knoppix <http://www.knoppix.org/>: distribution that runs from a CD, you don't need to install anything for this one.

- DistroWatch.com <http://www.distrowatch.com/>: find a Linux that goes with your style.

- ...

A.2.4 Software

- Freshmeat <http://freshmeat.net/>: new software, software archives

- OpenSSH <http://www.openssh.org/>: Secure SHell site

- OpenOffice <http://www.openoffice.org/>: MS compatible Office Suite

- KDE <http://www.kde.org/>: K Desktop site

- GNU <http://www.gnu.org/>: GNU and GNU software

- Gnome <http://www.gnome.org/>: The official Gnome site

- RPM Find <http://www.rpmfind.net/>: all RPM packages

- Samba <http://www.samba.org/>: MS Windows file and print services

- Home of the OpenLDAP Project <http://www.openldap.org/>: OpenLDAP server/clients/utilities, FAQ and other documentation.

- Sendmail Homepage <http://www.sendmail.org/>: A thorough technical discussion of Sendmail features, includes configuration examples.

- Netfilter <http://netfilter.samba.org/>: contains assorted information about iptables: HOWTO, FAQ, guides, ...

- Official GIMP website <http://www.gimp.org/>: All information about the GNU Image Manipulation Program.

- SourceForge.net <http://sourceforge.net/>: Open SOurce software development site.

- vIm homepage <http://www.vim.org/>

Appendix B
DOS versus Linux commands

In this appendix, we matched DOS commands with their Linux equivalent.

As an extra means of orientation for new users with a Windows background, the table below lists MS-DOS commands with their Linux counterparts. Keep in mind that Linux commands usually have a number of options. Read the Info or man pages on the command to find out more.

DOS commands	Linux command
<command> /?	man <command>
cd	cd
chdir	pwd
cls	clear
copy	cp
date	date
del	rm
dir	ls
echo	echo
edit	vim (or other editor)
exit	exit
fc	diff
find	grep
format	mke2fs or mformat
mem	free
mkdir	mkdir
more	more or even less

DOS commands	Linux command
move	mv
ren	mv
time	date

Table 11.2. Overview of DOS/Linux commands

Appendix C
Shell Features

This document gives an overview of common shell features (the same in every shell flavour) and differing shell features (shell specific features).

C.1 Common features

The following features are standard in every shell. Note that the stop, suspend, jobs, bg and fg commands are only available on systems that support job control.

Command	Meaning
>	Redirect output
>>	Append to file
<	Redirect input
<<	"Here" document (redirect input)
|	Pipe output
&	Run process in background.
;	Separate commands on same line
*	Match any character(s) in filename
?	Match single character in filename
[ ]	Match any characters enclosed
( )	Execute in subshell
` `	Substitute output of enclosed command
" "	Partial quote (allows variable and command expansion)
' '	Full quote (no expansion)
\	Quote following character
$var	Use value for variable

Command	Meaning
$$	Process id
$0	Command name
$n	nth argument (n from 0 to 9)
$*	All arguments as a simple word
#	Begin comment
bg	Background execution
break	Break from loop statements
cd	Change directories
continue	Resume a program loop
echo	Display output
eval	Evaluate arguments
exec	Execute a new shell
fg	Foreground execution
jobs	Show active jobs
kill	Terminate running jobs
newgrp	Change to a new group
shift	Shift positional parameters
stop	Suspend a background job
suspend	Suspend a foreground job
time	Time a command
umask	Set or list file permissions
unset	Erase variable or function definitions
wait	Wait for a background job to finish

Table C. 1. Common Shell Features

C.2   Differing features

The table below shows major differences between the standard shell (**sh**), Bourne Again SHell (**bash**), Korn shell (**ksh**) and the C shell (**csh**).

Shell compatibility

Since the Bourne Again SHell is a superset of **sh**, all **sh** commands will also work in **bash** - but not vice versa. **bash** has many more features of its own, and, as the table below demonstrates, many features incorporated from other shells.

Since the Turbo C shell is a superset of **csh**, all **csh** commands will work in **tcsh**, but not the other way round.

sh	*bash*	*ksh*	*csh*	*Meaning/Action*
$	$	$	%	Default user prompt
	>|	>|	>!	Force redirection
> file 2>&1	&> file or > file 2>&1	> file 2>&1	>& file	Redirect stdout and stderr to file
	{ }		{ }	Expand elements in list
`command`	`command` or $(command)	$(command)	`command`	Substitute output of enclosed **command**
$HOME	$HOME	$HOME	$home	Home directory
	~	~	~	Home directory symbol
	~+, ~-, **dirs**	~+, ~-	=-, =N	Access directory stack
var=value	**VAR=value**	**var=value**	set **var=value**	Variable assignment
export var	**export VAR=value**	**export var=val**	setenv var val	Set environment variable
	${nnnn}	${nn}		More than 9 arguments can be referenced
"$@"	"$@"	"$@"		All arguments as separate words
$#	$#	$#	$#argv	Number of arguments
$?	$?	$?	$status	Exit status of the most recently executed command
$!	$!	$!		PID of most recently

sh	bash	ksh	csh	Meaning/Action
				backgrounded process
$-	$-	$-		Current options
. file	source file or . file	. file	source file	Read commands in file
	alias x='y'	alias x=y	alias x y	Name **x** stands for command **y**
case	case	case	switch or case	Choose alternatives
done	done	done	end	End a loop statement
esac	esac	esac	endsw	End **case** or **switch**
exit *n*	exit *n*	exit *n*	exit (expr)	Exit with a status
for/do	for/do	for/do	foreach	Loop through variables
	set -f , set -o nullglob|dotglob| nocaseglob|noglob		noglob	Ignore substitution characters for filename generation
hash	hash	alias -t	hashstat	Display hashed commands (tracked aliases)
hash *cmds*	hash *cmds*	alias -t *cmds*	rehash	Remember command locations
hash -r	hash -r		unhash	Forget command locations
	history	history	history	List previous commands
	ArrowUp+Enter or !!	r	!!	Redo previous command
	!*str*	r *str*	!*str*	Redo last command that starts with "str"
	!*cmd*:s/*x*/*y*/	r *x=y cmd*	!*cmd*:s/*x*/*y*/	Replace "x" with "y" in most recent command starting with "cmd", then

sh	bash	ksh	csh	Meaning/Action
				execute.
if [$i -eq 5]	if [$i -eq 5]	if ((i==5))	if ($i==5)	Sample condition test
fi	fi	fi	endif	End if statement
ulimit	ulimit	ulimit	limit	Set resource limits
pwd	pwd	pwd	dirs	Print working directory
read	read	read	$<	Read from terminal
trap 2	trap 2	trap 2	onintr	Ignore interrupts
	unalias	unalias	unalias	Remove aliases
until	until	until		Begin until loop
while/do	while/do	while/do	while	Begin while loop

Table C. 2. Differing Shell Features

The Bourne Again SHell has many more features not listed here. This table is just to give you an idea of how this shell incorporates all useful ideas from other shells: there are no blanks in the column for **bash**. More information on features found only in Bash can be retrieved from the Bash info pages, in the "Bash Features" section.

More information:

You should at least read one manual, being the manual of your shell. The preferred choice would be **info bash**, **bash** being the GNU shell and easiest for beginners. Print it out and take it home, study it whenever you have 5 minutes.

See Appendix B if you are having difficulties to assimilate shell commands.

Glossary

This section contains an alphabetical overview of commands discussed in this document.

A

a2ps

Format files for printing on a PostScript printer, see Section 8.1.2.

acroread

PDF viewer, see Section 8.1.2.2.

adduser

Create a new user or update default new user information.

alias

Create a shell alias for a command.

alsaconf

Configure sound card using the ALSA driver, see Section 11.1.2.

alsamixer

Tune ALSA sound device output, see Section 11.2.2.3.

anacron

Execute commands periodically, does not assume continuously running machine.

apropos

Search the whatis database for strings, see Section 2.3.3.2.

apt-get

APT package handling utility, see Section 7.5.3.2.

arecord

Record a sound sample, see Section 11.2.3.

aspell

Spell checker.

at, atq, atrm

Queue, examine or delete jobs for later execution, see Section 4.1.2.2 and Section 4.4.3.

aumix

Adjust audio mixer, see Section 11.2.2.3.

(g)awk

Pattern scanning and processing language.

B

bash

Bourne Again SHell, see Section 3.2.3.2 and Section 7.2.5.

batch

Queue, examine or delete jobs for later execution, see Section 4.1.2.2.

bg

Run a job in the background, see Section 4.1.2.1.

bitmap

Bitmap editor and converter utilities for the X window System.

bzip2

A block-sorting file compressor, see Section 9.1.1.3.

C

cardctl

Manage PCMCIA cards, see Section 10.2.3.3.

cat

Concatenate files and print to standard output, see Section 2.2 and Section 3.2.4.

cd

Change directory, see Section 2.2.

cdp/cdplay

An interactive text-mode program for controlling and playing audio CD Roms under Linux, see Section 11.2.1.

cdparanoia

An audio CD reading utility which includes extra data verification features, see Section 11.2.1.

cdrecord

Record a CD-R, see Section 9.2.2.

chattr

Change file attributes.

chgrp

Change group ownership, see Section 3.4.2.3.

chkconfig

Update or query run level information for system services, see Section 4.2.5.1.

chmod

Change file access permissions, see Section 3.4.1, Section 3.4.2.1 and Section 3.4.2.4.

chown

Change file owner and group, see Section 3.4.2.3.

compress

Compress files.

cp

Copy files and directories, see Section 3.3.2.

crontab

Maintain crontab files, see Section 4.4.4.

csh

Open a C shell, see Section 3.2.3.2.

cut

Remove sections from each line of file(s), see Section 7.2.5.2.

D

date

Print or set system date and time.

dd

Convert and copy a file (disk dump), see Section 9.2.1.2.

df

Report file system disk usage, see Section 3.1.2.3.

dhcpcd

DHCP client daemon, see Section 10.3.8.

diff

Find differences between two files.

dig

Send domain name query packets to name servers, see Section 10.2.6.1.

dmesg

Print or control the kernel ring buffer.

du

Estimate file space usage.

dump

Backup file system, see Section 9.2.5.

E

echo

Display a line of text, see Section 3.2.1.

ediff

Diff to English translator.

egrep

Extended grep.

eject

Unmount and eject removable media, see Section 7.5.5.2.

emacs

Start the Emacs editor, see Section 6.1.2.2.

exec

Invoke subprocess(es), see Section 4.1.5.1.

exit

Exit current shell, see Section 2.2.

export

Add function(s) to the shell environment, see Section 3.2.1, Section 7.2.1.2 and Section 7.2.4.2.

F

fax2ps

Convert a TIFF facsimile to PostScript, see Section 8.1.2.

fdformat

Format floppy disk, see Section 9.2.1.1.

fdisk

Partition table manipulator for Linux, see Section 3.1.2.2.

fetchmail

Fetch mail from a POP, IMAP, ETRN or ODMR-capable server, see Section 10.3.2.3.

fg

Bring a job in the foreground, see Section 4.1.2.1.

file

Determine file type, see Section 3.3.1.2.

find

Find files, see Section 3.3.3.3.

firefox

Web browser, see Section 10.3.3.2.

fork

Create a new process, see Section 4.1.5.1.

formail

Mail (re)formatter, see Section 10.3.2.3.

fortune

Print a random, hopefully interesting adage.

ftp

Transfer files (unsafe unless anonymous account is used!)services, see Section 10.3.4.2.

G

galeon

Graphical web browser.

gdm

Gnome Display Manager, see Section 4.2.4.

gedit

GUI editor, see Section 6.3.3.3.

(min/a)getty

Control console devices.

gimp

Image manipulation program.

gpg

Encrypt, check and decrypt files, see Section 9.4.1.2.

grep

Print lines matching a pattern, see Section 3.3.3.4 and Section 5.3.1.

groff

Emulate nroff command with groff, see Section 8.1.2.

grub

The grub shell, see Section 4.2.3 and Section 7.5.4.

gv

A PostScript and PDF viewer, see Section 8.1.2.2.

gvim

Graphical version of the vIm editor, see Section 6.3.3.3.

gzip

Compress or expand files, see Section 9.1.1.3.

H

halt

Stop the system, see Section 4.2.6.

head

Output the first part of files, see Section 3.3.4.3.

help

Display help on a shell built-in command.

host

DNS lookup utility, see Section 10.2.6.1.

httpd

Apache hypertext transfer protocol server, see Section 10.2.3.1.

I

id

Print real and effective UIDs and GIDs, see Section 3.4.1.

ifconfig

Configure network interface or show configuration, see Section 10.1.2.3.

info

Read Info documents, see Section 2.3.3.1.

init

Process control initialization, see Section 4.1.5.1, Section 4.2.4 and Section 4.2.5.

insserv

Manage init scripts, see Section 4.2.5.1.

---

iostat

Display I/O statistics, see Section 4.3.5.4.

ip

Display/change network interface status, see Section 10.1.2.3.

ipchains

IP firewall administration, see Section 10.4.4.2.

iptables

IP packet filter administration, see Section 10.4.4.2.

J

jar

Java archive tool, see Section 9.1.1.4.

jobs

List backgrounded tasks.

K

kdm

Desktop manager for KDE, see Section 4.2.4.

kedit

KDE graphical editor, see Section 6.3.3.3.

kill(all)

Terminate process(es), see Section 4.1.2.1.

konqueror

File manager, (help) browser, see Section 3.3.2.1.

ksh

Open a Korn shell, see Section 3.2.3.2.

kwrite

KDE graphical editor, see Section 6.3.3.3.

L

less

more with features, see Section 3.3.4.2.

lilo

Linux boot loader, see Section 4.2.

links

Text mode WWW browser, see Section 10.2.3.2.

ln

Make links between files, see Section 3.3.5.

loadkeys

Load keyboard translation tables, see Section 7.4.1.

locate

Find files, see Section 3.3.3.3 and Section 4.4.4.

logout

Close current shell, see Section 2.1.3.

lp

Send requests to the LP print service, see Section 8.1.

lpc

Line printer control program, see Section 8.1.

lpq

Print spool queue examination program, see Section 8.1.

lpr

Offline print, see Section 8.1.

lprm

Remove print requests, see Section 8.1.

ls

List directory content, see Section 2.2, Section 3.1.1.2 and Section 3.3.1.1.

lynx

Text mode WWW browser, see Section 10.2.3.2.

M

mail

Send and receive mail, see Section 10.3.2.3.

man

Read man pages, see Section 2.3.2.

mc

Midnight COmmander, file manager, see Section 3.3.2.1.

mcopy

Copy MSDOS files to/from Unix.

mdir

Display an MSDOS directory.

memusage

Display memory usage, see Section 4.3.5.3.

memusagestat

Display memory usage statistics, see Section 4.3.5.3.

mesg

Control write access to your terminal, see Section 4.1.6.

mformat

Add an MSDOS file system to a low-level formatted floppy disk, see Section 9.2.1.1.

mkbootdisk

Creates a stand-alone boot floppy for the running system.

mkdir

Create directory, see Section 3.3.2.

mkisofs

Create a hybrid ISO9660 filesystem, see Section 9.2.2.

mplayer

Movie player/encoder for Linux, see Section 11.2.2 and Section 11.3.

more

Filter for displaying text one screen at the time, see Section 3.3.4.2.

mount

Mount a file system or display information about mounted file systems, see Section 7.5.5.1.

mozilla

Web browser, see Section 10.2.3.2.

mt

Control magnetic tape drive operation.

mtr

Network diagnostic tool.

mv

Rename files, Section 3.3.2.

N

named

Internet domain name server, see Section 10.3.7.

nautilus

File manager, see Section 3.3.2.1.

ncftp

Browser program for ftp services (insecure!), see Section 10.3.4.2.

netstat

Print network connections, routing tables, interface statistics, masquerade connections, and multi-cast memberships, see Section 10.1.2.5 and Section 10.4.2.

newgrp

Log in to another group, see Section 3.4.2.2.

nfsstat

Print statistics about networked file systems.

nice

Run a program with modified scheduling priority, see Section 4.3.5.1.

nmap

Network exploration tool and security scanner.

ntpd

Network Time Protocol Daemon, see Section 7.4.3.

ntpdate

Set the date and time via an NTP server, see Section 7.4.3.

ntsysv

Simple interface for configuring run levels, see Section 4.2.5.1.

O

ogle

DVD player with support for DVD menus, see Section 11.3.

P

passwd

Change password, see Section 2.2 and Section 4.1.6.

pccardctl

Manage PCMCIA cards, see Section 10.2.3.3.

pdf2ps

Ghostscript PDF to PostScript translator, see Section 8.1.2.

perl

Practical Extraction and Report Language.

pg

Page through text output, see Section 3.3.4.2.

pgrep

Look up processes based on name and other attributes, see Section 4.1.4.

ping

Send echo request to a host, see Section 10.2.6.2.

play

Play a sound sample, see Section 11.2.3.

pr

Convert text files for printing.

printenv

Print all or part of environment, see Section 7.2.1.

procmail

Autonomous mail processor, see Section 10.3.2.3.

ps

Report process status, see Section 4.1.4 and Section 4.3.5.4.

pstree

Display a tree of processes, see Section 4.1.4.

pwd

Print present working directory, see Section 2.2.

Q

quota

Display disk usage and limits, see Section 3.2.3.3.

R

rcp

Remote copy (unsafe!)

rdesktop

Remote Desktop Protocol client, see Section 10.4.6.

reboot

Stop the system, see Section 4.2.6.

recode

Convert files to another character set, see Section 7.4.4.

renice

Alter priority of a running process, see Section 4.3.5.1.

restore

Restore backups made with **dump**, see Section 9.2.5.

rlogin

Remote login (telnet, insecure!), see Section 10.4.2 and Section 10.5.2.

rm

Remove a file, see Section 3.3.2.

rmdir

Remove a directory, see Section 3.3.2.2.

roff

A survey of the roff typesetting system, see Section 8.1.2.

rpm

RPM Package Manager, see Section 7.5.2.1.

rsh

Remote shell (insecure!), see Section 10.4.2.

rsync

Synchronize two directories, see Section 9.3.

S

scp

Secure remote copy, see Section 10.4.4.1.

screen

Screen manager with VT100 emulation, see Section 4.1.2.1.

set

Display, set or change variable.

setterm

Set terminal attributes.

sftp

Secure (encrypted) ftp, see and Section 10.4.4.1.

sh

Open a standard shell, see Section 3.2.3.2.

shutdown

Bring the system down, see Section 4.2.6.

sleep

Wait for a given period, see Section 4.4.1.

slocate

Security Enhanced version of the GNU Locate, see Section 3.3.3.3.

slrnn

text mode Usenet client, see Section 10.2.6.

snort

Network intrusion detection tool.

sort

Sort lines of text files, see Section 5.3.2.

spell

Spell checker, see Section 5.1.2.3.

ssh

Secure shell, see Section 10.4.4.1.

ssh-keygen

Authentication key generation, management and conversion, see Section 10.4.4.5.

stty

Change and print terminal line settings.

su

Switch user, see Section 3.2.1, Section 7.5.3.2 and Section 10.4.6.

T

tac

Concatenate and print files in reverse, see *cat*.

tail

Output the last part of files, see Section 3.3.4.3.

talk

Talk to a user.

tar

Archiving utility, see Section 9.1.1.1.

tcsh

Open a Turbo C shell, see Section 3.2.3.2.

telinit

Process control initialization, see Section 4.2.5.

telnet

User interface to the TELNET protocol (insecure!), see Section 10.4.2.

tex

Text formatting and typesetting, see Section 8.1.2.

time

Time a simple command or give resource usage, see Section 4.3.2.

tin

News reading program, see Section 10.2.6.

top

Display top CPU processes, see Section 4.1.4, Section 4.3.5.3 and Section 4.3.5.4.

touch

Change file timestamps, see Section 7.1.2.

traceroute

Print the route packets take to network host, see Section 10.2.6.3.

tripwire

A file integrity checker for UNIX systems, see Section 10.4.5.

troff

Format documents, see Section 8.1.2.

tvime

A high quality television application.

twm

Tab Window Manager for the X Window System.

U

ulimit

Controll resources, see Section 7.1.2.5.

umask

Set user file creation mask, see Section 3.4.2.2.

umount

Unmount a file system.

uncompress

Decompress compressed files.

uniq

Remove duplicate lines from a sorted file, see Section 5.3.2.

up2date

Update RPM packages, see Section 7.5.3.3.

update

Kernel daemon to flush dirty buffers back to disk.

update-rc.d

Configure init scripts, see Section 4.2.5.1.

uptime

Display system uptime and average load, see Section 4.1.4 and Section 4.3.5.2.

urpmi

Update RPM packages, see Section 7.5.3.3.

userdel

Delete a user account and related files.

V

vi(m)

Start the vi (improved) editor, see Section 6.1.2.3.

vimtutor

The Vim tutor.

vmstat

Report virtual memory statistics, see Section 4.3.5.4.

W

w

Show who is logged on and what they are doing.

wall

Send a message to everybody's terminal, see Section 4.1.6.

wc

Print the number of bytes, words and lines in files, see Section 3.2.1.

which

Shows the full path of (shell) commands, see Section 3.2.1 and Section 3.3.3.2.

who

Show who is logged on, see Section 4.1.6.

who am i

Print effective user ID.

whois

Query a whois or nicname database, see Section 10.2.6.4.

write

Send a message to another user, see Section 4.1.6.

X

xargs

Build and execute command lines from standard input, see Section 3.3.3.3.

xauth

X authority file utility.

xawtv

An X11 program for watching TV.

xcdroast

Graphical front end to cdrecord, see Section 9.2.2.

xclock

Analog/digital clock for X.

xconsole

Monitor system console messages with X.

xdm

X Display Manager with support for XDMCP, host chooser, see Section 4.2.4 and Section 7.3.2.

xdvi

DVI viewer, see Section 8.1.2.2.

xedit

X Window graphical editor, see Section 6.3.3.3.

xfs

X font server.

xhost

Server access control program for X, see Section 10.4.3.2.

xine

A free video player, see Section 11.3.

xinetd

The extended Internet services daemon, see Section 10.3.1.2.

xload

System load average display for X, see Section 4.3.5.6.

xlsfonts

Server font list displayer for X.

xmms

Audio player for X, see Section 11.2.2.1.

xpdf

PDF viewer, see Section 8.1.2.2.

xterm

Terminal emulator for X.

Y

yast

System administration tool on Novell SuSE Linux.

yum

Update RPM packages, see Section 7.5.3.3.

Z

zapping

A TV viewer for the Gnome environment.

zcat

Compress or expand files.

zgrep

Search possibly compressed files for a regular expression.

zmore

Filter for viewing compressed text.